# HOLDING THE LINE

## WOMEN IN THE GREAT ARIZONA
## MINE STRIKE OF 1983

*Barbara Kingsolver*

ILR Press

New York State School of Industrial and Labor Relations, Cornell University

Cover and text design by Kat Dalton


Library of Congress Cataloging-in-Publication Data

Kingsolver, Barbara.
    Holding the line: women in the great Arizona mine strike of 1983
/ Barbara Kingsolver.
        p.    cm.
    Includes bibliographical references.
    ISBN 0-87546-155-7 (alk. paper).—ISBN 0-87546-156-5 (pbk. :
alk. paper)
    1. Phelps Dodge Corporation Strike, Morenci, Ariz., 1983–
2. Strikes and lockouts—Copper mining—Arizona. 3. Women in trade-
unions—Arizona. 4. Women in political activists—Arizona.
5. Women—Arizona. I. Title.
HD5325.M73 1983.M675 1989
331.89'28292'0979151—dc20                                    89-17422
                                                                CIP


Copies may be ordered through bookstores or from
ILR Press
School of Industrial and Labor Relations
Cornell University
Ithaca, NY 14851-0952

Printed on acid-free paper in the United States of America
5   4

*For the families who held the line,*
*and those who will have to do it again*

*"No nation is greater than its women."*
—Mother Jones

# Contents

Preface / *ix*

Acknowledgments / *xiii*

1. The Devil's Domain / *1*

2. On the Line / *22*

3. Hell and High Water / *49*

4. We'll Stay Here Until We're Gone / *64*

5. Ask Any Miner / *73*

6. We Go with Our Heads Up / *97*

7. Falling-Apart Things / *111*

8. My Union and My Friends / *123*

9. Women's Work / *134*

10. Up to No Good / *150*

11. If the Truth Would Come Out / *163*

12. Just a Bunch of Ladies / *175*

Epilogue / *191*

Bibliography / *197*

Index / *201*

# Preface

In the summer of 1983 I was working as a journalist, making frequent trips to the small strike-ravaged mining towns of southern Arizona in order to write articles for several publications. At that time I drove a light brown Nissan pickup truck. In these blue-collar outposts, the credo "buy American" was no platitude; it was food on the plate. The very first time I parked on Clifton's main thoroughfare, summoned up my reporter's nerve, and crossed the street to talk with a group of men standing outside the Steelworkers' Hall, they looked me up and down and asked pointedly if I belonged to that little Japanese truck. I answered defensively that it was put together at a plant in Tennessee. I couldn't read from these men's faces whether I'd given the right answer.

Two weeks later I was in the Clifton area again, talking to some women on the picket line near the mine's main gate. I knew nobody in town—before the strike I'd never had reason to set foot there. During a lull in the interview, while I was trying hard to take cogent notes, a young man teased me about driving a Japanese truck. Two other perfect strangers instantly admonished him: "It was made in Tennessee," they said.

By the end of that first summer I'd begun to write this book. In the years to come I would see a lot of Clifton, and I would never have to explain myself again.

This is an account of eighteen months, between June 1983 and December 1985, during which a strike against the Phelps Dodge Copper Corporation permanently altered the social order in several southwestern mining towns. In particular, the book is about the women in these towns: how they answered the challenge set before them, and how they changed. The strike proved to be an important moment in U.S. labor history, but more than that, it was one of those rare events that forces a turning point in many lives at once.

When it began, anyone who was paying attention believed this was going to be a brief and conventional strike. But within a month, things were happening that I'd never seen before, or heard of happening in my lifetime. People were being jailed for simply calling a neighbor "scab." Helicopters and squads of men with hefty-looking automatic weapons were coming in to break the strike, and strike supporters were answering back with extraordinary resistance. A fair number of the faces and hands on the strike's front lines belonged to women. All of this looked interesting to me, and terrifying, and it looked like history.

For the next year and a half I did my best to watch it happen. Some half-dozen mining towns were involved, but the focal point of the strike, over the long haul, was at the Morenci mine, and to a lesser extent the Ajo mine. The former is a four-hour drive, and the latter, three hours, from my home in Tucson. I put a lot of miles on my pickup, spending as much time as possible in Morenci and nearby Clifton and making briefer trips to the other striking towns in Arizona. (The strike also affected a few towns in New Mexico and Texas, which I was never able to visit.) I taped extensive interviews with about seventy-five people, mostly women, who were in some way involved with the strike; I talked with several of them again many times over the course of two years, tracking their changes of heart and mind. From my own observations and accumulation of taped interviews—which came to fill half a dozen shoeboxes and spill onto the floor of my bedroom/office—I've made this account of the strike.

The story of my Tennessee-Japanese truck, and the lightning speed with which its identity became known in Clifton, made me think twice about journalism and the nature of objectivity. I had driven into town thinking of myself as an invisible reporter, as anonymous to my subjects as they were to me. The fundamental myth of journalism, I now believe, is that the writer can convey events straight from the scene of action to the reader's mind without casting his or her own shadow across the page. I was not in any way important to the strike, but still I was a presence in Clifton; I cast a shadow on it, and it on me. Not by way of apology, but by way of clarification, I would like to explain the biases of this book.

It can't be considered the complete, scholarly, archival account of the strike. I've aimed toward readability, in the hope that any person interested in labor conflicts, mining, the sociology of women in the 1980s, life in the remote modern-day Southwest, or just a good human drama could have access to this story. But, of course, it's only part of the story. The Phelps Dodge mining towns affected by the strike were scattered widely across a very large desert. It was impossible for me to witness all or even most of the bone-grinding routine that added up, day by day, to one of the longest strikes there has ever been, anywhere. I relied on the participants to direct me toward the emotional and strategic landmarks of that great expanse of time. The events of the strike could fill several books of many different sorts; I've written only one.

Most obviously, I have left out much about the men. Their struggle was parallel to that of the women, equally difficult and often equally heroic, and their stories are no less deserving of an audience. But for several reasons I set out to write a book about women. The women's lives were transformed in more obvious and compelling ways. The dominant role they assumed in maintaining the long strike appeared to be one of the unique features of the conflict. And if it wasn't actually unique—if women have been shouldering the burden of labor struggles since time began—it still *seemed* very surprising to people both inside and outside the strike, leading one to believe that women's aptitude for this kind of work is a well-kept secret. And that, I felt, was another good reason for writing a book like this one.

It's also undoubtedly true that I identified more easily with the women of the strike, and they were generally more candid with me than were the men. This is one of the unavoidable biases of reportage. And since hidden biases are more dangerous than obvious ones, the reader should also know that I was, from the outset, sympathetic to the strikers' cause.

In addition to my own particular leanings, there were practical limitations to the illusion of objectivity in writing this account. Within a few months I was known to one and all in the mining towns, not only as the driver of the Nissan truck but also as "that gal that's writing the book"; this undoubtedly had its effect on what I heard. Anyone who has lived in a small town knows that anonymity in such places is a daydream. And what's more, anyone who has lived in a town deeply divided over a life-and-death issue knows that if you aren't willing to declare your allegiances, you're unlikely to get served a cup of coffee in a restaurant, much less engender anyone's trust. I decided early on that I wanted to write something more than the extended news analysis that so often lacks heart and depth; I wanted to be trusted.

By the time the strike was a year old, driving through Clifton, Arizona, was as perilous as steering a ship through the Persian Gulf, so I flagged my truck prominently with orange "Support the Copper Strikers" bumper stickers. I had extensive conversations with Phelps Dodge officials from time to time, with lawyers and police officers, and occasionally with people who'd crossed the picket line. But mostly I talked with those who sooner or later supported the strike. We talked in bars, in cars, in their kitchens and back-porch swings, and on the picket line. During those drawn-out days I developed a great admiration and fondness for some of the people whose stories are told here. I would like to think this has made the book better, not worse.

All the people and events in this book are real. In a few cases I've changed names to protect safety or family harmony; in those instances I've used a first name only. I also changed the name of the woman identified as Flossie Navarro, because she told me many things about her long and remarkable life on the condition of confidentiality. All others who speak here are identified by name. I've sometimes edited their statements for brevity and clarity, but I hope I've retained the letter and spirit of their testimonies.

When it came to reconstructing the dramatic events of the strike, sorting fact from fiction was rarely simple; tales ran rampant on both sides of the picket line, and while all of them would have made good copy, many of them simply turned out to be untrue. For example, during one of the showdowns between strikers and the police, a woman strike supporter who was eight and a half months pregnant was trapped inside the small store she owned, tear-gassed, and arrested. Some people said she was beaten then and went into labor on the spot. Some said she gave birth to a brain-damaged boy later and that her doctor (also a strike supporter) vowed to sue Phelps Dodge. Some said the police let her out of the paddy wagon as soon as they realized she was pregnant, while others insisted that she was detained. When I asked the woman herself, she put her head in her hands and said, "I don't want to talk about it." (I could hardly blame her.) The straight story, finally, is that she was gassed in her store, abruptly questioned, handcuffed, put into the paddy wagon, let out a little while later, and held overnight in the home of a police officer. Two days later she gave birth to a boy who developed meningitis but recovered fully. So all of the tales contained a bit of the real story, but only a bit.

Collecting rumors and trying to assemble truth, I sometimes felt like the foolish heroine of the Rumpelstiltskin story, whose brash confidence got her into the job of trying to spin straw into gold. I became obsessed with verification, because as the strike wore on, the truth was generally shocking enough without embroidery. On important events, even when I'd witnessed them myself, I gathered as many independent accounts as possible (including the "official" version in state newspapers—which occasionally was the wildest fiction of all) and looked for agreement on sequence and detail.

Many of the stories here are personal, though, describing an internal as well as an external landscape, and in those cases I simply had to trust the integrity of my sources. I believe that the people who survive a cataclysm, rather than those who stand by and analyze it, are nearly always the more credible witnesses to their own history.

# Acknowledgments

Literally hundreds of people helped bring this project along its way. Two stand out especially, because without them the book would not now be in your hands: Jessica Sampson accompanied me on many of the research trips, helped greatly with interviews, transcribed innumerable hours of tape, and provided valuable insights and unflagging friendship throughout the process of researching and writing. Frances Goldin, my literary agent, consistently and enthusiastically believed in the value of the book even when I doubted it myself.

I am deeply grateful to all those who took the time to talk with me about the strike or otherwise make material available to me. Phelps Dodge company personnel were universally helpful, as were the reference librarians at the University of Arizona and Tucson public libraries. I also owe a great debt of thanks to the many people who read and discussed drafts of the manuscript, including Anna and Jorge O'Leary, Tom Miller, Jill Barrett Fein (who first proposed the idea of the book), Janice Bowers, Pamela Portwood, and especially Joseph Hoffmann, whose wholehearted support was a cornerstone of the project.

Most of all, I'm indebted to the women of Clifton, Morenci, Ajo, and Douglas, Arizona—whose names essentially comprise the index of this book—who welcomed me into their houses and their lives. Their compassion, resourcefulness, and courage will be an inspiration to me for life.

# HOLDING THE LINE

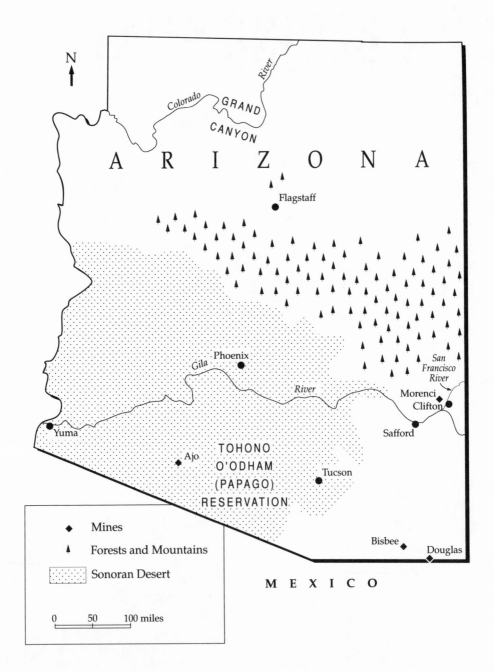

N

Colorado River
GRAND
CANYON

A R I Z O N A

Flagstaff

San
Francisco
River

Gila
Phoenix
River
Morenci
Clifton
Yuma
Safford

TOHONO
Ajo
O'ODHAM
(PAPAGO)
Tucson
RESERVATION

Bisbee
Douglas

♦ Mines
▲ Forests and Mountains
Sonoran Desert

0    50    100 miles

M E X I C O

# 1
# The Devil's Domain

lossie Navarro is a sturdy woman, strong-boned and handsome, with a
lightness in her bearing that has stood up to some seventy years of living
a rock-hard life. Those years have neither dulled her mind nor dented
her will. She says she isn't leaving Clifton, Arizona—not now, and not
ever. There has been talk of moving people out, but she and her husband,
Ed, are permanently settled here in their weathered-white frame house on the
floodplain of the San Francisco River.

But back in 1944, when she left her family farm in Arkansas and struck out
for Arizona, Flossie was footloose and on her own. She'd heard that the copper
mines out west were hiring women to keep the smelter fires burning while the
men were away fighting World War II. The rumors proved true: the Phelps
Dodge Mining Company promptly hired her on at the mine of her choice.
With a trace of lingering homesickness, she picked the one near Clifton
because someone told her—when she asked—that of all the Arizona mines,
that one was the closest to Arkansas.

The next day she embarked on the career of her life. "I did anything," she
says. "I'd get a shovel and shovel, push a wheelbarrow, load that wheelbarrow
and dump it on a belt, whatever they said. I was raised on a farm, and we
girls did everything there was to do on a farm, but not necessarily like that.
It was hard work, and when we went to the bucket room where they run the
samples, it was extra-hard work. We'd have to stand and collect mud and
water and put it in a bucket for eight hours straight. On our shift it was all
women, except for the floorwalkers."

A floorwalker, according to Flossie, is a man who "noses around and sees
what he can find out to go tell on people to get them in trouble." These were
the only men she ever saw in the concentrator and the ball mill. She declares
simply, "Those women kept that mine going."

Even so, the women who walked to work every morning in their coveralls,
hairnets, and hard hats, telling jokes and swinging their lunch buckets, were
tugging at the moorings of the status quo. Clifton was a traditional Catholic
town where a woman's world was quietly but firmly defined by the walls of
her home. Those who worked in the mine were considered unwomanly at

best, and at worst, unladylike. Some people hinted that they were prostitutes. It didn't slow Flossie down. "Well, sure, the men would call you a nasty name, but you'd learn how to call them one back, and go ahead. I always said if I wanted to go and do such things I would sure find a nicer place to do them than in the muck and the water on that ball mill floor!"

The notion that women don't belong in a mine still persists in the copper pits of Arizona and is just as likely to surface on the iron range of Minnesota or the Kentucky coal fields. In fact, the exclusion of women from mines is a tradition probably as old as mining itself, rooted in the mineral-rich soils of the Andes, where the Incas opened mines before European ships ever reached the shores of the western hemisphere. To this day, the miners of the Bolivian *altiplano* divide their world into two domains. The world of agricultural production, home, and family is overseen by Pachamama, a benevolent earth mother with an eye for continuity; the stony underground world, carved out by a hundred generations of miners seeking copper, tin, and silver, is the devil's domain.

Anthropologists who scour the world for pockets of ancient lore are unlikely to find a devil older than this one, whose name is Supay. He has ruled miners' lives from underneath their floors since before the Spanish conquest, and his age hasn't weakened his influence. When the mine shafts rumble and threaten to collapse, the miners assume it is Supay begrudging the ore they tap, little by little, from his glittering black veins.

The mountain town of Oruro, in the heart of the Bolivian mining region, was the ancient ceremonial center for the Incas. The high priests allegedly traveled from Peru through tunnels, passing secretly under the core of the Andes, and in full ceremonial dress leaped out of the ground in Oruro. The tunnel's mouth is blocked with boulders now, but the festivals celebrating the powers of Supay and Pachamama are still honored there, unaltered by centuries. During the week of Carnival, Devil Dancers in red-tipped shoes and horned masks jam the streets in a wild procession leading to the Church of the Mine Shaft. The festivities end with a ceremonial offering to Supay, held deep in the mine—where women can't go.

More than anything, the devil's domain is masculine, not just on Carnival days but on every working day of the year. June Nash, in her book *We Eat the Mines, the Mines Eat Us*, says that women in Bolivia may earn subsistence wages by picking through the slag heaps for overlooked bits of ore, but mining itself, the central economic pursuit of the region, is closed to them. According to persistent tradition, a female presence in this special corner of hell would anger Supay terribly and cause a cave-in. If a woman went into the mines, it's claimed, disaster would follow her.

The people of Oruro say their world wasn't always organized this way. Originally they were agrarian people like their northern neighbors in Guatemala, who still ask the earth's forgiveness for wounding her before they plant their seeds. But when the Incas came to the *altiplano* and forced the farmers into mining labor, Pachamama's earth and the subterranean world parted asunder, like some oddly vertical version of the Red Sea. Before this, there was no hell.

So the strict male-female dichotomy of Pachamama and Supay was already established in legend and in fact by the time the Spaniards reached Oruro in 1535. Ancient tradition has gradually been overlaid with a Catholic veneer, but the European conquerors had no reason to change the underlying beliefs that admitted only men into economic productivity.

In the open-pit mine in Morenci, Arizona, the steady motion of mechanized shovels raises a yellow haze of fine dust. Yielding 290,000 tons of metal in a good year, it is the most productive copper mine in North America. The smokestacks of the copper smelter rise like a pair of giant horns out of the mountain's granite pate. Below the horned promontory, the earth's entrails are laid open in a pattern of circular, descending steps, exposing the strangely delicate colors of a mountain's insides: lavender, pink, and blue-gray. If the miners who work there are in the belly of a beast, gutting it a little more deeply every day, then the beast is as tough as Prometheus, the fire thief in Greek mythology whose punishment was to be disemboweled every day for eternity. The twin stacks of the Morenci mine have stood over this scarred landscape for decades.

Around the mine and in the river valley below it lie the ordinary mining towns of Morenci and Clifton. Each has its high school, its main drag, its dust-coated, blinking neon signs, and its sundry collection of bars and drive-in restaurants. Nowhere could one be less inclined to look for vestiges of Andean tradition: no devil dances in these streets. But the germinal social order of Oruro that predates all other mining traditions in the New World seems to have influenced much of what has come after, even in Clifton and Morenci. A mine is a masculine enclave, not just in the Andes, and not just in Latin America—the exact same social prescriptions surface wherever the earth is scratched. Flossie Navarro heard many a time that female workers would jinx the mine. When women began working the Appalachian coal mines in the late 1970s, they confronted a centuries-old folk belief that a woman underground was bad luck and could cause a cave-in merely by her presence.

But, with or without a woman's presence, the history of mining is a story of inevitable disaster. Between 1961 and 1973, more than half a million disabling injuries occurred in mines in the United States—nearly twice as many as incurred by all U.S. soldiers in Vietnam. The mean death rate for miners during those years was approximately 1,080 per million, and for active-duty military personnel, about 1,270 per million (figures from the National Safety Council and Department of Defense Information). If war is hell, so is mining: underground shafts collapse, smelter furnaces explode, lung disease is endemic. In few other professions are the odds so stacked against living long enough to retire.

These odds aren't so much laws of nature as of economics. Many cave-ins could have been prevented had there been enough supporting timbers; extra drying time will keep damp ore from exploding inside a furnace. But every penny spent on such precautions is a penny robbed from the business of mining ore. Safety costs money; speedy production costs lives. The familiar formula has never yet been solved by cool algebra. Obviously, the miners have a strong interest in their side of the equation and have forever sought to organize for better working conditions, longer lives, and better-fed children. And this, too, is a history punctuated by disaster. Every country that has tapped its mineral wealth has also accumulated grisly stories of strikes, repression, and massacres. This part of mining tradition has been far less exclusive of women.

History tends to polish the marble surface of a wall and ignore the mortar that holds the slabs in place; likewise, the contributions of women to mining history are mostly invisible, but they are a good part of the reason the wall still stands. For the most part their participation must simply be taken for granted, but in a few cases it is well documented. The film Norma Rae, loosely based on an actual strike in a textile mill, popularized the image of a modern working woman devoted to her union. But at least three earlier U.S. strikes in which women played leading roles have been recorded or reenacted on film. With Babies and Banners documents the 1937 strike against General Motors in Flint, Michigan, in which women auto workers and workers' wives—dubbed the "Red Berets"—held the battle lines out front while male workers occupied the Fisher I and II automotive plants for more than a month. (Women workers were sent out before the sit-down, to avoid suggestions of licentiousness.) Similarly, in 1973, women sustained the ultimately disastrous coal strike at the Brookside mine in Kentucky on a steady diet of soup-kitchen stamina and political zeal; the strike was the subject of the documentary Harlan County USA. And at a point in time almost exactly halfway between the Flint and Brookside strikes, while McCarthyism burned white-hot, a militant strike led by women against Empire Zinc in Hanover, New Mexico, was immortalized at some peril both to actors (many of whom were strike supporters themselves) and filmmakers in the now-famous film *Salt of the Earth.*

It's tempting to wonder, after watching these films, if many other strikes would now be remembered as largely or partly led by women if a movie camera had been on hand. All three documentaries portray events very much like those of the 1983 strike against Phelps Dodge Copper in Arizona, in which the same forces again called women to the line: loyalty to the union, desperation over their families' living conditions, and the fact that men were legally or physically barred from action. The 1951 Empire Zinc strike, in particular, strongly foreshadowed the complexities of the Phelps Dodge strike, mainly because of geography. Like the strike in Arizona three decades later, it was shaped by the special conflicts of economics, ethnicity, and gender that are woven into the social fabric of these isolated, predominantly Mexican-American mining towns, where a woman's place is in the home, or on the line—depending.

Every tradition has its price, and most have been bought and sold many times over. Flossie Navarro and her companions, who a year earlier couldn't have gotten a job selling sandwiches in a mine, were gladly given hard hats when World War II simultaneously swept out the men and slapped a premium price tag on copper. There was nothing new about this contradiction. Fifteen years earlier, hundreds of Bolivian women had been recruited for underground labor in the infamous domain of Supay while their sons and husbands attended a war on the hot plains of Paraguay. If the Inca priests, the Spanish conquerors, and all subsequent religious and economic rulers of Bolivia had found it expedient for these mines to be off limits to women, those in command of the tin industry and the government at the time of the Chaco War, for the moment, did not. Thus, the supernatural order of a thousand years was eclipsed by government edict, though it promptly prevailed again when the war was over.

The use of female mine workers at convenient historical moments was not unique to the New World. Emile Zola's novel *Germinal,* written in 1885, tells of an actual French mining disaster that took the lives of women as well as men in the shafts of a coal mine. Women and children commonly worked underground in England also, probably as a natural outgrowth of the standard family economy in preindustrial society, until it was prohibited by law in 1842. (The gentle Victorians were mortified by the savage world of mining, which during this era spawned many Dantean fantasies, including John Martin's famous illustrations of *Paradise Lost.*) Angela V. John, in her book *By the Sweat of Their Brow,* documents the great Victorian debate on whether legally to exclude women from mine work, an argument fueled by the raging ambivalence of nineteenth-century attitudes toward working-class female employment. The "pit-brow lasses," who sorted coal and performed other above-ground tasks at British mines, were viewed as the very essence of degraded womanhood—a view that failed to take into account the realities of life for working-class families and the appetite of mining companies for low-cost labor.

Vivian Vallens characterizes this ambivalence very well in her dissertation on working women in Mexico during the rise of industrialism under the regime of Porfirio Diaz (1880–1910):

> Women provided an inexhaustible pool of cheap, docile labor drawn as needed from the rural communities. From the beginning, factory owners displayed a splendid indifference to the question of women's proper place. They believed that the proper place for poor women was in the factories running looms, sewing shirts, or making cigars at wages from a third to a half of those paid to men.

The women who rolled cigars in Mexico and mined ore in England or Bolivia were just a few of the many who have been picked up on a wave, carried into the current, and beached again like driftwood, swept by the tides of deficit and profit. The process is familiar to any subordinate population in a so-called "expandable labor force." During the nineteenth and early twentieth centuries in what became the U.S. Southwest, women and men of Hispanic descent experienced such contradictions in every form.

When eastern investors under the aegis of the Phelps Dodge Corporation began to develop a profitable copper industry in the region, the anti-alien laws they constructed were as utilitarian and malleable as the metal itself. In 1913 at the Copper Queen mine in Bisbee, Arizona, the underground shafts gave access to precious deposits of silver and gold as well as copper. Mining here was regarded as a highly skilled and well-paying (albeit hazardous) craft; Mexicans were explicitly forbidden to work underground. But the rules changed in other mines throughout the state, where geology called for different methods and attitudes. In the Clifton-Morenci district, during the same era, the mechanics of the mine required a large, unskilled labor force. Workers for the Morenci operation were imported from Mexico en masse. According to James Byrkit, Morenci mine records from 1917 show the makeup of the labor camp to have been 80 percent Mexicans, 15 percent Spaniards and Italians, and only 5 percent "whites"—a designation that included European Anglo-Saxons.

The Mexican laborers were regarded as beasts of burden and were paid only slightly better than the average mule, even though their descendants now living and mining in Morenci say that many who crossed the border from Sonora were skilled miners and smelters. The *mineros* from the south brought along more than strong backs and a residual memory of Supay. Outside the mining museum at Jerome, Arizona, for example, sits an old "Chilean wheel"—an efficient ore-crushing technology that was used extensively in Latin America before being introduced into Arizona, probably by Mexican miners. Their stories have been lost, in the main, but their knowledge enriched the industry.

For better or for worse, workers of Mexican heritage have continued to serve as the spine of mining operations in the Southwest. Today in Arizona mining towns, Spanish surnames are as ubiquitous as the *mesquite* and *palo verde* trees that root in the baked-brick soil, unroll their leaves, and wait for water. It's hard for an outsider to understand how either the trees or the miners have survived. In the early days in Morenci, Mexican laborers earned as little as twelve cents per day and were obliged to buy their necessities from company stores, where prices were inflated. Payroll records of the Jerome-Verde Copper Company show that in 1916, a better-paid Mexican laborer typically received about nineteen dollars for a six-day week, before hospital and store deductions. Employees with English surnames, listed as "miners" rather than "laborers," were paid thirty-three dollars for the same week's work. Mexicans were discouraged, generally and specifically, from aspiring to skilled positions. A Mexican miner who touched a locomotive would be fired on the spot.

Mike Baray was born in 1921 within a stone's throw of the Morenci smokestacks. When he married his wife, Stella, in 1939 he was already a miner, as were his father and his grandfather, two of the "Mexican imports" of 1915. Stella remembers their wedding day well. "We didn't go on any honeymoon, because Mike was working seven days a week. He didn't get off work."

Stella preferred to let her husband do most of the talking on the afternoon we sat in the Steelworkers' Hall in Clifton. Mike, an energetic man with a deeply creased face and hands, let his memory roam with a certain hungry anger over those early years before unions. There were two kinds of wages, he said: one for Mexicans, and one for Anglos. "There were very few Mexicans who ever got to be tradesmen. If you were Mexican they thought you didn't have any skills, so they would put you on as a laborer. We used to get $2.80 a day."

Of the four categories of laborers, most worked under Classification D, otherwise known as Pick and Shovel. But there was little incentive to rise through the ranks; a worker's fate was pretty well sealed with the "laborer" brand. "If you worked real hard and got promoted to Labor C, they would give you a broom and two cents more," Mike explained. "For Labor B you would be helping some carpenter or somebody." And so on. Regardless of the classification, it was hard work, low pay, and Mexicans who did it. Anglos could work in the machine shop or other trades, and often they started there without previous experience. The machine shop in particular, according to Mike, had what was known as the "family deal"—sons of the men who worked there automatically moved into their fathers' positions when they came to work in the mine. "Their daddies broke the fall, gave them their classifications. So we could never get in there."

Scenes from South Africa that have shocked the international conscience— destitute, dusty shanty towns where black children grow up in the shadow of a privileged life they cannot touch— are not so different from what Arizona mining towns looked like when Harry Truman was president or, for that matter, John Kennedy. As late as the 1960s, segregation was absolute, extending to housing, schools, movie theaters, and social clubs. The first interracial couple in Morenci—a white woman who married a Mexican man—couldn't rent a house for decades. As one woman who grew up there put it, "There was a separate everything." In Ajo, Mexican-Americans were allowed to swim in the public pool once a week, on Wednesdays, just before the water was changed.

For a very long time this way of life was accepted on both sides as more or less unassailable. Eddie Marquez was born in Clifton in 1920 and has lived there most of his life; to him, discrimination is as tangible as geography. He pointed out its hills and valleys to me one morning from his back yard. "When P.D. built new houses up there in Morenci, we knew they would be for Anglos. We Mexicans lived in a part of town called Tortilla Flats. And the poor Indians! They had a place across the river called Indian Town—you can still see where it was—that was nothing but tents and shacks." It was difficult to bear in mind, during this graphic travelogue through recent American history, that Eddie was not talking about squatters' camps and homeowners' neighborhoods, but official company housing provided by Phelps Dodge for its employees.

In these isolated towns where "The Company" dictated virtually every physical aspect of life, the confines of race were inescapable. In this context it is easy to understand why Mexican-Americans were a crucial component of the union movement: it provided their only recourse against injustice.

Arizona miners began their slow, steady effort to organize around the turn of the century. Phelps Dodge has held dominion among the state's copper companies since 1900, when James Douglas bought Arizona Copper—the only copper mining company in the region that was then showing a profit—for the Phelps Dodge interest of New York. The corporation's history has been marked by some well-known clashes with its employees, many of which are described in George Leaming's *Labor and Copper in Arizona,* James Kluger's *The Clifton-Morenci Strike,* and James Byrkit's *Forging the Copper Collar.* The most notorious of these confrontations boiled over around the time the U.S. economy was mobilizing for World War I. In 1916, thanks to the booming demand for communications cable and copper shell jackets, Phelps Dodge enjoyed more than a 200 percent increase in net profits over the previous year. The meagerness of their wages, by comparison, rankled the miners, and their unions gained broad support. But in 1917 their broadside collided with superior force: in the quiet of an early July morning, a posse of sheriff's deputies and vigilantes rode into the streets of Bisbee, arrested some two thousand striking miners and sympathizers, forced them into waiting boxcars of the El Paso and Southwestern (a Phelps Dodge subsidiary), and hauled them over 173 miles of desert to a detention camp in central New Mexico, from which few ever returned to Bisbee.

The story of the Bisbee deportations has its place, though perhaps not a very public one, in the historical record. It is less well known that much of the labor leadership of this era was provided by Mexican-Americans. At that time the American Federation of Labor (AFL) sought to exclude minorities from the craft unions to avoid driving down wages. In fact, the Industrial Workers of the World (IWW) had organized in 1905 because of the general conviction that the conservative AFL would never represent the entire working class, including women and minorities. (This is discussed in *Women and the American Labor Movement* by Philip Foner.) So Hispanic workers had little to lose by taking their organizing efforts in an independent, militant direction. One of the state's first labor disputes, in July 1915, was a work stoppage known as the "Strike of the Mexicans" in the Ray, Arizona, mine. The strikers demanded and won a more equitable wage standard and the right to organize. The Mexicans in the Morenci mine followed suit in September, with the additional demand that white foremen cease harassing workers. The strike, which received little national support, was carried out under the banner of the Western Federation of Miners.

The following year this union rechristened itself the International Union of Mine, Mill and Smelter Workers, better known as "Mine-Mill." As a laborers' union, its Arizona membership was predominantly Mexican-American. In 1935, when the union affiliated with the Congress of Industrial Organizations (CIO), Bisbee had an officially recognized local charter and most other Arizona miners were looking toward the day when they would have the same.

The miners could be fired for union talk, so they organized in secret. A prominent rabble-rouser in the Morenci mine was David Velasquez. He'd started work there in 1937, and by the mid-1940s he was operating a bulldozer, as one of the few Mexican-Americans who'd managed to get into a better-paying position. Nevertheless, he was told by white co-workers that the only union he was entitled to join was the laborers' union, "with the other Mexicans." Velasquez wanted a union, so Mine-Mill it would have to be.

He and a handful of co-workers began calling meetings. "We had to meet up the river, in the cemetery," he recalled. "There was an old church up there, just four walls with no roof, that was our first meeting place. Or sometimes we would meet up on the mountains behind the mesquite bushes." When they felt they had enough support to risk an election, they called one, and Mine-Mill Local 616 was born in Morenci.

Their organizing efforts were severely limited by World War II, which called virtually every young miner to another front. The company, though, would find a way to go on extracting and selling copper. "During the war," Mike Baray explained, "there weren't hardly any men, so they brought in a bunch of Jamaicans, and a lot of women started working there too. They started some of the women out in the concentrator, operating the machinery, because they said the jobs were easier. But some worked in the pit, too. After, I think, about eight months, the Jamaicans left. They said the work was too hard. But the women stayed."

The old-time mining men speak of these women with rare and unmistakable respect. Eddie Marquez concedes that they were among the bravest and best mine workers Morenci has seen. "They were *tough*. You take Flossie Navarro and her sister Sue, they were a couple of toughies. And Rosie Patterson was tougher than heck, too. I knew them. They were good, hard-to-earth women, and they didn't take no bull."

Flossie Navarro is undeniably a toughie. She doesn't hesitate to explain how she felt about holding down what others considered a man's job: "Why, you didn't have no choice, you just did it. You couldn't say 'let a man do it.' You had to get right in there and lift and work right beside them. If the men gave me trouble, I'd just say, 'Well, damn ya, I'll show you I can do it if you can.' And that's what you had to do. You couldn't be a kiddie-baby and cry for them to give you a easy job. You had to pull your weight."

For most of the war years, the women in the Morenci mine had no union. They were organized briefly under the auspices of, oddly enough, the Amalgamated Clothing Workers of America, because it was considered a women's union. But by all accounts the women miners were militant. They pulled off a wildcat strike for better working conditions. One of their demands was for "women's things" (sanitary supplies) in the bathrooms. But according to Flossie, the incident that precipitated the strike was the firing of two sisters for allegedly "flirting with the floorwalkers." When a hearing was called, women packed the hall to testify about sexual harassment from the foremen. The strike lasted only two or three days; the women won their demands.

When the boys in uniform returned at last, nearly everyone—including, presumably, the company—expected the women to go home quietly. "Phelps Dodge gave us a pretty good round," Flossie says. "It wasn't the bosses up there in the front offices, it was the floorwalkers that gave us the trouble."

Eddie Marquez agrees. "The company was trying to push them out more or less on the sly. They said a woman couldn't lift those sample buckets, that they couldn't shovel on chains, and all that. They never said that *during* the war, just afterwards."

But by this time the Mine-Mill union had been officially chartered in Morenci, and it had a clause stating that "all people are created equal." The women joined, and the union stood behind any woman who wished to keep her job in the mine. Flossie Navarro and many others stayed on until they retired.

Marquez, who fought to get Mine-Mill organized in Morenci, says the union held onto its radical reputation during the postwar years. In 1946, Mine-Mill led a 107-day strike that ended with the signing of its first contract, which included equal pay for all new hires. The union had shown proof that three Arizona mining companies were hiring Anglo males as "helpers," at $6.36 per shift, and "other employees" (Latinos and Indians) as "laborers," at $5.21 per shift with no hope of raises or promotions.

Mike Baray feels that the presence of the union made a world of difference to Mexican workers, and eventually to all the workers. "After we got our union, other unions started coming in: the pipe fitters, the machinists, the electricians—all the craft trades. But we Mexicans were really the fighters. We used to call those others the 'me-too' unions."

Marquez confirms this view. In fact, it's his recollection that the craft unions, which had a primarily Anglo constituency, rarely even negotiated a contract. "We would negotiate, then the Anglos would come along and say, 'Just sign me, too.' The Mexicans fought harder because we were discriminated against—these other guys had all the cushy jobs. After we got the union it got better and better."

But with time the tide ebbed. Women retired from the mines, taking home the memory of their wildcat strike. The organizers of the original Strike of the Mexicans were also gone. The red-baiting started. In 1950, Mine-Mill was ousted from the CIO for refusing to denounce communism. Ed Marquez believes this happened because their union was getting too strong to control. "We had the whole Phelps Dodge chain organized. They figured there were too many of us Mexicans in there who were not going to give up, so they started calling us Communists. They even took it to the schools. Our kids suffered. We were always having to sign things, and I would ask, 'How can I be a Communist, when I don't even know what a Communist is?' A lot of the Anglo workers were playing the company's end of it. They thought they were the 'real Americans.' " Eventually members of the predominantly Anglo unions were also called Communists, but this came later and was generally less extreme.

And so, even if the Wild West had grown tame by the 1950s, the tradition of discrimination in the Arizona mines was apparently too tough to die. Roy Santa Cruz came into the Phelps Dodge mines in the mid-1950s, on what was called the "rustling shift." "It was like herding cattle. They would put everybody on the stage, where they could look you over. They would pull out ten guys in a group, and the foreman would say, 'You got a job for a day. I want you to take a big drink of water, because I don't want to see you at the fountain. All I want to see is asses and elbows.' All Mexicans went straight to the track gang or the smelter. There were no clean jobs for us."

In spite of previous agreements, which, on paper at least, had ended the dual wage scale and other overt forms of discrimination, inequities persisted. In 1967 the unions tackled segregation. Since housing is a condition of employment in a company town, it slowly dawned on miners that segregation was a union issue, not necessarily a permanent fact of life. By the end of an eight-month strike, they had scored a significant victory over housing discrimination in Phelps Dodge towns.

Eddie Marquez, by then a twenty-year veteran of his union, led the 1967–68 negotiations. "We met in the Steelworkers' Hall in Douglas: federal housing people, Phelps Dodge, and the union negotiating committee. By that time we had the Unity Council [a coalition of all thirteen unions in the Morenci mine], so we got the others to go with us: the machinists, the United Transportation Union, everybody. Those UTU guys were all Anglos—P.D. didn't let Mexicans on the trains at that time—but they were with us all the way."

Marquez says he'll never forget the climax of that meeting. "Pat Scanlon told the government officials that the reason the company could not let us into the better housing was because the Mexicans—this is what he said—the Mexicans were very dirty. He said it right in front of us. The negotiating committee was mostly Mexican-American. We all went wild, including the Anglos. Some of the UTU guys got up and said, 'If they're dirty, we are too! You go to a Mexican house and you won't see anything but *clean.*' We were *really* mad. Old Gonzalez started yelling, 'Remember the Alamo! We Mexicans don't quit!' "

M. Pat Scanlon was at that time assistant director for labor relations in Morenci. When I asked him twenty years later about the remark Marquez attributed to him, Scanlon denied having made it and did not remember the meeting in question. "I do remember some bargaining sessions in which that was discussed," he said. "Housing discrimination was a big subject at that time, because that was the period when things were changing in the U.S., and it was occasionally discussed with some heat. But I never would have said that."

By the time of the 1983 strike, Scanlon was vice-president of finance for the Phelps Dodge Corporation.

Some of the mine's most symbolic battles have centered around, of all things, locker rooms.

Well into the 1960s, Mexican and Anglo men still changed in separate facilities. The "Mexican locker rooms" were often inferior, and sometimes had only cold showers. In Morenci the change rooms consisted of one original facility divided by a specially constructed barrier. Such was the importance of segregation.

"The day they finally broke that wall down," recalls Mike Baray, "everything changed." A white co-worker complained that he would have to stop showering after work because he didn't intend to do it in the presence of a Mexican. Baray told him, with a smile, "Well, that's up to you."

But a new brand of discrimination was about to emerge. In the early 1970s, in response to a union-backed equal opportunity lawsuit, the mines at Ajo and Morenci agreed to hire women for the first time since the 1940s—this time without a declaration of war. It was a fight, nonetheless. Many women say they had their applications in to Phelps Dodge for years without acknowledgment. It took most of them more than a decade to make their way into skilled jobs in the Phelps Dodge mines. But they had families to support, and these communities offered a woman little else in the way of financial security. Clifton, for example, had car-hop jobs at the Sonic Burger, work at the laundromat, a handful of secretarial positions at the courthouse. It's understandable that many young women held out for work in the mine, in spite of the odds, which were rather daunting. All the old battles of discrimination, inequity, and harassment were resurrected.

Janie Ramon, a small woman with long dark hair and a cheerfully defiant disposition, was hired at the Ajo mine in 1973. She applied for the job after her father's death in an automobile accident cut short her college career; she was twenty years old. Janie was the first woman hired there as far as she knows (Ajo is a postwar mine), and she says without hesitation that it was terrible. She was shuffled around and harassed. "They didn't really know what to do with me. They asked if I would mop floors and clean bathrooms, which I did." Eventually she landed in the paint shop.

The following year, Betty Copeland and nine other women joined Janie at the Ajo pit. Betty weighed ninety-two pounds when she was hired as a laborer. While many men gave her a hard time, she found that some of her male co-workers were at first surprisingly encouraging. Later on, her father told her why. The men had placed bets on whether or not she would last two weeks. Some of them lost money; ten years later, Betty still hadn't quit.

As women's numbers in the mine continued to grow, Phelps Dodge handed them a place of their own—the old, inferior "Mexican locker rooms." Though it was probably not calculated, the statement was clearly symbolic; it was as if the Mexican men had handed their female co-workers a baton in a relay race and the next leg of the long, uphill run was going to be theirs.

In the years since, one fact has become apparent concerning these women: one should be careful about betting against them. Probably no one knows this better now than Phelps Dodge Copper. It was the clearest moral of the 1983 miners' strike.

Long before their contract expired at midnight on June 30, 1983, a consortium of more than twenty miners' unions attempted to reach a settlement on basic contract issues with all the major copper-producing companies. The practice of arriving at a standard set of terms for workers throughout an industry (known as pattern bargaining) has been used in mining for years. The miners knew times weren't good for the company, and they offered what they felt they could give: frozen wages for the duration of the next three-year contract, provided that they would continue to receive cost-of-living protection tied to the consumer price index. Four of the companies—Kennecott, Asarco, Magma Copper, and Inspiration Consolidated Copper—settled with little delay. The fifth, Phelps Dodge, refused the offer, asking the miners to accept further cuts in wage scales, benefits, holiday and vacation time, and an end to cost-of-living protection. Deciding that it was less than they could live with, Phelps Dodge miners at Morenci, Ajo, Bisbee, and Douglas walked off their jobs one minute after midnight on July 1. The normal cacophony of mining and smelting noises went dead still. Outside in the hot desert night, supporters waited along the road to clap and cheer as the strikers trailed away from the mine gates in a long caravan of cars and pickup trucks.

But Phelps Dodge didn't intend to let its operations be closed down. When the company began bringing in workers to replace them, striking miners lined up at the mine gates in protest. A few days later, when Phelps Dodge won a court injunction barring the miners from assembling at the gates, women strike supporters began holding mass pickets of their own. When the National Guard and riot troops from Arizona's Department of Public Safety (DPS) were summoned to occupy Clifton and Morenci, no one expected the strike to last much longer. The women organized rallies, pickets, and more rallies. They were tear-gassed and arrested. They swore and screamed and sometimes threw rocks, and *always* they showed up for the picket. Thirteen months later, when they were still on the line, a DPS officer remarked, in what was to become the most famous summation of the strike, "If we could just get rid of these broads, we'd have it made."

Fina Roman, president of the Morenci Miners Women's Auxiliary, responded to this statement before a gathering of supporters and the press. "They'll never be rid of us," she declared with controlled anger. "Do they ask us to forget the elderly being tear-gassed? Do they ask us to forget the beatings and arrests? To forget the past generations who handed down a sacred trust to preserve a dignified way of life won through tremendous sacrifices? Many did not live long enough to benefit from those sacrifices, yet because of them we enjoy those benefits today. Do they ask us to give them up without a fight?"

Anyone who expected a quiet surrender underestimated the stakes. Vicky Sharp, the wife of a Morenci miner and a former miner herself, explained, "They were asking us to take a step backward, and we said no."

If Vicky's words sound easy, they aren't. "Saying no" in these circumstances means putting earnings, possessions, friendships, and sometimes even lives on the line. Mining history is bound together with a long chain of strike martyrs and an even longer chain of bereaved families left behind to fight for their daily bread.

News media are often attracted to the external drama of a strike but rarely examine the personal stories that are dragged along beneath the surface: wages are lost, with no guarantee of when, or if, they will resume. Sofas and station wagons are repossessed. The arrival of the mail becomes a dreaded event, since it brings utility bills that can't be paid, shutoff notices, foreclosures, and eviction papers. Children's outgrown school clothes aren't replaced, and their birthdays pass without presents. There is little glamour in impoverished lives.

Given the risks, it's hard to believe the decision to strike has ever been made lightly or that it could be a simple gamble on big money. Mainstream news media have frequently managed, intentionally or not, to create a caricature of strikers that associates the words "overpaid" and "greedy" with "labor," as surely as Florida has oranges and Arabs have oil. In fact, wages—when they are even at issue in a strike— are generally secondary to other considerations such as safe working conditions, health care, and retirement benefits (and sometimes, as in the case of the air traffic controllers' strike, the claim that working conditions affect the public safety). In recent years especially, strikes in the United States have not been "for more" but rather, as Vicky Sharp said, against a step backward.

Five days after the Arizona copper strike began, an editorial in the *Arizona Republic* (the state's largest newspaper) pronounced that the days were gone when labor could get away with "bloated agreements that merely passed along the costs of lower productivity, higher wages and golden fringe benefits to the captive and unquestioning U.S. market." It continued, "Jobless Butte [Montana] miners undoubtedly would be very happy to accept what Phelps Dodge's miners have refused." The public seemed willing enough to go along with this assessment: as long as someone, somewhere, was willing to settle for less, the miners were wrong to ask for what they had. Virtually no attention was given to the fact that the miners had already volunteered to freeze their wages.

Spokespeople for the other copper companies continued to express contentment with the unions' proposed compromise, but Phelps Dodge officials pointed to the company's $75 million losses in 1982 and maintained that they could afford to offer nothing but cuts. Tom McWilliams, assistant director of labor relations for Phelps Dodge, told the *Arizona Republic*, "We are a separate company and have no connections with those [other copper-producing] firms. We feel we can't continue on the same road we've been on for the last 15 years, making settlements not consistent with the economic condition of the industry." Vice-President Pat Scanlon knew a strike was coming, because the unions were committed to the pattern-bargaining precedent. He admitted later, "If you'd asked me, at that point, what would be the likely outcome, I'd say, 'Well, the unions will see that we'll be able to operate in the face of a strike, and they'll find some way to come to an agreement that gives us what we need, and will be face-saving for them. We'll work it out, once they see that the alternative is that we're going to keep the place running.' "

On their side of the fence, as Fina Roman so eloquently pointed out, the miners saw the erosion of their standard of living as not only personally dangerous but as an insult to their ancestors. In their tiny, isolated towns they had been steeped for half a century in their own labor traditions and had extracted a sense of pride that preserved them through hard times. When asked about their reasons for striking, most mentioned before anything else the community's self-respect and the parents who struggled all their years for a decent living. The miners also had a sophisticated awareness of pattern bargaining and the connections between themselves and other workers: if they gave in, the miners in other towns and other states, the railroad workers, and the auto workers would suffer.

The women who carried their own flag into this battle were miners' wives and daughters, and a few were miners themselves. Their grandfathers had walked out of the Morenci mine in 1915 or left Bisbee by cattle car in 1917. They had grown up with the union, a tool as familiar to them as a can opener or a stove. They knew exactly where they would be without it.

Jean Lopez, an outgoing, youthful-looking mother of teenagers, immediately described herself to me as "just a mom" but gave the impression of being a great deal more. Jean spent her entire childhood in sight of the smokestacks of the Morenci smelter. Her grandfather Brigham Hernandez fought to get the Mine-Mill union in Morenci; before that, he was railroaded out of Bisbee in the 1917 deportations. Jean, who was active in the Morenci Miners Women's Auxiliary, learned about unions from her father, who's retired now from P.D. "The thing that really sticks in my mind about growing up here," she said, "is that every three years there was a strike. *Every* three years. We had to make sacrifices to keep going. We were a family of six, and they didn't make much money at that time.

"This was just part of life—life in a mining town. After the strike would end, my family would start planning for the next one. When another strike was coming up, we knew we would be eating beans and tortillas again, for as long as it would take. But it didn't really bother us. My memories of all that are not bad. I admire my father, never being a scab, never even thinking of it. The unions were tight here. Almost everybody in the area was raised that way.

"It wasn't until I got married that I really understood the importance of a union. I married a miner, of course. He and I went to high school together. My husband was also born and raised here—his father worked for the company, and his grandfather; it goes on and on and on. So after we got married, then *I* was in charge of the finances. I would ask my mother, 'God, how did you make it?' I only had one kid then—she'd had four! And she'd say, 'Well, you know God will never let you die of hunger. But you have to have the guts to stand up for what you believe.' "

The strike of 1983 turned out to be in every way more difficult than any she had known before. Like everyone who supported the strike from the beginning, she gave up a great deal for her beliefs. She also can't imagine having done otherwise.

Lydia Gonzalez Knott weathered the strike with her mother, son, and two daughters in a sea-blue house on a street that, like most streets in Clifton, is never called by name. The street sign is wrong anyway. The hill is so steep and cut with gullies that a small footbridge leads from the street to the house. The front porch, with wrought-iron railings and floorboards worn smooth by generations of neighborhood children, overlooks the steep valley that holds the San Francisco River and the town of Clifton. Up at the head of the valley is the entrance to the Morenci mine. Lydia has lived in this house all her life.

She is a miner's daughter, a miner's sister, and, since 1979, a miner herself. "When I was twenty-five and divorced with three kids to support," she explained, "I knew it was time to go to work for the Company."

Lydia was initially hired as a laborer in the mill and was later promoted to mill repair, the only woman on a crew of sixty-six. "I enjoyed the work, because I was learning to do a lot of new things. I worked with jackhammers, sledgehammers, air wrenches that weigh 100 pounds. I can operate a 160-ton crane."

But when the strike came, there was no question about her course of action. "My dad was president of the Boilermakers for over twenty-five years. He worked for the company for thirty-four years—my mom is a union widow. My dad was strong in the union, and gave it all he had. When the unions went out on strike, my brother and I didn't have any choice. We knew if we crossed that picket line, Dad would come out of his grave and pull on our feet at night."

Gloria Blase, like Lydia, is a miner who feels rooted in her small town. Her mother is a Papago Indian, and her father a Mexican who spent his life in a Phelps Dodge mine. When the strike was called, Gloria was clear about where her loyalties would lie. "I'm a striker," she says, "because I believe in what my dad fought for. He worked as a crane operator for fifteen years before P.D. gave him the same benefits as the white operators." She also learned about unions from her father. She, too, grew up knowing that for several months out of every third year, there would be nothing but beans and tortillas.

For all they have in common, Gloria has never met Lydia or Jean; nor is she likely to, because she lives in Ajo, Arizona. It's possible, barely, to drive between Ajo and Clifton in a day. It's a stunning drive, crossing through boulder-filled canyons and deep blue mountain ranges that rise up from the desert like coral reefs out of an ocean floor. It's also a spectacularly hot and wearisome drive, and the traveler's patience with stunning natural beauty is apt to wear thin. But it's probably the only way to get a genuine feeling for the distance between these towns—a distance I never could quite believe in, for on reaching Ajo I always found it cloaked in the same yellow haze of dust that rises over Morenci. I found also that on striking up a conversation with someone like Gloria Blase, her words would match to the letter those of Jean or Lydia, someone I'd talked with two hundred miles ago.

It's a mystery. The mines are remote: far from one another and from anything else. Bisbee, the old stronghold of the Arizona copper industry, is in the southeastern corner of the state, barely six miles from the Mexican border. Douglas hugs the border several miles to the east. Clifton and Morenci (big-city newspapers tend to connect their names with a hyphen) lie more than a hundred slow, winding miles to the north. These sister towns, and the mine that served as birth canal to both, are tucked into the mountains at the edge of the Colorado Plateau, a great rim of high, forested rifts and valleys curving across the state toward the Grand Canyon. Far to the west of Clifton and Morenci lies a vast, dry stretch of Papago Indian land. (In 1986 the tribe changed its name to Tohono O'odham.) On the other side of the reservation is Ajo; the word is Spanish for "garlic," though no one remembers much of anything green ever growing there. It may be a corruption of the Papago word *au'auho*, or "paint," since in earlier centuries the mines there were a source of ores the Indians used for making red body paint.

The nearest city of any size, Tucson, is roughly in the center of the Ajo-Morenci-Bisbee triangle of mines, and a long drive from any. For the most part, people who live in the Phelps Dodge towns don't leave, unless it's to work on one of the ranches in the outlying areas. The women, especially, tend to have little mobility. As Stella Baray put it, "It's a family town. We stay here."

In nature there is a phenomenon called convergent evolution: through time, similar forces acting on unrelated organisms in widely separated places manage to create similar-looking creatures. Thus, for example, deserts on nearly every continent are home to some animal that looks like a sand-colored gerbil and some plant that looks like a cactus.

History has done something like this to the copper-mining towns of Arizona. In spite of their isolation from one another, the same force has wrenched and sanded each of them into a shape that is noticeably the same. Identical themes surface in the lives of the people rooted there. That they haven't somehow conferred with one another like witnesses to an accident, to synchronize the story, is unbelievable. It seems more likely that the great mineral hole that gapes open into each of these towns leads down into the earth like those ancient tunnels under the Andes. You could almost believe a person could walk down into one of these mines one day and surface in another, a hundred miles away.

The women who walked the line thirty years earlier in Grant County, New Mexico, and, for that matter, in Harlan County, Kentucky, would feel at home if they were to show up here. They would certainly have had stories to swap on the picket line during the strike of 1983. Basically, it had all been done before. No one can claim that the history of the Arizona copper strike was the first story of the coming of age of women in a mining town; they had grown up a long time ago.

But there were differences. Virginia Chacon, one of the women who razed stereotypes in the *Salt of the Earth* strike, said thirty years later that the status quo returned after the strike. Even the film—which was ostensibly about these women's newfound pride in their accomplishments—didn't make any big difference, she told writer Tom Miller in a *Cinéaste* article. "A lot of the women are still very much oppressed by the men. There's no difference in the home, I'm sorry to say. That's the way it was, and that's the way it's going to be. It didn't change my life. You can't teach an old dog new tricks."

The women who held the line in Clifton, Morenci, and Ajo in 1983 and 1984 are whistling a different tune. They say their hometowns will not be the same again, ever. It's true that women have been assaulted by police and jailed before and have seen their children threatened. Even in the U.S.A., women have stood up to martial law. But this was the 1980s. If a woman can run for vice-president, they said, then a woman can hold a strike together, even if it means her husband has to iron his own shirts. They gave the impression that if the old dogs around here didn't learn some new tricks, they'd be left tied to the post.

These are the same women who say they now understand what "solidarity" means, and that it isn't just in Poland. Their unions and union auxiliaries mean more now than they ever did—at a time when unionism seems pale and barely breathing in the United States —and they've found organizational skills and leadership capabilities they never suspected they had. Women who used to be too shy to speak up at a PTA meeting have now crossed the country addressing crowds of thousands. To them, what happened in 1983 was much more than a strike. It gave them a new perspective on a power structure in which they were lodged like gravel in a tire.

Shirley Randall is the kind of person who doesn't speak until she's sure of what she's about to say. She is tall and quiet, with an angular body undisguised by a union cap and T-shirt. Her demeanor is modest in the extreme. During the strike she was elected to be responsible for very large sums of money, as treasurer of the Morenci Miners Women's Auxiliary. In the past, she says, she didn't think of herself as a capable person. She dropped out of high school and didn't collect the nerve to go back for her diploma until she was twenty-eight and a mother of four. "I thought I was dumb, I really did. When I took those classes, I never did speak up and ask questions." But she got the diploma.

Soon afterward, in 1975, she was hired as a general laborer in the Morenci mine. Four years later she quit because of continuous sexual harassment. "Men in this town . . ." she says simply, in a tone that explains a whole way of being born, living, and dying. "I put up with so much from the men. They thought the wife's place was in the home.

"But when a lot of those same men went out on strike, you better believe they were glad to see me out there on the line."

# 2

# On the Line

**A** visitor to Clifton soon learns there is no such thing here as a street address. Instead, residents happily offer elaborate, mind-boggling directions: "Turn down the next road after the double-wide trailer, it's near the old water tank, not the new one, then you pass through two dips and then just look for her old T-bird." The principal compass points are "up toward the mine" and "down toward the freeway, like you're going out of town." In between lies a maze of landmarks significant only to the trained eye: dry stream beds, bends in the road, wheelless vehicles propped up in perpetuity on concrete blocks. In Clifton, whole lives are lived in relation to these things.

A stranger passing through is apt to feel like a conspicuous and slightly embarrassed foreigner. Not unwelcome, by any means—any friend of a friend of a resident of Clifton will not want for hospitality there. A pot of *menudo* is always simmering on somebody's stove in case of drop-in guests, and a spare bedroom waits, still adorned with Michael Jackson posters and 4-H Club ribbons collected by a child now married and gone. But a visitor to these homes can never completely blend in. A great deal is assumed, on both sides, and the assumptions simply don't overlap.

"Oh, sure, you know Louise," a Clifton man insisted to me one afternoon. "She's the one that drives around in that truck with the dogs in the back." He could tell me the names of her dogs but not the streets that would take me to her house. The roads and hills were as familiar to him as the features of a grandchild's face, and as impossible to describe objectively.

Stranger that I am to the territory, I can give it official delineations: Greenlee County, eastern Arizona, fifteen miles as the crow flies from the New Mexico border. Arizona Highway 666 trails northwest through the valley, following the snaky course of the San Francisco River through Clifton, winding six miles up the hill to Morenci, skirting the mine, and finally striking a shadowed path through the high pine forests of the White Mountain Apache reservation.

According to *Arizona: The Land and the People*, the Morenci area belonged to the reservation at one time, having been deemed useless enough to give to the Apaches. The U.S. government promptly took it back when Anglo prospectors hit pay dirt there. The Morenci pit has since proven to be one of the richest, longest-yielding sources of copper ore in the world.

Modern-day Morenci, a prototypical company town, has no city government, no elected officials, and no police force. All municipal functions are in the hands of the Phelps Dodge Corporation, as are the town's only shopping plaza, bowling alley, and snack bar; even the books in the library are subject to approval by P.D. management. The high school football field, the water and electricity, the houses and the land under them, the cacti, the stones and the dust belong to Phelps Dodge. An old-timer in Morenci once told me, "This town only has two laws." He led me by the elbow into the street where we could get a clear view of the twin stacks of the Phelps Dodge smelter, and he pointed: "There they are."

Clifton is another story. Here Phelps Dodge owns the part of the ground that begins twenty-five feet down and continues, presumably, to China. But from the topsoil up, the town is independent and has fought for nearly a century to stay that way. Clifton's shallow roots imply anything but impermanence.

Clifton sits in the river valley with its back to the canyon wall. (Historians think the name is a slurring of "Cliff Town.") The city hall is on a hill across the river, but the pulse of Clifton beats in Chase Creek. The street is aptly named: after any heavy rain it is, for a brief spell, a creek. Chase Creek is flanked on either side by an uninterrupted row of brick buildings, aged but solid, built at the turn of the century. High above the street, doves and pigeons pass deftly through broken windows to their roosts in attics. There's a combined air of medieval Europe and the cinematic Old West; the street is narrow and steep, and each building shares its wall with the next so that no alleys run between them. If you turn onto Chase Creek from Highway 666, you have no choice but to proceed uphill past the imposing facades of the Wagon Wheel bar, the steelworkers' and machinists' union halls, two Mexican restaurants, and a dance hall and tavern known simply as the Social Club. Also called the "Mexican Elks," it was established years ago when the Elks Club wouldn't admit Mexicans.

Inside the Social Club, booths surround a large dance floor, and a long window opens onto the bar. Elk and deer heads glower above it, each with a plaque bearing the name of the man or boy who took it down. Over the front door a remarkably large, shiny stuffed fish leaps through a bright blue sea painted on the wall.

Technically one must be voted into the Social Club by the membership.

Once, years ago, someone was blackballed—Clifton's priest, for reasons now vague. A parishioner said, "Okay, who volunteers to tell him he can't join the Social Club?" Another vote was quickly taken, and the priest was admitted.

The Catholic Church is a hundred yards farther up Chase Creek. Beyond it, the brick structures give way to frame houses with upstairs porches, honeysuckle vines, borders of dahlia and marigold, concrete urns, and handmade signs announcing the family name. The yards and porches have been planted and trellised to the lawless, resplendent extreme. In contrast to the long tracts of identical Phelps Dodge houses in Morenci, homes in Clifton are spectacularly individual.

While people in distant cities clamp iron grills over the windows and warn their children about talking to strangers, Clifton's front doors have gone for generations without being locked. Four men comprise the police force—about one per thousand residents. The telephone directory could be torn in half by a small child. When people here try to describe what happened in 1983, they quickly become exasperated. "It's hard to explain this to somebody who doesn't live here," one woman told me. "You just can't understand what we felt."

How *does* it feel to someone who's at home in a neighborhood of unlocked doors—who calls every police officer in town by his first name—when the governor marches in four hundred armed state troopers, armored personnel carriers, Huey helicopters, and seven units of the National Guard?

Clifton was stunned. Diane McCormick shook her head, remembering the day they came in. "All I could think was, this isn't Russia. We're supposed to be a free country here. I couldn't believe what was happening to us, and I still can't. We were under martial law. I just couldn't understand *why.*"

Diane and her sisters—Berta, Lolly, and Cindy—are an energetic quartet, dark-eyed, direct, quick to laugh and slow to get mad. Their parents raised them to be good Catholic girls, but also to act on their beliefs, and this they do. During the strike and after, mention of the "Delgado sisters" was likely to provoke a woolly reminiscence from anyone in town.

None of the sisters is a miner, but Phelps Dodge could no more be separated from their lives than could honey from a bee's. Their father is a retired miner; Cindy and Berta married miners; Berta and Diane have worked in the company store. They were all active in the strike, they say, "even before day one."

Berta is a born organizer. Diane says that for weeks before the strike started, Berta talked constantly about reviving the Morenci Miners Women's Auxiliary, which had existed since the 1940s but always died down between strikes. After meeting with union officials, they and three other friends convened the auxiliary. According to Berta, no one paid much attention at that point. Once, several weeks into the strike, during a meeting attended by nearly the whole town at Clifton's American Legion Hall, someone asked if the auxiliary was around. "I stood up—I was way in the back—and I yelled, 'Yes, it's still around!' I gave them my phone number, which got a big laugh, because I told them, 'It's unlisted, so here it is.' " After that, Berta's phone began to ring.

But revival was slow. "The women didn't want to be involved in anything," Diane said. "Their husbands would say, 'No, you can't go to the union hall.' It was always a place for just men, see? They didn't want the women going in there. All the time we were trying to recruit women into coming, they would say, 'Go into the union hall? With all those men?' We told them, 'Get off it. Jeez, wake up. It's a new generation!' "

"It wasn't like later in the strike, where all you saw was women on the line," Berta agreed. One of the women's first and most enduring tasks would be to get people out on the line for the shift changes.

Holding a picket line is a simple act with many levels of consequence. It's the strike's public face, meant to elicit support, discourage would-be strikebreakers, and serve as a constant reminder to the company that the union is alive. But it is far more than a symbolic protest: if it's respected by outside unions, the picket can be as functional as a tourniquet. Until the strike is settled, the Teamster driver is honor-bound not to bring in smelter parts from Detroit or to haul out ore. No matter what the railroad boss wants, if a picket is on the tracks, a union engineer can't take the train across.

Picketers who hold up their signs at the gate know their strike is as fragile or as strong as their interlocked arms. For as long as it lasts, holding this line is the striker's job. Sometimes it doesn't amount to much more than passing the time with co-workers and friends in the long, uncharted days of waiting to work again. And sometimes it is a harder, more dangerous job than mining ore.

At the 5:30 A.M. shift change on July 1, the first day of the walkout, a company convoy of more than 150 vehicles rolled up to the Morenci gate with Phelps Dodge security guards in the lead. The company had drafted office workers and foremen into service as replacements for the 1,400 workers who left their jobs. Company officials announced that this makeshift crew, along with the 600 nonunion personnel who remained, would work in twelve-hour shifts to keep the mine and smelter operating at 40 percent capacity. It was a bold gesture; Phelps Dodge hadn't kept its gates open through a strike since 1959.

Strikers lined up on the roadside shouted amiably at first as the parade approached: "You don't want to go in there, they'll work you like slaves. Come on out, we'll buy you breakfast." As cars continued to pass through the gate, the mood darkened. Friendly dissuasions turned to succinct cries of "scab!" Men pounded on car hoods, and a few were asked to stand clear of the traffic. But apart from these flares of temper, the morning remained calm.

Even so, by the following day Phelps Dodge officials had asked the Department of Public Safety to increase its presence in Morenci and were discussing a restraining order to limit picketing. Vice-President Scanlon conceded that there had been no violence, but according to an article in the *Arizona Republic* of July 2, he justified the request on the basis of the "large and unruly mob" that had congregated and said there had been "threats" and "repeated incidents of mass picketing." P.D. also organized shift-change convoys and greatly enlarged its force of security guards, moves that Dick Boland, personnel services director, said were meant "to make workers feel more comfortable about crossing the picket lines."

In Douglas, 150 miles south, an injunction naming five individuals and two hundred "John Does" was served on strikers, ordering them to appear in court and restricting their presence on the picket line. By the end of the week Phelps Dodge had won similar injunctions in Morenci and in Ajo, where several hundred strikers had lined the entrance roads blowing whistles and ringing cowbells to discourage workers from crossing the picket line.

In Ajo the restraining order not only limited gate pickets but also, according to Scanlon, prohibited "setting up a gauntlet of persons or automobiles" along the roads to the mine gates (in a town where essentially all roads lead to the mine gates). Furthermore, the order stated that "unless defendants' illegal or nonpeaceful acts are restrained, inhabitants of Ajo may be deprived of electrical energy or water." These utilities, naturally, are owned by Phelps Dodge.

Caught in the bind of the company town, the Ajo strikers felt blackmailed. Obviously, the company was better prepared for a strike than they were, and it had the power to cut off the flow of basic necessities to their homes and families. Strikers complained that they were being denied their rights to assembly and free speech. But they obeyed the restraining orders, playing for time. A settlement couldn't be far away. The unions were trying desperately to find a compromise to which Phelps Dodge would agree; the United Steelworkers of America hired a prestigious New York labor consulting firm to help form a plan that would lead to a settlement. Union spokesman Cass Alvin assured strikers, "What we'd like to have happen is to end this thing before it takes on a life of its own." In the meantime, union leaders said, with Phelps Dodge's mines and smelter lines limping along on a fraction of the normal work force, it couldn't survive long without them.

The company had other ideas. "For the first six weeks," recalled Vice-President Scanlon, "we were remarkably successful in operating, and we were waiting for the phone call from the unions that would say, 'Can you meet me off the record so we can settle this thing?'

"But six weeks into the strike, our supervisors and engineers and clerks, who were out there running locomotives and so forth, were pooping out, and their work wasn't getting done. So even though we were getting more people returning every day, it was beginning to level off. We saw that in order to get back to more normal arrangements we were going to have to start hiring permanent replacements for the strikers."

Berta Chavez recalls that about that time they began picketing the employment office. "P.D. had ads in the paper, so people from Colorado and places like that would read it and say, 'Oh, there's a good job,' and they'd come down. We figured if we picketed there nobody would come in for the applications. I think we changed a lot of people's minds. When they found all of us picketing—there must have been a hundred or more—they'd say, 'You're on strike?' They didn't realize P.D. was advertising for scab labor.

"I remember this one couple that came and asked where the employment office was. They had a family and everything there in the truck. We said, 'You don't want to go up there.' We told them the situation and they just turned around and went back to Nevada."

Phelps Dodge stepped up recruitment on all fronts. In Arizona, one of twenty right-to-work states, employees in a unionized industry aren't required to join a union, and, conversely, employers need not honor picket lines, union jurisdiction, or the sanctity of a striker's job. A letter mailed on July 7 stated: "If you are a present employee and want to be sure of having your old job back when the strike is over, you should return to work immediately, before your job is given to someone else."

Patience turned to panic: a striker's labor is his or her only bargaining chip. Skeleton crews of foremen and secretaries weren't a threat, but if Phelps Dodge planned on massive recruitment, the strikers couldn't stand by and watch.

Early on the morning of August 8, busloads of workers were spotted going into the Morenci mine. Word ran through town like a grass fire. Carmina Garcia, a retired school bus driver married to a retired miner, was at home in

Clifton. To her mind the danger was clear: "We knew if P.D. got all those people in there, they weren't going to give us a contract," she explained. "It was 11:30 in the morning when Beaver came and told us, 'Hey, we wanna close down the mine—we *have* to close down the mine. Something's going to happen. They're taking in mattresses and taking in food, so we'd better have some people up there.' "

Carmina went. Her husband, Willie, was away for the morning, so she called her friends Jessie and Velia, the mayor's wife. "We went around the side to check the Columbine gate and saw that the trucks were coming in and out through the back, bringing in food, cots, and whatnot. Then they told us there were more people going through the main gate, so we went to the main road and there we saw the people were coming in *buses*. They were scared to come to work. Don't you see, they shouldn't have been working— there was a strike! So P.D. hired those buses to bring in the scabs from Safford, and even a few from Clifton. They would stop and pick them up and drive them around back.

"We had to put a stop to it. People from Duncan, Safford, *everywhere*, were coming in to help us close it down. They said in the papers there were one or two thousand, but it was more than that, I know. As time went on you started seeing a little bit more and a little bit more.

"And P.D. was bringing in stuff left and right. The helicopter was coming in with food, because a lot of them were going to stay in the mine, once they got in. P.D. was telling them, 'They're going to kill you.' I know this because there was a guy working in there that my husband and I know real well—later on he quit. He told us that his foreman told him, 'Here, go kill those sons of bitches! Look at that mob, they're going to kill you anyway!' And threw a gun in his truck! David didn't want it— he threw it out of his truck and left it there. But they were trying to get everybody scared.

"We weren't going to kill them, honey. All we were asking was for them to *get out* of there. That's all we ever asked."

Berta Chavez and her sisters were there, of course. Berta was up above the mine. "We could look down into the mine where the scabs were. They had their hats over their faces; I guess they were afraid, because we had control. And they'd come in disguises. One guy came in with a paper sack over his head, with holes cut for the eyes. They were ashamed because they knew they shouldn't be in there scabbing for P.D.

"Outside, there were people from the mine gate all the way to the general office. It was full of people. A couple of thousand, I'd say. We had our trucks there—we backed them up—and we had our beer and our ice chests—it was just like a picnic. We were just waiting. We gave them till 12:00 to get the scabs out. We said after 12:00, nobody comes in or out."

Diane was on the opposite side of the crowd, closer to the road. "P.D. did send people home," she said, "and we were happy. Our union leaders said 'Okay, let them through.' We let them through, yelling 'hurray!' and laughing and screaming. That's exactly what we wanted, all the scabs out. But I started looking around and said, 'Hey, wait a minute. Not everyone is out of there, not even half.' We were there in the morning and saw all those cars going in, and not that many, really, were coming out. Tom Aguilar, the mayor, had been sitting and counting the cars, going and coming. So what they did is they kept some in. They said they needed a 'skeleton crew,' that they couldn't just shut it down, they had to do it gradually. I said, 'Uh-uh.' "

The crowd, a whole town threatened with the loss of livelihood, was as volatile as kerosene-soaked tinder. This last news was enough to strike the spark. Plans of action sprang up spontaneously and began to roar: the crowd was ready to march into the mine and take it over. Berta asked her friend Liza, who worked in the mill, "What should we do, once we get in?" Liza said, "Just follow me and push all kinds of buttons."

At noon, P.D. officials appeared at the gate, conferred briefly, and agreed not to bring in the next shift. Diane said, "Our union leaders told us, 'They've given us their word, they're going to shut down. We have to be peaceful, we have to maintain.' But I heard Berta up on top, saying, 'No, don't believe them.' I was yelling, 'No! They've lied to us before! Don't trust them.' "

Berta said, "Sure, I knew better. They've messed us up so many times. But our union president said, 'Brothers, let's wait and see what happens.' In my mind I kept thinking something was going on. See, we could have had full control of the mine, taken it over. We could have made them close down until we settled, the way a strike is supposed to go. But the guys were saying, 'Let's show them our word is good, that we're good people standing behind our company.' That's what they decided, so we obeyed. We had our hopes high so many times. That was one of the times."

The company had agreed that nothing more would be brought in. Word passed down the hill, and the crowd was jubilant, though not quite ready to believe that no more busloads of workers, food, and cots would be coming up the road. They stayed to watch. Carmina and her friends were in the middle of the throng. "We got stuck," she recalled, laughing. "DPS closed the highway. There were a lot of tourists coming from up north, campers coming down from Springerville—we were on the main highway, 666—but they wouldn't even let them through. DPS cars were all along the highway, and in the P.D. parking lot, hundreds of cars."

Carmina, who is something like the force of a typhoon packed into a polyester pants suit, never fails to get excited as she relates the events of that day. She produces photos from her scrapbook to confirm her estimates of crowd sizes, numbers of cars, weapons carried by DPS officers. Frequently, she leans forward and yells to emphasize a point.

"So then a WHOLE BUNCH of officers marched down the highway, like an army. They marched DOWN with their riot sticks and guns and told us to move OUT of the road. They kept marching back and forth, back and forth; they made us so mad. But we couldn't move because there were people and cars EVERYWHERE, and it was getting dark. We were stuck. My husband was down here, and we were up there, and there was no way to get out.

"By around six o'clock it was raining and pouring but we STAYED there. The DPS parked their cars and closed the highway. It was 9:30 that night when I got back home. My husband knew I was up there; he had gone to see the horses that day, and when he came back he kept waiting and waiting. He tried going up, but a deputy told him, 'No need to go up there, you can't get through.' A lot of people were going through anyway. They would say, 'We live up there,' whether they did or not. Everybody I knew that wasn't working was up there—kids, husbands, wives, everybody.

"When I finally got home my husband said, 'What's happened, what's happened? I tried to get up there but I couldn't; they wouldn't let me.' 'You should have gone up there!' I said. But he said, 'Oh, they told me . . . ' He's the type, you know, that wouldn't dare. Whatever they told him, well, that's it. Now I'm the type that I don't care what they tell me, I'm STILL going to go through, one way or another. I'll tell them *something!*

"That night Bert Drucher called from Governor Babbitt's office. They couldn't get hold of Tom Aguilar, the mayor, or Eddie Marquez, or none of the Democratic party—they were all over there at the courthouse. The only name they could find, after those guys, was me. I belong to the Precinct Committee Women.

"So he said to me, 'Carmina, can you please get hold of Lalo [Eduardo] Marquez and tell him to tell the union that Governor Babbitt is on his way; he just had trouble on account of it's been raining. He says everybody has to have a ten-day cooling-off period—the unions, P.D., everybody.' I says, 'NO WAY! I just came from up there. Tell Babbitt to get here, and we're NOT COOLING OFF. He has to close it down until the unions sign a contract.' "

Laughing, Carmina remembered that Drucher was not amused. "He said,

'Carmina! You just pay attention to what I'm telling you!' Oh, he hollered at me. He was wanting to set up the ten-day cooling. I told him to FORGET it.

"But I guess P.D. had already called them, and they had already planned it that very night. We all went home, and in those ten days the union officials tried to talk to [Vice-President] Bolles, trying to meet together, and waiting and waiting. The unions wanted everybody out of the plant. They met at the conference room down here at the Clifton courthouse, and there was Governor going back and forth."

News of the Morenci shutdown crossed the state in record time. Janie Ramon, the first woman in the Ajo mine, was now reporting secretary for her union, the International Chemical Workers Union Local 703. She took it upon herself to try and stir up some resistance to Phelps Dodge in Ajo.

I met Janie several weeks later in the Ajo Union Hall—a mobile home equipped with a few chairs and a rickety aluminum table, an ancient coffee machine, and a TV. "On August 8, when things started happening in Morenci," Janie said, rapping her knuckles precariously against the table, "the strikers up there claimed we didn't have any courage, that we were meek little mice. I was with a girlfriend and my boyfriend that day, and the three of us went around to the Ajo bars to tell people what we were doing on the line. There were a lot of scabs in some of the bars, but I thought if I talked to them and told them what harm they were doing the union, it might make them change their minds. But they weren't having anything to do with me. We ended up getting into a fight. We left.

"The next day, August 9, was when the women blocked traffic at the mine gate." The men, she said, were away from the gates trying to stop individual cars. "Everyone had bats, but no one used them. We didn't hurt anybody. We were there again the next day. I was on a side gate. All of a sudden six cars pulled up and a driver got out of every car with a machine gun—an M-16. That was ridiculous. Not one of us had any weapon."

Gloria Blase was there too and clearly remembers the M-16s. "It was the state troopers, the DPS. They jumped out with their machine guns pointing straight at us. They kept telling us, 'Move, you're next, go ahead. Just try us.' There were three women where I was standing, and they [DPS] were aiming right at our heads. A striker grabbed a camera and started taking pictures, so they pulled the machine guns back to their shoulders.

"I hadn't done anything; I was just at the picket line. Earlier, some guy threw a beer can at a DPS car. It was after that that all the DPS showed up.

Then, later on, some windows were broken out of a scab van going by, so the cops came again, in four cars. They all jumped out with their batons, but they didn't know what to do. One of them said, 'Somebody without a shirt did it.' But all four guys had taken off their shirts, so they couldn't arrest anybody. It was just a show of force."

Later that morning Janie Ramon left for the union hall. On the way she was stopped and arrested for assault, as a result of the fight in the bar two nights before. "I just couldn't believe it. My boyfriend made a remark, and they said he was obstructing justice, so they arrested him too. That afternoon we were to be arraigned. They brought me in the hallway, and I stood there for an hour, and then they said the *paperwork* wasn't done and I couldn't be arraigned until the next day, so I had to spend the night in there. I was released the next day at 9:00 A.M. They told me if I touched the people who filed charges against me I would be thrown in jail for sixty days. No appeal."

The judge, Ajo Justice of the Peace Helen Gilmartin, was widely regarded as a Phelps Dodge employee, and Ajo strikers complained about conflict of interest. They found it a bit galling that she drove around town in a car with vanity plates reading "PD AJO." When I called Gilmartin's office to ask about this, I was told only that prior to her appointment to the bench six months before the strike, she had indeed worked in the security division of Phelps Dodge. (Eventually, in September 1983, she agreed to excuse herself from hearing cases involving strikers.) According to Janie and others arrested at that time, the judge offered jailed strikers the choice of crossing the picket line or staying behind bars.

Judge Gilmartin and Janie Ramon are relatives, a fact that increased Janie's bitterness. "I told her, 'Don't tell me I'm going to sit in jail or go to work, because I'll sit in here and I'll rot before I cross a picket line!' I have two kids, six and nine, and they understood. I told them we were fighting for our rights—I've always told them we shouldn't be led around by the nose. If I crossed that picket line, it would be like letting the company slap me in the face every day. I wouldn't have any respect for myself. I told my kids it would be like bowing down to someone, and you don't have to bow down to anyone. You're a person, and everyone has rights. I've always taught them that.

"On August 19 I received a suspension letter from P.D. for strike misconduct on August 10. That's the day I was in jail. A few days later I was terminated for 'blocking mine gate traffic.' I'd been standing at gates that were already locked and chained. Nobody went by there, or through, or even attempted."

Gloria Blase was also terminated for alleged strike-related misconduct. "I was supposedly carrying a wrench. I wasn't—it was a crowbar that I picked up and put in my truck. I wanted to correct them, so I went to see the films at the general office."

Because the company couldn't legally fire strikers without cause, Phelps Dodge kept a file of films documenting activities for which they were being terminated. When Gloria viewed the films, she realized she wasn't in the cast; on the day for which her warrant had been issued, she wasn't even on the line. She had witnesses and decided to fight the termination.

Seventy-four other strikers in Ajo were fired and ordered to vacate their company-owned homes during the next weeks. Eleven Ajo strikers, including Janie, were arrested on charges of rioting, obstructing traffic, or "interfering with the judicial process."

Pat Scanlon felt that on balance the firings were good for the company. "We discharged throughout Arizona 188 of the strikers for strike-related misconduct," he commented later. "Our perception of that group is that in general it included a lot of the less desirable employees that were working, either because they were general troublemakers, or unreliable, or drunks, or whatever. So it had the effect of purging the work force of a lot of people who were not really on the company's side . . . so in that respect, we upgraded the work force."

Soila Bom, in the very first arrest of the strike, was jailed for using her telephone to tell a former friend that she now considered him a scab. Those arrested were booked into the Ajo annex of the Pima County Jail, but most were later moved to a jail in Tucson. For the three-hour drive they sat handcuffed in the back of a van without water or air-conditioning. The arrests were a shock, and the extremely high bonds set—up to $20,000—bankrupted union coffers overnight. Union attorney Duane Ice reported that the unions planned to fight back and would seek jury trials. Years later, Soila and the others would be vindicated by appalled juries. But at the time, and in the months to come, being legally in the right did them no more good than if they had been pedestrians run down in a crosswalk.

In Clifton, the mood of the day was wildly upbeat. The Morenci mine was closed for ten days: long enough, surely, to negotiate a contract and settle the strike. A celebratory racket rang from the Wagon Wheel bar, the Social Club, and the union halls, echoing up and down the high brick facades of Chase Creek.

"That was the start of the ten-day cooling-off period," Diane McCormick explained. "Phelps Dodge told us no one was in there, so we didn't go back up to the mine. There was *nothing* for those ten days. We were just down in Chase Creek, hanging out at the union hall and that kind of thing. We really felt good that first day. But now, looking back, we can see that it was just to give them time to bring in the National Guard, to get protection for the scabs. That's what they were doing with those ten days, not cooling off! All this time they knew that, but still we were so trustful. Never again. God, I wish we'd done something when we had the chance."

Berta said that at first they just heard rumors. "There are a lot of guys around who are in the National Guard [reserves], and they were hearing things, but we didn't believe it. We said, they're not going to waste money on that!"

The following day Diane was sitting on her front porch overlooking Highway 666. This memory still makes her stomach hurt. "All of a sudden we saw these caravans passing. I said, 'Oh, God, they've betrayed us.' "

Carmina heard the bad news from her brother-in-law Clyde, who lives in Safford, half an hour to the south of Clifton. "He lives right by the road," Carmina said, "and he saw all of the trucks, and trucks, and *trucks* coming through town. Then the tankers. He called and said, 'Are they going to fight another world war?' He's older than my husband—they've been in the service—and you know what he said? That it reminded him of when they were overseas. He said he feared for us.

"It *was* like they were going to start a war—with the TANKERS. A whole ARMY coming in to this little community, can you imagine? And there were helicopters coming in, dropping men off, and then the trucks, with water, the machine guns, and everything. We thought they were going to have a machine gun at every home. They started gathering down by the drive-in that's closed. People passing by kept saying, 'There's a lot of National Guards coming in.' We were just waiting.

"At the beginning, we didn't know what it would come to. I thought probably somebody would get killed. I was born and raised here, and I've never seen anything like that day. Just on TV. If somebody gets run over, that's a big thing here in this town, you know. It's a small community. When some kids got killed in the Marines, that was the saddest day. That was the worst we could think of."

Diane and her children watched from the porch. "I thought, we've had it. This is it. What were we going to do, throw rocks? Against their machine guns? It took a couple of days to get them all in here. We felt like we were being invaded. You couldn't do anything. You'd wake up in the middle of the night and hear the helicopters."

Berta drove down into town to watch them come in. "We couldn't figure out where they were going. My friend and I went all the way to the freeway, because we thought they were going to be posted there, but they weren't. They were putting them up on top, on P.D. property! Way up on top of the mound, where nobody could see them."

Soon, though, the troops were too numerous to hide. They swarmed over the little town like hornets, with about the same effect on its inhabitants. Cleo Robledo says she was less frightened than furious. "It was just the fact that they had done such a thing, you know? You'd go in a store to get your milk and your eggs and look around and it was National Guard and DPS all over the place. It was unbelievable. You'd have to walk right by them in the stores."

Lydia Knott, her mother, and her children watched from the porch of their sea-blue house above Chase Creek. "It was bad," Lydia agrees. "They had snipers on top of the hills, and tanks. They had SWAT teams all over here. I remember one case where they had a whole SWAT team on two picketers."

Nancy Hicks went each day to the American Legion Hall to help with the distribution of donated food for the strikers. One day while she was there, eight armed DPS officers surrounded her home and knocked on the door. Her twelve-year-old son was home alone. The officers asked the child for the whereabouts of his father, Clifford, for whom they had an arrest warrant. The DPS office would give no comment on the incident, but Nancy believes her son was threatened; it's obvious that at the very least he was intimidated. He told the men where they could find his father, who was helping a relative set fence posts. When Clifford was subsequently arrested, the boy felt responsible and became extremely upset, requiring psychiatric treatment.

Everyone in Clifton knew of friends or family members who were taken from their homes and arrested, sometimes literally bound in chains while they were watching TV. "I can't understand why the governor sent the DPS and the National Guard," Lydia said, expressing the universal sentiment. "Most of these men who came up here, they intimidated and they harassed us."

Outside the company towns, many applauded the show of force, saying it was necessary to control a volatile situation. Twelve days earlier in Ajo there had been an outbreak of gunfire, and the three-year-old daughter of a miner who'd crossed the line was injured when a bullet pierced the wall of her bedroom, and then her forehead, as she slept. Both sides acknowledged that little Chandra Tallant was the victim of an undirected (perhaps drunken) midnight fracas; she recovered, but the accident was fateful. Governor Bruce Babbitt paid a high-profile visit to her hospital room, and the dramatic scene was invoked repeatedly as justification for any strike-suppressing action the governor might take.

Babbitt defended his decision to send in the National Guard, saying that the strikers had violated the anti-assembly injunctions and would have to accept the consequences. When the unions charged that he was in the hip pocket of Phelps Dodge, he responded, "I'm in the hip pocket of the judicial system of the United States, and Arizona, and the Constitution of the United States and Arizona. . . . As far as I'm concerned, when a judge hands down an order about how the peace is to be maintained, that's the law of the land. If we can't, as individuals and elected officials, understand that that's our first obligation, then this whole society falls into anarchy, and you have politicians and elected officials siding first with lawbreakers on the management side and then lawbreakers on the union side."

Granted, it's hard to argue civil rights when visions of anarchy are dancing in taxpayers' heads. Since Arizona's population is primarily urban, the majority of the governor's constituents couldn't easily relate to the inhabitants of remote blue-collar mining towns and were probably inclined to distrust the bred-in-bone union loyalty that led the strikers to seemingly desperate measures. But the people of Clifton and Morenci saw Babbitt's "first obligation," a frightening military occupation of their town, as excessive; the punishment didn't fit the crime. They felt that the anti-assembly injunctions had been unfairly invoked in the first place. What they saw more than anything was a clear alliance between their governor, the troops, and Phelps Dodge. When the mine gates reopened on August 19, National Guardsmen were lined up on Phelps Dodge property, guns pointing out. Patrolling activity was stepped up for the shift changes when, after the ten-day "cooling-off" period, Phelps Dodge again began bringing busloads of nonstrikers in and out of the mine. When Phelps Dodge reopened the employment office, armed National Guardsmen were standing on the roof. The sensation of being stared at through a riflescope is unsettling, to say the least. When strikers and their families walked the picket lines, uniformed sharpshooters followed their movements with automatic weapons. Strike sympathy still ran high in the town, and the memory of the shutdown—the astonishing power of their numbers— was fresh in the strikers' minds. But they reluctantly came to understand, as many have learned before them, that a majority opinion means nothing against guns.

Trudy Morgan, the wife of a striking miner, summed up the town's emotions. "I felt defeated, just lost. I think we all felt that way. I have to say our town was raped."

Flossie Navarro's memories of the occupation are vivid. Having survived clamorous days as a union miner during World War II and after, she never expected to see the same battles fought again, like a rerun of an old war film, in her retirement. She didn't care for the show.

"I was here when the National Guard came in, yes, ma'am. I saw them helicopters come in. We had eighteen up here in the air—*eighteen helicopters*. We went out there in the yard, and I counted them as they went over. They circled and circled; it was just like a battle. You'd just like to have got a gun and shot 'em all down! That's really what I'd like to of done. All night you'd hear them—brrr, brrr, brrr, like they was taking the top of the house off. At night, and of a day, for the three o'clock shift change. And of a morning, when the early-morning shift was coming up, them helicopters would wake you up, here they'd come. It was as bad as during the war when those planes would come down drilling. That's just what it put me in mind of. Just like war.

"When those National Guard were here I kept the grandkids right with me every minute cause there was no telling what was going to happen to them. One time we went up Old Chase Creek to the fruit stand up there. While we was there at the truck stop, there was a cop car come down, one of those DPS, and there was six of them in that sucker. They stopped right over here and got out, and they took off their shirts and put on those bullet-proof vests. Then they got in the car and come on down the highway. Right there, *ignorantly*, in front of us. I didn't say anything to them, but I sure would have liked to. But I was just one woman there; they probably would have beat the hell out of me. Now, why couldn't they have done that in a motel room, up in Morenci? At least I have the guts to drive through town without no bullet-proof vest!

"They was all over the place, all up the road and on top of the stores, pointing their guns down at people like it was a battle. They had all their jeeps, whatever you call them, and those old stupid-looking outfits. At the lines they'd have four or five of them ganged up on one striker. That's not fair, is it? Why didn't they take them man to man? Why didn't they give them both a gun, stand them up there, and let them go at it—if it was a war they wanted?"

Jean Lopez had been away from Clifton, visiting friends in California, during the ten-day shutdown. "When I came back," she said, "I was driving into town and saw a caravan of the National Guard in full gear, and *trucks*, and *tanks!* I said, what is going on in this little town, what could possibly have happened? Right away I was scared. I didn't know what to expect. I stopped at my mother's house on the way in, and she was very upset. They're elderly;

my dad is retired. The helicopters had been going around all night and woke
them up, and they were so scared.

"I stayed there with Mother for a while and told her not to worry, nothing
was going to happen. People are not dumb, to try to go against the National
Guard! It's ridiculous. We're not armed. We're not allowed to carry anything
that even resembles a gun. A tire-iron in your car is enough to get you
arrested."

That afternoon Jean went up to the plant gate to see if there was going to
be a picket line. "It looked like the whole town of Morenci was under siege.
That's all you could see: the trucks, the National Guard with their rifles over
their shoulders, the bullets hanging across their chests. They were walking
around in their helmets, with their rifles or their machine guns, just all over
Morenci. At the front gate I saw about a hundred DPS officers in complete
riot gear, just outside the entrance. And they were all over everywhere—in
the stores, in restaurants. If I needed to go in a store but saw them in there,
I wouldn't go in. I wasn't scared, really, I was angry.

"The governor sent the National Guard in so that P.D. could open the
plant without any incident. It was as simple as that. People knew it wasn't
just an ordinary strike, and they were scared. The newspaper said they were
being trained up here at the National Guard armory in Safford, practicing
their . . . whatever it is they have to practice. It just wasn't *necessary*. These
people all grew up here. You *know* the people here, and they're not bad
people. I was so angry when I saw all these guys here, and we pay for that
with our own tax money! I called Governor Babbitt, and I told him I do not
appreciate that he sent these people up here, against us, and *my* taxes are
paying for *them* to threaten me and my people? I say that's wrong!

"I was angry that our own country would turn our own people against us.
A lot of these strikers are Vietnam vets; they fought for this country—for
what? I had an uncle who got killed in Vietnam. It just doesn't make sense
to me. This is an American against an American. That didn't seem like it
should be happening here. These are horror stories you hear from somewhere
else—South America, Poland, or someplace—but not here in the United
States. We like to think we're better off—you know, patriotism and all that.
I'm not saying I'm not glad I'm an American, but at this moment I don't feel
that I'm 100 percent. I'm sorry, but that's the way it is."

Fina Roman, head of the Women's Auxiliary, expressed similar doubts
about truth, justice, and the American Way. "I think this has been a learning
process for us. We have always been proud of our country and believed in the
democratic system. Try to imagine the disappointment of having had such

faith in that system that's turning against us now. We taught our children that if you do right and don't break the laws, the system in place is your defense: you can't lose if you work within that system—you can defend what you think is right, and not be punished for it. But we *have* been punished, and that's been damaging to the values we tried to instill.

"This town has been here over a hundred years, and for all that time we have been law-abiding citizens who raised our children, supported our town, and produced many valuable, worthwhile human beings. All of a sudden, as soon as we stand to defend what we believe is right, they call us law-breaking animals."

Fina confided these thoughts one evening as we sat in the Machinists' Hall in Clifton, after she'd spent a long afternoon standing on the picket line and trying to organize some emergency relief for a striker family with five kids in danger of having their home foreclosed. The huge, dimly lit hall, which ordinarily buzzed with people and projects as the nerve center of the strike, was nearly empty now as people went home to supper. Fina looked worried and tired.

"The greatest disappointment for me was that I campaigned for Governor Babbitt door to door. I thought he was the best thing that could happen to Arizona. Now I feel betrayed. He was a guest at our graduation, in May of last year, and applauded unions. Three months later he sent in troops to destroy them. We remember these things.

"It was such an excessive show of force. It's frightening. We're facing people armed with destructive weapons, and we don't know—would they take our life? Our children are impressionable. They go out and taunt them, sometimes acting immature, thinking they're defending their parents, and one day they might overstep." She paused for a minute as four small girls in blue jeans, their long black hair flying, tore into the union hall and chased each other up the stairs, screaming and giggling. Fina asked me, as if I knew, "Would these men shoot our kids away? People think about it every day. Would they shoot them for throwing a rock? We don't know."

The occupation of Clifton and Morenci left indelible marks. The character of the strike, and the tactics of its supporting organizations, were forced to change. The Women's Auxiliary in particular hardened its core.

According to Jean Lopez, the auxiliary used to be "a group where the ladies would get together and air their complaints." She says it made them feel better to see that other families were in the same boat. "You'd come feeling depressed and leave feeling great. And it was kind of a support group for the men—the women would get together and make tortillas to take to the picketers up at the mine. And parties for the children at Christmas, that kind of thing. This is basically what it was. But it changed. The women were forced to take a stand. We were always behind the lines, and the men were up in front. But in this strike, the women had to move to the front."

Fina Roman explained how this had come about. "Everybody was on the line at first, including the women. But the women are the ones who have never stayed away from it. Partly this is because there was an injunction against the men, but also because it was very important to us to keep that picket line active. The men, after the injunction, were in danger of being arrested for just being there. The women took over."

The injunction against the unions said that no more than five miners could be at the picket shacks, and not more than a hundred on the line at the main gate. "We argued with the unions that that meant there could be ninety-nine," Fina said, "but the men were hard-pressed to come up with those ninety-nine, so the auxiliary took it upon themselves to be on that picket line."

And this they did. As Trudy Morgan put it, "We went up there to hold the line, and we *held* the line."

"The Women's Auxiliary would say they were going to meet up there," Diane McCormick recalled, "and we would just go and do it. A *lot* of us would show up, just us women. P.D. was threatening the men, saying they were going to fire them for being on the line, and they were taking pictures and all that. But they couldn't fire us. So the women would go."

"Believe me," Berta added, laughing, "they would love to have fired us if they could!"

And so, in the face of a considerable army, the women of Clifton and Morenci began rolling their groggy children out of bed at 4:00 A.M. and making their way in the predawn light to the top of the hill. Most of them now groan remembering the difficulty of organizing their households around this strange new schedule—Phelps Dodge's "state-of-emergency" twelve-hour shift change—but they also agree that the all-women pickets were "kind of fun." It had never been their habit to go anywhere but the grocery store without their husbands—socializing spots like the bar were traditionally off limits to women alone or in groups—so the female camaraderie on the line was a heady discovery.

The Women's Auxiliary received notice that it was technically barred from the lines along with the strikers, because of its legal affiliation with the unions. Undaunted, the women organized under a new title, "Citizens for Justice," and refused to stay home. Carrying hand-painted signs that declared such things as "WHO IS GOVERNOR, PHELPS DODGE OR BRUCE SCAB-BITT?" housewives, waitresses, mothers, and daughters came out to the roadside to make the most public stand of their lives.

"We had to try and keep the number *down* to ninety-nine," says Shirley Randall. "All women. We knew we couldn't just quit. We asked the men not to go, so they couldn't say we were doing anything wrong. The men were more rowdy—the rock throwers."

This last point is debatable; Cleo Robledo said the opposite. "You better believe the women turned out. And oh, they were brave! The scabs, the DPS, all of them hate facing the women worse than they hate facing the men. Even if there were just five, seven women up there in that little island, they'd call out the DPS. Oh, yes. 'Get them up here, we can't stand these women!' They were afraid of the women because I think we're much more . . . verbal."

Their "verbs" were sharply curtailed, though, by the presence of armed guards. "When we were on the line," Diane said, "you really had to maintain. You couldn't be rowdy—you knew they were watching. I remember one time we were on the line and I looked up and said, 'They have snipers on the hill!' Everyone turned and, sure enough, they were all up there, right above the mine. There's a little shack up there. Always before we had just seen the Guard and the DPS when they were right there near us. When I saw the snipers up there, with their guns ready, I felt like, man, we don't have a chance; don't do anything. I felt they would shoot us, I honestly did—that they wouldn't hesitate.

"They said we were dangerous. But none of us, even when the guys were there, not one of us was *ever* armed. Sometimes bats, or chains. But bats and chains against machine guns? We couldn't even defend ourselves. No way." Still, Diane said, the all-women pickets were as rowdy as they could be, under the circumstances. "We kept getting court injunctions put on us for this or for that, so we couldn't flip anybody off, no bad words or whatever. Finally they had us to where all we could do was just wave."

This was hard to take. "To stand there and smile and wave at the scabs!" Berta said. "When we were so angry!"

They stayed on the line in spite of the accumulation of both legal and physical barriers, which included immense piles of sand that had appeared at the main gate early in the strike, entirely smothering the roadsides where the picket lines had been in the past. "When they put those piles of sand up there," Berta said, "we moved the picket to the Federal Market. This was when the National Guard was still here. The next day they had signs up saying it was private property and that you couldn't park there unless you were going to buy something. So everybody would park and go buy a piece of bubble gum or something before coming back out to the line." Eventually they won a court order that allowed them to stand on top of the "berms," or sandpiles, by the main gate.

As had happened in Ajo, the arrests and termination notices came in sobering numbers. In the last two weeks of August, twenty-four Morenci strikers and supporters were arrested on rioting charges, and ninety-five received termination notices. Sixty of these also received notices ordering them to be out of their Phelps Dodge homes by September 22.

The picketers complained that they were under constant surveillance. When questioned by reporters, Frank Navarrette, director of the Arizona Criminal Intelligence Systems Agency, confirmed that he had sent agents into the strikers' communities to work undercover. Such activities might seem outside the official line of duty for the agency, which is a special intelligence unit established to fight organized crime, but Navarrette justified the move saying, "What happened during the strike doesn't fall within the definition of organized crime, but from my perspective, it's organized labor. . . . Our main emphasis is to explore the possibility of deep-rooted criminal conspiracies with respect to the strike and the potential threat of violence."

Most of the surveillance activities were laughably obvious. Suffice it to say that undercover agents had some trouble with their assignment of "blending in" with the local residents. Berta Chavez responded in her own fashion: "They started taking pictures of us, so I figured I'd get them nervous—I'd start taking pictures of them. Me, Bev Cole, Nancy Hicks—we'd all do stuff like that. We didn't even have film in the camera most of the time, since we couldn't afford it, but they didn't know that. They'd look away; it really made them nervous. Once I went up real close to a DPS officer and took a picture of his belt buckle, because his number was on there. You could say he was, uh, uptight."

The women were quick to learn exactly what rights they and the police did and didn't have. They were surprised to realize how little they had thought of such things before. They also learned to be extremely careful. "Nobody wanted any waves," said Jean Lopez. "It's stupid to think anything else. These people here, going up against the National Guard? Forget it, it's not worth your life."

The press, however, portrayed the strikers as a bloodthirsty, immoral mob. In their coverage of the early weeks of the strike, the state's newspapers seemed to go out of their way to provide photos of strikers drinking beer on the picket line. After the shutdown on August 8, the editorial pages fairly rang with bestial adjectives. "Mobs seem to be in control," proclaimed an editorial in the *Arizona Republic* on August 11. "The ultimate capitulation came when Phelps Dodge closed its Morenci plant when 1,000 wild-eyed strikers and their supporters—most armed with baseball bats—delivered an ultimatum: if the company doesn't close the plant, the herd-like mob, baseball bats and all, would." And a day later, in the same newspaper: "If the union leadership cannot be depended on to assert control over the rabble on the picket line . . . can the public rely on law enforcement authorities to prevent mob rule from compromising public safety? Whether the mob or law prevails in this ugly dispute will be tested again next week, when Phelps Dodge plans to reopen the Morenci operation, and the bat-swinging strikers, some slurping beer for courage, plan to close it by force." This observation was printed beside a large cartoon featuring beer-slurping, bat-swinging, ape-shaped men in union caps, with the caption: "S.C.A.B.S. (Striking Copperworkers Anxious to Bash Skulls)."

The women on the picket lines never appeared in editorial cartoons, but they did begin to receive notoriety, which alternately embarrassed and amazed them. Berta and Diane said their cousins periodically called from Washington to say they had seen them on TV. Gray-haired, feisty Pearl McBride refused to be embarrassed when her picture was "splashed all over the front page" of the *Arizona Republic.* "My sister called me from Phoenix, and she says, 'My goodness, girl, what are you *doing* up there?' And I says, 'Nothing.' She says, 'Why, Pearl, you're sprawled all over the front page.' Well, I'm telling you the truth, I didn't do anything except stand there and hold a sign: BABBITT TALK TO US. That's all. I thought if he really wanted to know what's going on up here he could come and talk to us, and we could tell him the true facts of it. So that's what my sign said." Pearl laughed. "It could have been a lot worse!"

Many of the women said seeing themselves on the news made the experience more real to them, and much more frightening. "We knew it was happening, of course," Berta said. "But when I saw it on TV, that's when it really sank in, what they were doing to us."

If calling in the troops was meant to intimidate strikers and their supporters, it ultimately had the opposite effect. Townspeople who were initially neutral grew infuriated by the display of force and placed their hearts and their feet behind the strikers' side of the line. It was soon impossible to find a person in Clifton who had not been drawn into the strike. "At the beginning," Cleo Robledo explained, "we didn't know exactly what was going on, so we just sat back and watched things. Then it really hit us. Then we got involved."

Obviously, not everyone supported the strike. Most of the workers who crossed the picket lines each day were from Safford, Duncan, and other small ranching towns in the area, but many were from Morenci, and a handful were from Clifton. Strikers watched bitterly as friends changed their minds. One of the five original members of the Women's Auxiliary withdrew in support of her husband when he decided to go in to work.

Some women didn't support their husbands' decision to strike—like Vivian, who says she just got fed up with having no money for her kids and, against her husband's wishes, went to work in the Phelps Dodge store. Others refused to support their husbands' decision to cross the line—such as Rosemary, whose husband dropped her off at the picket line each morning on his way into the mine to work. Both of these arrangements soon ended in divorce.

The women felt they had substantial influence over the men's decisions. Alison Rainbelt says her husband went in for exactly one day, in August. "And that was the lowest day in my life. I cried all day. I told him, 'If you can go up there and be proud to do it, fine, but you *can't!*' You can't feel proud to be a scab. It's like stabbing your friends in the back; that's the way I saw it. After that, he couldn't do it.

"The funny thing is that he was the one that was always all for the union and all this, but you get to a point where you wonder if you're making the right decision—especially with house payments and stuff like that. We have two little kids. But I just couldn't see it. How could we face our friends?"

Janet Fullen, of Douglas, didn't have the same certainty in the beginning. "When my husband talked about the strike, my first reaction was panic. He'd been laid off for most of two years and had just gone back for two months. You think, why now? But the unions have been very supportive, and I'm happy to see him stand up for something he believes in. We can't just think of the money—there's safety on the job and other matters. There are transfer rights. They're going to close the Douglas mine in '87, and without a union contract there's no guarantee they'll transfer the workers to another smelter, so that's an important thing down in Douglas. I understand these things much better now."

Janet's comment about the decision to strike—that they couldn't "just think of the money" and go in—flies in the face of every truism equating labor, strikes, and greed. Holding out for a contract was going to mean *less* money, not more. By September there was probably not a striking family in the state who deluded itself on this issue. The contract dispute revolved around issues more important than cash.

One of the most serious doubts about the contract Phelps Dodge had offered

(and, by this time, withdrawn again) was that it would have ⌐
tradition of pattern bargaining, which averted the need for individ⌐
and lost work time at all the mines. Had the unions accepted Phe⌐
counteroffer, they would have set a new, greatly lowered standard for the
entire industry.

One of the concessions the unions found unacceptable was the proposed
establishment of a dual wage scale, something they had finally eliminated
thirty-seven years earlier. When new hires are paid a substantially lower wage
than workers hired under the old contract, as when Mexican workers are paid
less than Anglos, the work force is effectively divided. The unions felt this
would undermine the unity needed for effective bargaining.

Also, the unions didn't like the company's demand that they cancel the
cost-of-living allowance (COLA), which the workers had won in 1969. Since
they had already offered to freeze wages, COLA was the only protection
against the runaway inflation rates that recent history had impressed upon
their memories. Every dollar that Arizona miners earned in 1980, when they'd
signed their last contract, was worth about eighty cents by the contract's end.
Setting a precedent for the general abolition of cost-of-living protection would
be a heavy cross to bear.

Phelps Dodge officials had calculated that killing COLA could save the
company some $25 million over the three-year contract, and they wanted to
do it. What other producers had settled for, they said, was immaterial: the
market was down, imported copper was cutting into profits, and the workers
would have to help swallow the loss. Vice-President Scanlon said that as
divisions of large multinational corporations, the other major copper producers
were not under the same pressure as Phelps Dodge to make a profit from
mining and smelting.

It's true that Phelps Dodge made its profits entirely from enterprises related
to mining and metals, and it was worse off than many of its domestic competi-
tors, having sold off some of its assets. But its ad in the 1984 *Financial Times
Mining International Year Book* didn't paint such a bleak picture: "Phelps Dodge
is the second largest producer of copper in the U.S. In addition, we produce
silver, gold and molybdenum as by-products of these copper operations. Our
copper refineries treat our own copper and that mined by others. . . . Our
manufacturing divisions roll and continuously cast rod, draw wire, and produce
electrical wire and cable, tube and pipe, fittings and valves, magnet wire,
communications cable, and solar absorber plates. We also have interests in
companies that manufacture electrical wire, cable and related products . . .
in a number of foreign countries."

Phelps Dodge came into 1983 with roughly $2 billion in total assets, including mills and mines or mining interests in Peru, South Africa, Mexico, Australia, Chile, and the Philippines. The company was also involved in domestic uranium mining and exploration for oil and natural gas.

Some analysts argued that the company's decisions to close and then reopen its mines had traditionally had little, if anything, to do with the price of copper and everything to do with breaking unions. Phelps Dodge had most recently closed its operations in Ajo, Douglas, and Morenci in February 1982, laying off thousands of workers. In the few months before that shutdown, many of these workers had been given company housing, which they kept on credit during the layoff. They were also allowed to continue shopping on credit at company stores. A year later, less than five months before their contract would expire, Phelps Dodge reopened and called back many of the laid-off workers. According to union spokesperson Cass Alvin, the strategy was a powerful one: "We never said that some people who've starved for a year were not going to cross the picket lines."

Ray Isner, chief steward of Operating Engineers Local 428 in Morenci, said it was clear, in retrospect, that Phelps Dodge had been planning for a long time to get rid of the unions. "More than a year before the strike, they hired psychologists to map out a strategy. The long layoff that ended just a few months before the new contract was to come out was part of this strategy— to make the miners hungry for work." They were not only hungry for work, but also obliged to begin paying off the huge company housing, store, and utilities debts that P.D. had let them accumulate during the layoff.

The combination of psychological and strong-arm tactics did not pass unnoticed by the rest of the corporate world. Myron Magnet noted in *Fortune* magazine (August 22, 1983): "Phelps Dodge is set on breaking this strike. Tough tactics like these haven't been seen since the 30's. . . . Companies whose contracts have yet to expire could well be emboldened by Phelps Dodge's example." On July 1, after the company announced its intentions to bring workers through the picket lines, Phelps Dodge stock rose a quarter, to 28½; by the end of the month it was up to 29½.

Pat Scanlon said that the Monday morning the Morenci mine was shut down was a psychological turning point: "Once that occurred, then that hardened the attitudes of people on the management side. We said, 'By God, we're going to show these thugs that they can't do that to us.' So we proceeded to hire replacements. Not withstanding the outlawry and abuse they took, there were plenty of people willing to come to work. We gave each one of them a certificate, if you will, saying we would not lay him off to make room for a returning striker; he was a permanent replacement as that term is defined by the law. It just happened that during that period the Supreme Court had decided that an employer's agreement to do that is an enforceable contract. If the employer then violates the agreement and does lay him off, then the laid off replacement has a personal right of action against the employer. So what we were doing was burning our bridges."

I asked Mr. Scanlon, to make sure I understood, if he meant that as far as this strike was concerned, Phelps Dodge had burned its bridges after forty-two days. He replied, "That's about right."

The stakes were high on all sides. Angel Rodriguez, president of USWA Local 616 in Clifton, said that P.D. was seeking to terminate every agreement they'd had for the last forty years. "Contract language, working conditions, medical and insurance, things that have taken many strikes to win," he told *Village Voice* reporter Joe Conason. "We couldn't give those things away— they weren't ours to give. Our fathers and grandfathers won those things."

Liz Hernandez-Wheeler, head of the Tucson Union Support Committee, explained: "The labor movement is going to suffer considerably if this strike is lost. It will establish a precedent for many companies in this state, and in the country, to engage in this type of union-busting tactics. We're already seeing it."

As the "union-busting tactics" grew more overt, defense of their civil liberties became as much of an issue to the strikers as their contract. "I definitely think there's more than a strike happening," said Fina Roman. "The blatant violation of civil and human rights that is running rampant here is an indication that more than the strike needs to be defended. More than the strike needs the attention of the people who can bring solutions to this community.

"For just innumerable years Clifton was a safe community; people knew everyone else; everyone looked after everyone else's children. There was just a family atmosphere throughout the community. Now that no longer is true. Unfortunately it isn't always those who have crossed the picket line, but the law enforcement agencies, who are causing the problems. They are forever questioning people who they meet walking down the street. We're used to walking everywhere—it's a small community, and people enjoy walking. Now we're questioned when we are found walking. This is strange to us. I think an investigation has to be undertaken to find the reasons for our rights being violated. There is a right-to-work law in Arizona, but that doesn't mean that we must forfeit all other rights."

What they were being asked to forfeit had no apparent limits. Strikers in Clifton were questioned not only for walking but for standing, driving, and speaking. They were issued traffic tickets for driving too slowly, and arrested for carrying tire-changing tools in their cars. Their homes were watched at night by armed officers. Ray Isner told the press, "We've had countless individuals arrested in their homes. The show of force is excessive. Women have been arrested in front of their children. As many as a dozen DPS officers have encircled homes."

Most residents of Clifton can't say exactly how long the National Guard occupation lasted, because the effects stayed with them long after the olive-drab convoy pulled out. Diane McCormick's assessment was typical: "They were here forever. I guess it must have been about two weeks."

Also, many people didn't make a clear distinction between the National Guard and the DPS, since all were outsiders and the sense of invasion was the same. The so-called "siege" by the National Guard lasted approximately ten days. "But really," said Jean Lopez many months later, "we've been under siege since then. They pulled the Guards out, but the DPS have been here all along. The storm troopers—you can see them up there on the picket line any day. I knew it was going to be a long strike, but I never expected anything like this. I don't think anybody did."

In Ajo, too, strikers felt their town could never return to normal. They no longer knew what to expect from a future that had always seemed exceedingly predictable. Personal rights they'd spent a lifetime taking for granted had vanished along with their paychecks. But still they were sure the strike would be resolved. Like most red-blooded Americans, they had utter faith in the notion that justice would prevail. "I know the unions are going to win," said Janie Ramon, "and that P.D. is not going to get away with what they're doing to us. I realize it's going to take awhile. But to me it's worth it."

The sentiment among strikers was the same everywhere. "We *are* going to see the end of this," Carmina Garcia declared. "Come hell or high water. The river can take us, but we're not giving in to P.D."

# 3

# Hell and High Water

Like most Arizona rivers, the San Francisco is a friendly ephemeral stream. It swells with the rainy seasons and recedes with drought, exposing mats of algae that whiten in the sun and curl up at the edges like an old carpet. Children make their way through the shallows to fishing holes by memorizing the positions of stepping-stones embedded in the mud.

People in Clifton talk about the "Frisco" as if it were an eccentric, beloved uncle. In summertime they love to go down to its banks for quiet visits. Sometimes in bad winters it gets cranky and causes trouble, but come springtime they are generally willing to forgive it. When it rained in Clifton for a solid week at the end of September 1983, no one was especially worried. Floods had come to dampen their doormats before, and the town had always dried up afterward, little the worse for wear.

On Saturday, October 1, striking miners and friends were down at the American Legion Hall, a few yards from the river. There wasn't a meeting or any other special reason for congregating there, except that they were three months into the strike and had grown accustomed to one another's company. Gloria Armijo explained, "We were just down there drinking beer and looking at the river."

They weren't expecting a flood. The river was high, but it had crested and stayed at the same level for about three hours. Then it rose another few inches. People who lived near the riverbank began to think about going home to get their trucks across the bridge to higher ground, just in case. Then, while they watched, a six-foot wall of water came down the canyon, and they understood that if they went for their trucks now, they wouldn't come back.

"When we saw it coming we knew this was it," Gloria said. "All we had time to do, really, was run out of the hall. We almost got trapped in there; we had to wade across. I took my kids and some ladies that were there, and I told the rest of them you better get out. My husband and Fina, the president of our auxiliary, were the last ones, and it took all their strength to get across. They almost drowned.

"We ran up the mountain. I guess we must have stayed up there for two or three days. It wasn't just me and my husband, there were thirty or forty people up there sitting on blankets, just watching everything. You see your ice chest, your refrigerator, your camper coming down the river—everything gone. I could just see the top of my house. The rest was underwater.

"We were soaking wet, of course, and didn't have food. We'd come down to the Circle K to eat something, to feed our kids or whatever, and then go back. I stayed wet for two days—you're not thinking, you don't even feel the cold. It's like you're in a trance, that you don't want to leave. You think if you watch long enough, some miracle is going to happen."

They watched as the big iron bridge caught uprooted trees in its cables and then began to collect mud and debris, building a nightmarish dam. The water that swelled behind it was forced to seek another path, finally surging over the banks. Houses were engulfed and dragged into the current. The flood whistle, warning Clifton to evacuate, howled faintly over the roar of the water. As they kept watching, the force of the current overcame the resistance of the dam. In what seemed like slow motion, the bridge broke in half and fell into the river.

"When you're in something like that, you're not thinking about your stuff— it's gone," Gloria said. "You're just praying to God nobody's drowned. In North Clifton you have a lot of retired people, so you're thinking about Granny, or about Mrs. Smith, you know, hoping all these people got out. One little old couple, Warren and Irma, had to be pulled out. They were sitting in their house with water up to their chests, and they didn't want to leave. They had to tie them with ropes. They were worried about their damned dogs, little tiny dogs. They were probably taken by the first crest that came.

"My *tia* [aunt] Julia, the heliocopters had to take out. The older people, you see, are very stubborn. They've lived there for so many years they don't believe that something like this is going to happen. People were just in a state of shock."

On the day of the flood, even Fina Roman—the calm, articulate spokes-woman for the Women's Auxiliary—lost her cool. She was worried about her grandchildren and called her daughter across the river just before the phones went dead to ask her to send them over. "A helicopter was evacuating people, and at ten o'clock in the morning I saw these two little pathetic figures out in the pouring rain. It was my two grandchildren—they're three and six years old—on a ledge over the river. The little one, Jessie, had a terrible cold.

"From ten in the morning until six that evening, I watched my grandchil-dren on that ledge waiting to be evacuated. They kept on waving their arms. I was going into hysterics in front of the Circle K. I called the sheriff's office and said, 'When are you going to get those babies off that ledge?' They said,

'As soon as we finish the *shift change.*' They were taking the scabs in and out of the plant!"

At six that evening, Fina's grandchildren were brought down off the ledge and delivered to Fina, shivering and soaked to the bone. She couldn't find a dry blanket in town to wrap them in. The Red Cross had flown in hundreds of blankets, but according to Fina, on that first day everything went straight to the Morenci Club, where the scabs were being housed.

"We complained to the governor, but he said we didn't have enough documentation. Sure, I should have asked for the name of the person I spoke to, who told me they were giving priority to the shift change. But I wasn't thinking about documentation right then. I wanted those kids off the mountain!

"So that's my story. I can't say, 'Officer Jones said . . . ' It's just one more lesson we learned."

Berta Chavez had left town that morning and driven to Globe, Arizona, to get government surplus cheese for the strikers' food bank. During the long drive back she stared through the heavy rain on the windshield and worried about Clifton, having heard rumors of flooding. Just outside town a DPS officer flagged down her truck, saying she couldn't get through to Clifton. Being Berta, she wasn't persuaded. She told him she had perishable food to deliver, and he reluctantly let her pass.

She couldn't believe what she saw. The town was engulfed. The food bank building, where she had planned to deliver the cheese, was entirely underwater.

When Berta got to her house, which is high above the canyon a few miles outside Clifton, her mother was standing in the front yard in her nightgown. Her father was missing. Berta's sister Diane had been with her mother when Mr. Delgado disappeared. "He works for the city, and had been driving the front loader," Diane explained. "We were standing on this side of the river watching the loader go down the road on the other side, a long way away. All of a sudden it tipped into the water. The last time we'd seen Dad he was driving one of those, so we were sure it was him in there. We were in a panic."

They searched for hours among the crowds of refugees in churches and other makeshift shelters, hoping he hadn't been in the loader after all. When he didn't turn up, they made up their minds to search flood zone. Berta's husband, Candy, insisted on getting into one of the rescue helicopters. He and Berta agreed to signal with flashlights if anyone found him. "They didn't want to take Candy in that helicopter, but they did," Berta said, "over to the

other side. When he got out he stopped the first truck he saw, to ask whoever
was in it if they had seen Dad. He opened the door, and there was Dad inside.

"We must have been on that bank for twenty minutes, jumping up and
down and signaling with the lights. We were so happy."

All through the night and the next day, the same drama was played out
hundreds of times as lost friends and family members were recovered. Morenci,
six miles up the hill, became a refugee camp for dazed survivors. If Gloria and
the others huddled on the mountain were waiting for a miracle, perhaps they
got it. In the wholly inundated town of 4,200 people, not one life was lost.

They kept their spirits up however they could. Gloria tells a story about
some friends who were stranded above the river for more than a day without
food or water. "They had rope, so they were trying to lasso ice boxes as they
went by. They just happened to rope a big ice cabinet from the Oasis bar,
packed full of beer and wine. They didn't have one other solitary thing to eat
or drink. What else could they do? They had a party!"

The return of National Guard helicopters to Clifton, ostensibly for humani-
tarian purposes this time, was naturally an uncomfortable sight for the strikers—salt in a still-open wound. Many of the flood victims, like Fina, say they
were told Phelps Dodge had top priority. Gloria Armijo says it was a TV
station helicopter, not the National Guard, that brought food and water to
people on the mountainside where she was. "P.D. and the National Guard
weren't helping us. They were just flying their scabs in and out. They didn't
give a damn about the people that were trapped."

There is substantial evidence that National Guard helicopters were not
only used to run Phelps Dodge errands but that they did rescue operations as
well. (In addition, Phelps Dodge officials say the company doled out whatever
emergency supplies it had, to whomever asked for them.) But townspeople
felt that diverting *any* emergency resources to keep the mine open, during
such a crisis, was morally questionable. "They flew the scabs in the helicopters
to *work*," Diane McCormick said angrily, "while people were still stranded.
That's why everyone's so bitter. People were in trouble, and P.D. was worried
about losing a day's work.

"It's really hard to understand unless you were here. If you just came here,
you would think, 'God, these people from Morenci are sure angry.' Well, this
is why. This is what we've been through. We've seen where the priorities
really are."

On Monday the water started to recede. A strange calm settled over the
town as people moved from crowded shelters out into the tentative sunlight.

Tarantulas driven from their burrows huddled together on dry patches in the road, their legs twitching nervously. Shell-shocked residents of Clifton slowly returned to their homes, on foot or by boat, and began to sort out the wreckage.

Some found their houses had literally gone down the river. For others, the remains were beyond repair—more than a third of the town's 1,800 homes were "totaled"—but they wouldn't know this for weeks, not until they'd dredged out the waist-deep mud from their living rooms and wrenched vehicles and splintered trees out of the eaves where they had lodged. Then they would be able to see what the Frisco had left them.

Gloria Armijo, who owned and ran the Wagon Wheel bar with her husband, Macy, is a woman who in her time has leaned on her elbows to listen across the counter to many a litany of sorrows. Her hair is streaked with gray, and her face looks tired—whether from other people's troubles or her own, it's hard to say, since she's seen plenty of both.

The flood, like any spectacular act of nature, had made all the papers, so I'd seen what Clifton looked like. But now I sat facing Gloria across the bar, listening and trying to understand the scope of the disaster in human terms. She told me what she had lost.

Her bar, like the rest of the old brick buildings along Chase Creek, was flushed of its contents but left structurally intact. With her home she wasn't so lucky. She has photos, taken by a friend from Morenci, that show what was left of her house when the floodwaters pulled out. The Victorian eaves, with white gingerbread trim, contrast absurdly with the rest of the picture: a front porch clotted with a six-foot-high mud-colored mass of tree branches, vehicle parts, furniture, dead animals. Someone's silver-white mobile home has come to rest like a beached aluminum whale, its nose embedded in the upstream wall of what used to be Gloria's kitchen.

Another photo shows the back yard. In this swamp of mud Gloria once tended a flower garden and built a patio and a barbecue pit. Only after she pointed them out did I recognize the outlines of the roof of a camper and two other vehicles, completely buried in mud. "We were walking that day," she laughed, with unconvincing levity. "We've been walking ever since.

"I have, I had, a real big house. High ceilings. The water was up to the tops of the doors, about eight feet. This was the lower mark." She pointed to a dark line on the floral paper of the living room wall. "At about four feet. That's where it stayed and wouldn't go down. We couldn't go in for three days. When we finally did go up in a little rowboat, we saw we'd lost everything. It was full of mud. There was even mud on the inside of the TV. You'd sink to your waist in mud, and you couldn't walk. You're in shock at first. You start by throwing everything out the door. You don't save anything.

"I tried to look for my rings, things I thought *maybe* I could find. You don't find them. You just find other people's stuff. I found furniture that wasn't mine in my living room. We found Virginia's jewelry box stuck on the fence between my yard and the Smiths'. Virginia lives four or five houses up. And we found Margaret Skidmore's ice box, full of food. The food was still frozen, so we took it up to her.

"The hell of it is, you got to pack everything in bags and get rid of it in a dump or something. You can't just throw it out in the yard, because in four or five days the smell would be ridiculous. Some people did, and that's where all the contamination came in. And then the sewers were all over. If you had asthma or hay fever, anything like that, there was no way in hell you could stay there working more than a few hours because of the filth and the stench. You could smell it from here. I caught pneumonia from the moisture and filth. I stayed wet for so long.

"I think the National Guards gave us a few shovels, but the first equipment we got was from the Red Cross. They were wonderful. They came in with brooms, shovels, disinfectant, and those fungus killers. You've got to have that, because the moisture creates big green fungus—it just moves in. And then St. Vincent de Paul brought clothing and food. We had help from people from out of town and even out of state. There was this one group, ten women and ten men, that travel around and help people in disasters. The women would all wear dresses—in that mud! They were beautiful, always singing. The women would even clean out the appliances. We'd tell them they were no good, but they would leave them clean and shiny anyway. They would just leave a room spotless. It was some kind of a religious group, but I can't remember what they were called. You know, sometimes you're just so confused you don't think of taking names or anything. I wish I would have thought about it."

Gloria was probably referring to a group of volunteers from the Sun Valley Mennonite Church in Phoenix, who arrived to help shortly after the flood.

Gloria's insurance, like virtually everyone else's in Clifton, didn't cover floods; what's gone is gone, they told her. And because her home was pronounced 59 percent damaged, she could never get a permit to reconstruct it.

Flossie and Ed Navarro fared better. When I visited them a few months after the flood, they had moved back in. The doors, woodwork, and walls were all faded up to doorknob height, giving the eerie impression of a room still half underwater. But we sat comfortably on odds and ends of furniture—

some from the Red Cross, some from friends on higher ground—and watched a small black-and-white TV that sat on top of a much larger color console left blind and mute by the water that had invaded its innards.

At the time of the flood, Ed was up north fishing with friends in Alpine. When the river began to rise, Flossie left. "After it was over," she said, "I came back to the house and oh, it was all full of muck. The first thing I did was I sat down and cried. That didn't do no good, so then I got up and beat on the cabinets awhile, and that didn't do no good either, so then I got to work. We shoveled it out, me and my daughter Edwina— she was pregnant— and whatever other help we had. I put a door on the bed to sleep on. I slept on that for a month.

"That big TV wasn't even a year old. People ask me, 'Why didn't you move that TV up on top of something, when you knew the water was coming?' Now where were we supposed to put it, on the refrigerator? How were we supposed to do that, me and Edwina, with her pregnant and me old? We just had to leave it all."

During the weeks of cleaning up, Gloria and Macy Armijo slept in a truck. Others stayed where they could. Cots were set up in churches, and the Red Cross set up soup lines. The Women's Auxiliary set up a clothing bank, looked after medical needs, and coordinated outside agencies. In the church kitchen in Morenci they cooked truckloads of bean burros and brought them down to where people were working. It was at that time that Fina Roman became president of the auxiliary. "That was when we first fanned out a little from our original role," she said. "We became very involved, because it was a life-or-death situation. Supplies that were being flown in—blankets, everything—were flown first to the scabs in Morenci, because they couldn't come through Clifton. We were without food and water for two days while supplies were being flown up there."

The disaster left 3,500 residents of the little town in need of some kind of emergency aid. Most went for days without running water, electricity, natural gas, and sewer service. According to Stuart Spaulding, Greenlee County emergency services director, Clifton suffered more than $8 million in damages to its homes and businesses and another $4 million to roads, bridges, and other public property. Public health officials warned about the threats of diptheria, tetanus, hepatitis, and respiratory and gastrointestinal infections. In a particularly draconian gesture, P.D. chose that week to announce that it was cutting off all medical coverage for strikers. Ironically, an overwhelming share of the flood damage was suffered by striking families, most of whom lived in low-lying Clifton rather than the company town of Morenci, high on the hill near the mine gate. It seemed to strikers that even God was on the side of P.D.

Immediately after the flood, authorities imposed a curfew on Clifton: 10:00 P.M. till dawn. Gloria was told this also meant no liquor sales. "They were probably afraid that if the strikers got drunk they'd kill somebody, we were so mad," she said. The ban on liquor struck the strikers as patronizing and—some felt—tinged with racism. (Most Clifton residents, and the majority of strikers, were Mexican-American.) Gloria was furious. "I said, 'Forget it!' If I couldn't sell it, I was going to give it away, and that's what I did. I loaded a Datsun truck with all the beer that was left in the bar, and I took it down to my people. Hell, those people were working ten, fifteen hours in the mud, and crying all the time, and they couldn't even have a beer? That's crazy."

Newspaper reports at the time created a portrait of men and women slogging through mud, crazed with the loss of their homes, and lashing out at anyone who passed by. In truth, the anger was extremely directed. The tanks and troops that had been so quick to arrive two months earlier, to contain a potential threat, were not much in evidence now that there was a real disaster. When Governor Babbitt visited on the Tuesday after the flood he was not well received. One indignant woman confessed, "You think we were glad to see *him?* We mud-balled him!"

Ed Marquez lodged his grievance with more restraint. "People around here are mad at you," he told the governor. "We've got nothing here—water, lights, gas, nothing. You've put the National Guard in to fight us before, and now we can't find them when we need them."

The DPS did arrive soon, eager to keep the peace, but they further infuriated the already bilious strikers with their apparent deference to the needs of Phelps Dodge. Their first order of business was to clean up the road to the mine. Vicky Sharp gave this account: "During the time we were cleaning up our town, the DPS would keep the main highway blocked off—we had to take detours—until it was time for the scabs to come through at shift change. Then they opened it up. Our own county employees, anyone driving a dump truck to clean up the muck, were stopped. They'd have to park, stay off the road, and wait for the scab parade to come through. If they went back on that road, the DPS informed them, they would be ticketed. Just for driving on that highway to help clean up."

Phelps Dodge countered that it was doing its part to help the community. Plant manager John Bolles said the company had loaned a house to union leaders for the storage of supplies, had sent cots, sheets, and rubber mats to the Catholic Church, and was handing out other relief indiscriminately to strikers and nonstrikers.

Not surprisingly, a good number of strikers said they would float down the river before they would knock on the doors of the Morenci Club to ask for a P.D. cot. The bitterness ran deep. Gloria Armijo said, "Phelps Dodge thought at that time that the strike was dead. They figured, 'This is it, they've got no homes.' And it's true, we were homeless, most of us. Without no place. People were staying at the Elks, at the gym, at the courthouse. But, by God, people got back on that picket line. That's when the women started picketing down here, right in front of the Circle K and the American Legion, so we wouldn't have to go so far. Because we didn't have time. The women would be cleaning up the houses and then, when the shift change came, they'd turn right around and picket. Those scabs, they'd stop here and laugh because we were all muddy."

Nancy Hicks remembers people yelling at her, "You got no paycheck, and now you don't have homes either." Terri Martinez says they shouted, "Hey, losers, we got your jobs!" Neither of these women denies that at that moment they had violence in their hearts. "They threw *pennies* at us," Terry said. "These were the people the DPS was protecting as they went back and forth to work. There was a lot of cruelty imposed on us."

The strikers' emergency food bank, organized by the Women's Auxiliary, had been housed in a grocery store called the Sanitary Market. It was inundated. Berta Chavez says one of the saddest cleanup chores was facing the horrific stench and, while so many people had nothing, throwing away all the ruined food. The job wasn't made any easier by the scabs who sat on a wall nearby, laughing.

"People were angry," said Fina Ramon, wildly understating the case. "While we were on the picket line, scabs came through carrying cups of water and saying to the kids, 'You want water? Here's water.' They would pour it out in front of the children."

Nancy Hicks said it was the mistreatment of children that finally got her goat. "I was out on the picket line in front of the bank, where there was mud and crud all along the highway. A little boy was kicking his feet in the water and it splashed on the pants of a DPS officer. I know it wasn't intentional. The child was just a baby. But the officer said, 'You stop that, you dirty little maggot.'

"I pushed my way through the people and I says, 'What right do you have to call those babies dirty little maggots?' And he says, 'I have the right to do and say whatever I want to say in your little county here.' I said, 'Personally, I think it takes a son of a bitch to say something like that.'

"I was so mad I was bawling. A person, a piece of garbage, talking to a child that way. I had vowed and declared when they done my little boy the way they did, surrounding my house and forcing him to tell where his father was, that I would never see an officer mistreat a child again while I'm alive. I said, 'Are you one of those son of a bitches that surrounded my house and scared my son?' He said, 'No comment.' I said, 'You son of a bitch, I think you were.' And then he grabbed me and shoved me against the side of a police van that was parked there.

"Later he tried to deny it, but it turns out there was a TV camera there— I had no idea. It was on the national news."

The officer was told to leave town, but the damage was done. Any respect picketers may have had for law enforcement was long gone, and the strikers had been pushed beyond human limits. "That," said Fina Ramon, "was when a lot of people made up their minds about the situation."

Many, many people in Clifton told me, "If you're writing a book about us, say this: if we were the violent people they say we are, somebody would be dead by now."

Mrs. Delgado is not one to take the limelight. While her daughters, Berta, Diane, and Cindy, told me stories in her living room, she stayed near the kitchen door, listening, examining the hem of her apron. Only once did she come forward with her own story, which began, "Let me tell you about the worst night of my life."

She paused for a long minute, and we all listened to the steady thrumming of the swamp cooler—a low-cost form of air-conditioning used in Arizona homes—and the whine of a chainsaw outside. Then she spoke. "I had a real awful experience. Berta, Cindy, and my son-in-law, Candy, were all arrested on the same night. They called and said they needed a thousand dollars for each one, to get them out. My son-in-law called about ten, I think, from the jail. I asked him to tell me why they had been arrested, and he said, 'We don't know why.' Cindy, my baby girl, was shackled. They brought over my granddaughter, Cindy's little girl, and she was oh, so scared. I have never seen her like that; she was white. She said, 'Some big guys arrested my mother and took her, I don't know where.'

"Where was I going to get three thousand dollars to get them out? And they wouldn't let me talk to them. I was scared to death. Is this how the people in Russia and the people in Poland feel? My kids were taken. I didn't understand what was going on, and nobody would explain anything to me. I tried to call back, but I couldn't find them. They wouldn't tell me where they were. I called Mike, Cindy's husband, and told him I thought they might be in Safford. So we went to Safford, but they wouldn't let us see them. I asked them at least to let Cindy out on her own—whatever you call it, her own recognizance— because of her poor little girl. So she could see her. They said no they wouldn't, because she is dangerous.

"Finally I talked to somebody from the union, and they helped me. That was the most terrifying night I ever had."

The three were arrested soon after the flood, following a rock-throwing incident on the line. "That night they just started picking people up," Berta said. "They would pick up just a few to get everybody else worried that they might be next."

The officers who arrested Cindy said they had seen her throwing rocks at cars. Cindy contends that she wasn't in Clifton on that day. "I was up in Morenci, taking a shower at a friend's house. We'd just gotten flooded. I was usually on the line, but not that day. I think they picked me out because I like to yell and tell the DPS what I think. Because I'm not afraid of them. They were always pointing at me."

"That's true," Diane said. "Even when she would be just standing there, they would point. We're always together, all the sisters, and they would specifically point her out from across the street. Because she's tough. She has a special name for each one of them. But still, that's no reason!"

Cindy, the youngest of the sisters, is twenty-five years old and looks younger. She wears tight jeans, sports a collection of gold studs in each earlobe, and has a smart mouth and the devil in her eyes. She's also a wife and a mother. Underneath the cool facade she seems a little astonished when she tells the story of her arrest.

"We were watching the World Series the night they came to get me. It was around nine o'clock. Six DPS came up to the house and said they had a warrant for my arrest, for doing damage to a vehicle. I told them I didn't do it. They said, 'Would you mind getting your shoes?' So I went and got them and they followed me all around the house, to make sure I didn't run off, I guess. Then I went down the stairs in front of the house with my husband and my little girl right behind me.

"At the bottom of the stairs they handcuffed me and wrapped me up in chains. They cuffed my hands to my sides, and then they got a chain and put it through each of my belt loops, and wrapped it around and around my legs, all the way down to my feet. Then they took these padlocks and locked the chain—one on the side, one on the back, and one through the handcuffs.

"My little girl, Michelle, was five at the time. When she saw them put the chains on me she started crying. I asked them, 'Can't you wait? Do you have to do this in front of her?' They said, 'You're supposed to keep her inside.' Here I was bound up in chains and they're telling me to take care of my daughter.

"The guys that chained me up thought the whole thing was funny. Officer Fink and another guy at the police station watched me trying to get out of the car and just started laughing. They said, 'She's under the influence of THC.' Then they said we couldn't stay here in Clifton because the facilities weren't working, that the water wasn't any good. But I don't get it—the DPS were drinking water out of the fountain. They took me down to Safford for the night. I think they took me just, you know, to take me.

"But I was chained up all this time. What could I do? Not much. They had me stretched out across the back seat and handcuffed to the doors. That's how I was when they read me my rights. I thought, 'Well, here I am.' "

She didn't know that her sister and brother-in-law were also being arrested at the time. "We were charged with throwing rocks," Berta recalled. "I wasn't even in town. Candy went in that day, I remember, to the Western Auto, to get a battery, I think. But he didn't get off the truck.

"This scab reported our names and said he had seen us throwing rocks. P.D. was encouraging them to put in complaints—it's a tactic they were using to get the people who were rowdy on the line. They wanted to get us, so when there was trouble I guess they just figured we were probably there, and charged us."

"I was there that day," interjected Diane, who would have to be considered the most demure of the sisters. "But they weren't! I was on the list, but I never got arrested."

"The list" was a product of Clifton's grapevine, which was remarkably efficient even for a small town. A woman who worked in the courthouse and was sympathetic to the strike always knew when a warrant was issued and managed to alert certain contacts. These were households with short-wave radios, which would broadcast the list of arrest warrants along with any other information gleaned from the police frequency. Through this elaborate system, Berta first heard that she and Candy were "wanted." "We'd come down to the Wagon Wheel, and we heard it on the scanner. We got panicky and didn't know where we should go. We were worried about the kids.

"Candy said, 'Oh, no, we're on empty'—we're always on empty—'do you think it's safe to stop at the Circle K and get gas?' I didn't see any DPS around, so we drove in, and the next thing I knew, Candy was arrested. He asked why, and they said, 'We don't know, but we're taking your wife, too.' I asked them if they could get me a babysitter. He said no, but I made him call up to make sure! We were lucky—it was the Clifton police. They do this because they have to. I guess they take orders from DPS.

"They took us down to Safford, and we were talking back and forth to the other criminals that were in there. One of them yelled, 'What are you in for?' And I said, 'For calling somebody a *scab!*' Those guys couldn't believe it." Berta never saw a warrant and says she was never read her rights.

With the union's help, Mrs. Delgado and her one free son-in-law arrived in Safford with enough money for Cindy's bail. "But they told my husband they couldn't accept the bond," Cindy said, "because I was dangerous. Then they let me out the next day, all charges dropped. Nothing ever came of it. I think they did the whole thing as a joke. It's just made me hate the DPS. As soon as I got out of jail I went right to the picket line."

Phelps Dodge appeared extremely eager to shut down these all-women picket lines. Paid television broadcasts claimed that any further mass picketing or violence of any kind would result in federal disaster aid being pulled from Greenlee County. Suspicious, several women checked with the government agency in charge of the aid and found the claim untrue. A far more serious scare tactic was the string of random, often terrifying arrests that followed the flood. "The list" seemed to have just about everyone's name on it.

"You didn't know where you were going to be when they got you," Berta said. "We had to explain it all to our kids. My son was always worried—my oldest, the ten-year-old. He would ask me, 'How are they going to pick you up? Are they going to give us away? Who's going to take care of us?' I would say, 'You have your dad, and your grandmother.' "

Diane felt especially vulnerable because she was a single parent. This was the hardest thing—preparing the children for the possibility of her arrest. "We had to discuss it. I told them I might get arrested, and that if I do, it's for something I believe in. I told them I was doing this so they wouldn't have to go through it all again when they were older."

On her fiftieth birthday, several months after the flood, Maggie Castañeda confessed she'd been worried sick that she would be arrested when the warrants came out. Yes, she had been down at the river helping with the cleanup on that famous day of what she describes as "almost a riot," when gravel and insults flew. She worried about what her parents would think if she were arrested.

"I talked to my oldest son, Johnny, he's twenty-six, and told him, 'Well, the warrants are coming out tomorrow and my name might be on the list.'

He said, 'Go for it, Mom!' Once I knew my kids were behind me I didn't feel so bad." Because her husband had gone deer hunting, she asked some friends to stay near the phone in case she needed to be bailed out. Fortunately, she didn't.

Maggie is a part-time schoolteacher whose house abounds with family pictures and her grandchildren's toys. She is as kindhearted and generous a woman as you could ever wish to have for a neighbor. I had brought her a loaf of zucchini bread for her birthday; cake would have seemed an extravagance—à la Marie Antoinette—at a time when people were counting eggs and measuring out milk with a teacup. As we sat in her kitchen I asked her whether she had ever before blown out candles with the wish that she'd stay out of jail. Maggie threw back her head and laughed till she cried.

With time, the sensational photos—people rowing among rooftops, cars standing on their noses in the mud—faded from the front pages of the state's newspapers. The victims of the San Francisco were no longer news, but their lives trudged on.

People who have lost an arm or leg often experience what is called a "phantom limb." A knee that's no longer there will ache anyway; a nonexistent hand will reach out to try to catch an overturned glass. After a lifetime of sending and receiving neural messages, the brain has trouble breaking the habit. In the same way, people in Clifton experienced "phantom homes." Time after time, cars made wrong turns down a road that no longer led home. In conversation, household items were discussed, borrowed, and loaned before anyone remembered they were gone.

"You forget," Gloria explained, "because you had it for so many years. Somebody will need something, to go camping or whatever, and I'll say, 'I've got one you can use.' Oh, I had everything, you know. And now . . . "

She and Macy had spent twenty-five of their twenty-seven years in the house the flood took, and it contained their history: their children's baby pictures, for instance. "Sometimes," she said, "you're looking for something a long time before you understand that it's gone down the river."

They also lost all the documents they needed to qualify for federal disaster aid. "You go down to the government office and they say, 'Okay, I need your marriage license, your kids' birth certificates, your deed to the house,' and you say, 'Damn it, you know we lost everything!' So they tell you, 'Okay then, we'll postpone your meeting till a month from now.'

"That was the hardest thing, those forms. Having to put all your life in papers for every Tom, Dick, and Harry that asks you. You get so angry. Why couldn't you just fill out one form and let them pass it around? The government people had all these tables set up, and you had to go to each and every table and answer the same damn questions. Some people really got mad; others would just cry. Some of the older people can't express themselves very well in English, and the agent would laugh. You're not in the mood for anybody to laugh at you.

"They said we needed to document all our damage with pictures. Now I ask you, what are you going to take a picture with? I worked five days to make a list of everything I'd lost, from underwear to appliances; they wanted everything. You have to sit down and remember each thing, and it hurts. Everything you won't have again. When it was all done, they gave me five thousand dollars and said I was lucky to get it. Why couldn't they have said, 'Just write down one thing you had that was worth five thousand dollars,' and then been done with it?" Gloria and her family were now living in a very empty government trailer in York valley, five miles from town. Their only income was Macy's strike benefits—forty dollars a week.

Flossie and Ed Navarro also lost nearly everything, but they still had their home and didn't plan to leave it. Flossie, like Gloria, was grateful for the Red Cross assistance that came immediately after the flood but didn't think much of the bureaucrats who came in later. Her complaint was that they seemed to be missing the point when it came to people's needs.

"Now they've got some big plan to get some money and move everybody up to Table Top," Flossie said wearily. "They say we can get a new house up there and have it paid off in thirty years. Thirty years! Now, anybody ought to know I'm not going to be around that long. We can't start over now. No, we'll just stay here until we're gone."

# 4

# *We'll Stay Here Until We're Gone*

No one, not even the strike supporters themselves, could explain how their resolve had solidified like cement around the brickbats fate threw their way. But no one doubted it. Nor was anyone denying by this time that one of the solidest ingredients was the statewide network of women's auxiliaries. Annie Jones, head of her auxiliary in Ajo, spoke proudly of her friends on the picket lines, who—when all else seemed to have failed— managed to throw a wrench into the strikebreaking machine. "Phelps Dodge doesn't know how to deal with us women," she said. "We come back fighting every time they try to slap us down."

In Clifton the strike's endurance was celebrated in its own song, "El Corrido de la Huelga"—the ballad of the strike. Marta Lopez, who worked as a nurse in nearby Safford, had written and recorded the song in her spare time on her own label, Lopez Records. Now her voice belted out the familiar verses from every surviving antediluvian jukebox in Chase Creek:

> . . . there are dismal mornings
> when we watch so many go in,
> all that their parents fought for
> is going to pass away. . . .

> Many of us will be poor,
> many will be left homeless,
> but we will have respect
> for the union that binds us all . . .

Not the stuff of great poetry, perhaps (and it does sound better in Spanish), but the words fell sweetly on the ears of the righteous. In spite of everything, confidence ran high in the union halls and bars of the mining towns.

On the first day of October, the Phelps Dodge strikers had been joined by two thousand brothers and sisters who walked out of the Duval Corporation mine, twenty-five miles south of Tucson. Duval, following the lead of Phelps Dodge, had asked its miners to accept reduced or frozen wages, no sick pay, reduced medical coverage, and an end to COLA. In addition, the new contract called for "cross training" for job combinations—a program union officials said could result in one worker doing the jobs of two or more people.

Within four days the Duval miners had signed the contract and returned to work. Many P.D. strikers felt betrayed by the quick turnaround. How could these miners accept a contract that was even worse than the one they'd refused? The strikers in Clifton, Ajo, and Douglas were famous by now for the hard times they had endured; how could Duval workers give in without a fight? The answer, if it exists at all, is a lesson in history, geography, and human spirit.

The Duval copper pit is a relatively new mine. It has no community fringing its open jaws, and it is unlikely to develop one; because of its proximity to Tucson, miners commute from there. They drive home at night to spend time with friends and live in neighborhoods where most people are not copper miners. Their co-workers are scattered like buckshot over a glittering city where choices are as abundant as traffic lights and convenience stores.

A Phelps Dodge town, by contrast, is a frontier phenomenon. When the company established its mining camps in Arizona's rocky back country, it created a model of choicelessness. There was exactly one career available. Miners were often paid with scrip that could be exchanged for goods only at company-owned stores. The mining town—as described by James Byrkit in *Forging the Copper Collar*—was designed as a colony, a closed social and economic entity where the company could control housing, law enforcement, medical care, and presumably workers' ambitions, since the laborers were isolated from national trends.

The plan succeeded in the early days but seems finally to have backfired in 1983. Now, their isolation was precisely the reason so many people were willing to go to extraordinary lengths to hold a position in the company and the community: they had everything to lose.

In the worst times every person must have considered it: I asked Carmina Garcia, "Do you think you'll ever leave Clifton?"

She squinted warily at the horizon, then answered for herself and everyone she knew. "Leave? Goodness, I don't think so. Where else can you go?"

Carmina, luckily, lives high above the floodplain in an old settlement called Shannon Hill. Her house is pleasant and smallish, settled like a hen into its nest of wrought iron and profuse vegetation. Honeysuckle and queen's wreath twine over the porch to create a shady grotto around the front door.

Inside there are shelves, ceiling to floor, housing old books and a museum of family memorabilia. Three ceramic ships—the Pinta, the Niña, and the

Santa Maria—sail across the expanse of bookshelf in front of the encyclopedia. There are antique bottles and kerosene lamps. "Oh, my house is full of junk," she laughs. "These are stuff I won at the Elks Club raffles." She indicates a dozen or so whiskey bottle likenesses of Elvis, John Wayne, and other assorted luminaries. "Looks like we're always winning, doesn't it? People say if Carmina buys a ticket, don't sell us any more! I drink it once in a while, but mostly I just leave it up there."

A pair of tiny, rotund poodles romp over the living room floor while she goes to get her photographs. Her prize is a very old panoramic view of Old Morenci that looks to be a composite of daguerreotypes. It hardly resembles modern Morenci. She points out all the parts of town that are gone now, buried under mine tailings. Carmina's roots in the area are deeper even than P.D.'s copper veins.

"Sometimes people will say, 'Go back to Mexico,' you know. What they don't understand is that we were always here, even before it was Arizona. I grew up at Eagle Creek. All our families owned this property—the Navarretes, the Nuñez, the Joaquins, the Lunez, the Marquez—all along the river. Some of them had horses, some of them had cows. My dad used to have donkeys and horses and bulls and cows to live on. But the majority of our living was the vegetables and fruit he grew—apples, apricots, peach, pomagrams, quince.

"My father just had one hand, so he couldn't work with WPA. This was during the Depression—back then it was P.D. or WPA. What could he do, with just one arm? He would sell vegetables. He used to bring them to all these little houses, all around P.D. He would go from house to house with the donkey and a little cart. Then in the wintertime he would bring wood. He would chop up mesquites, because everybody had a wood stove. There was no gas back then. The people up at Eagle Creek had just always been living there, even before P.D. was here.

"Now, if you went up there to Eagle Creek you would see the river that came down. The water would run, and everybody had a little canal to water their vegetables and orchards. So what did P.D. do? They made dams, up above, so they could shut the water off. They told everybody to get out of there. First my father sold his horses, then he sold his cows, but the trees were dying. How was he going to survive? They offered my dad a thousand dollars for all that land, and he took it. What could he do?

"Later on, people kept telling my mother, 'Why in the world didn't you get a lawyer?' Well, who would have thought of a lawyer? Who knew about water rights? So he took the thousand dollars to pay bills, and that was it. They moved to Morenci. My mother was tired of washing in the river, so she thought anyway the town might be better. But in Morenci we still had to haul water about two miles, take it up there in buckets. It wasn't any easier.

"And, oh, what a lot of discrimination. We couldn't even go to the bowling alley. The only place we could go was to the post office, to mail a letter. We thought that was a big deal! And then at the theater in Morenci they would let us in, but you had to go over to one side.

"The schools were segregated, too. They put us in 'Class B.' 'Class A' was for the white kids. We had white teachers, and they'd care less if we did our homework or not. A teacher would never call me Carmina. Now, even little kids in kindergarten that rode the bus that I drove would call me Miss Carmina. But back then those teachers called me Carmamina, Carmela, Carmanella—everything else but my name. They just didn't care.

"We used to have our own games, go trick-or-treating together and all, but only right there in Newtown or A. C. Hill, where the Mexican people were living. We could never go to Stargo, where, we used to call them, the big shots lived. We had to stay together because they didn't want us.

"It was in '38 that we moved to Morenci. Three years later my father died. My mother didn't have any income—she never did get social security. So my brothers worked in the mine. And, oh, bad things happened. One brother lost his arm. He worked in the smelter, where they had to keep throwing pieces of ore from around the conveyor. They didn't have good safety conditions up there; they would just have them using a board to keep the coals going into the crusher. One of those times the conveyor jerked that board and took his arm in. The conveyor pulled his arm out of the socket and threw him back. He kept on looking for his arm. The other men came along and found him there and took him to the hospital."

"Another brother was burned up in a car, and another one, Max, was killed working for P.D. It was on the last day of work before his vacation. He had always promised his wife they were going to take a real vacation when all the kids grew up. They had had three girls that were already grown, and then they had *twins*, mind you, a boy and a girl. He promised that after they raised the twins he would take her to Hawaii.

"Max was a pipefitter. That's the only thing he had been trained for, fixing pipes and things in the hospital and in P.D. homes. That day somebody called in that their swamp cooler wasn't working. That was a job for an electrician, don't you think? No. Instead of paying an electrician, they sent him to fix it.

"Someone had stuck pennies in there—they had tried to fix it themselves—and there was a short. They don't have nothing grounded in those P.D. homes. He went up there and got electrocuted. He died instantly.

"The union members all come to the funeral when one of them dies. There's a kind of insurance the Mexican people have, called *beneficio propio.* In case somebody dies we donate a dollar, so there's about a thousand dollars. That goes way back, as long as my mother can remember.

"My brothers were still young when they were living at Eagle Creek. They loved the outside life. Now, the ones still living say, 'If we only could have kept that place.' "

It was Carmina's opinion that, by busting the union, Phelps Dodge was trying to turn back the clock to the days of rampant discrimination. For evidence she brought out a newspaper article describing a brand-new P.D. policy forbidding employees of the company store from speaking Spanish (the preferred tongue of most Clifton residents) either to customers or one another.

"Do you see what I'm saying? The union is the only thing we have here that's *our own.* P.D. likes to tell us what to do, where to live. But I don't think they're going to run us out of Clifton. This is our home and we are staying, regardless."

Berta Chavez and her sisters also have memories of a childhood home lost to Phelps Dodge. They think it was the habit of literally pushing people around that first eroded their trust in the company.

"We grew up in Old Morenci, in a part of town called A. C. Hill," Berta recalls, "in a house my dad built himself. One year they told him he had to tear it down. They wanted to expand the mine, so they paid the people off. But they didn't give them hardly anything. My dad is real good at carpentry, and he put a lot of work into that house, and in the end they gave him nine hundred dollars for it. They said, 'Here's the money, we'll give you another house.' Which was a P.D. home, of course, so it's not like it was our own. And it was very small, too, considering all the family we had. They had new homes, but they weren't giving them . . . to everybody.

"P.D. owns everything in this area. You have to leave when they say so. The lease you sign is for twenty years *or* when they need the land, whichever comes first. It used to be ninety-nine years. People said, 'Ninety-nine years, okay, I'll build a house.' They thought they would be there forever. But when they looked at the small print it said, 'Ninety-nine years or tomorrow.' Nobody realized."

Relocation is as much a part of the culture and history of the Morenci mining community as it is to most Native American tribes. Subdivisions, whole towns, even cemeteries have been buried as Phelps Dodge rearranged the earth in search of copper. Just about every life history here is some variation on the theme of Jean Lopez's: "We used to live in Metcalfe. That's not there anymore. They tore it down and moved everybody to Chase Creek."

And like any other population that has seen its homeland jeopardized time and again, the people of this community love it fiercely. They are well aware that their community is monopolized by Phelps Dodge and that it is incredibly, anachronistically, limited; they love it anyway. It's hard to say whether people are attached to the place in spite of its isolation, or because of it.

Fina Roman acknowledged this. "You just simply have to love this community to live in it. It's not like other places, and it's not a place you can bring families into from the city and expect them to be happy. You're going to bring a little wife from Los Angeles to shop at the Circle K? It's not realistic. We have the Circle K, and we have the Yellow Front. If you want to eat out, you go to the Sonic Burger. You can't go to the theater because we don't have one. There's no other form of recreation except what we do—go fishing, spend time with each other. You just have to love to live here."

And they do. They love the mountains, the canyons, and even the river; by the time the flood was six months past, they no longer spoke of the San Francisco as a behemoth that had marched through their town like General Sherman but as the gentle, nature-loving saint it was named for.

Maggie Castañeda's family has gone camping in the nearby forests since the kids were small. Pete, her husband, plays the guitar, and they sing. They used to have a dog named Barney that sang along. "And we fish in the Frisco," Pete said. "We fish with lines until we get tired; then we reach in and catch them by hand." Maggie pointed out that people in Clifton would never starve; after five months without a paycheck, that's a significant consideration. "It's the people in the cities I feel sorry for. We catch cats out of the river. We have fish, venison, the vegetables we grow. We even have that weed, lamb's quarters—do you know it? We eat that."

The Castañedas and their neighbors resent the pollution from the mine. Trace copper and other minerals can be extracted from mining waste by means of a leaching process wherein mounds of the waste—sometimes whole hillsides—are saturated with a sulfuric acid solution. The runoff contains dissolved copper in the form of copper sulfate, a blue compound that is deadly to most living things. The sulfate should be recovered and processed, but according to Maggie, the waste stream Phelps Dodge puts into the San Francisco is deep, telltale turquoise. She cried indignantly, "They're dumping that into *our* river!"

While everyone seemed attached to the community, it was the women who saw themselves as inseparable from it. Maggie said she didn't want Pete to work for P.D. again, even after a settlement; he could find work in Phoenix or Tucson and drive home on the weekends, until retirement. But she didn't want to leave Clifton. ("Won't" is the way she put it.)

"I grew up here, on this very street. The house we live in belonged to the parents of one of my girlfriends, and we played all up and down these staircases. Pete's family lived up at the corner. They were just a whole bunch of boys. We'd see them coming down the hill, going to school, but I never really noticed Pete at that time."

Later she married him. During the strike, between picket duties, they celebrated their thirtieth anniversary.

Janet Fullen and her husband both grew up in Douglas. The bilingual, bicultural colors of a border town don't seem exotic to them; it's just a hometown, the only one they know. Now their five children feel the same way.

Janet's husband worked as a pipefitter in the smelter for fifteen years before the strike. "Hopefully," she said, "one of these days life can get back to normal. But we will stay in Douglas no matter what. It's our home. The people here feel the union has worked too many years and too hard just to give up everything. I know one man who only had two months to retirement, but he felt there was so much at stake he couldn't go in. He would risk losing everything. People outside the strike don't seem to understand that it's not just a matter of wages."

Janet's friend Merci Escalante knew of a similar case, a man with twenty-two years' seniority who was terminated because of the strike. "And do you know what?" Merci asked. "I don't think any of them have any regrets, because they feel that without a contract they'd have no guarantee of retiring after thirty years' service.

"We all know that if this strike isn't successful other companies will follow suit, trying to do the same thing: dividing the people and breaking the unions. Forcing their ways of operating on the people. It's a women's issue, too—not just in the mine, but also outside it. Our homes are at stake."

Merci and Janet believe that the highest stakes of all are in places like Ajo and Clifton. The border town of Douglas, with its old brick *barrios* and modern downtown storefronts, has a slightly more cosmopolitan feel to its streets. From the top floor of the grand old Gadsden Hotel in Douglas you can see the fancy white ironwork of the railway station in Agua Prieta, Mexico.

Each morning, housewives pass both ways through the border station seeking packaged dry goods or freshly baked *pasteles*. Phelps Dodge is a big cheese in Douglas, according to Janet, but not the only cheese in town. "There are other jobs, a little something extra to keep people going. It's not like in Clifton where the mine is the lifeblood of the town. I think that's why there's so much more action there."

This assessment held true for the duration of the strike: the more isolated the community, the stronger the resistance to the company's pressure. The people most dependent on P.D. felt their tradition, families, and homes were most threatened by an injury to the union. In retrospect, many of the women believed this was why they suddenly found themselves on the front lines.

At a meeting of the Morenci Miners Women's Auxiliary, Jessie Tellez declared, "Women have continually persuaded men not to cross the picket line, have kept them from disgracing themselves. Women are the center of the home, and that's why they are also the heroes of this battlefield."

One of the prominent heroines was the auxiliary's president, Fina Roman. But she didn't consider herself exceptional. "These are my family, my friends. I've *always* been very concerned with what happens to the community. I think 'union' is so closely related to 'family.' We refer to each other as brothers and sisters in the union, and that's how I see unionism—as people joining together for one cause that benefits everyone.

"The strike we're experiencing now is a unique situation for us—for the women," Fina said. "So many other things have come into play: violations of human and civil rights, our worst flood in recorded history. We've lost so much. To these women, defending the union is a means of defending family and home, because through the union they've elevated living standards and brought dignity into those homes. Homes where the children can have their teeth fixed if they need it, where they can look forward to going to college, where the wages permit these things. We're striving so the children are not wholly dependent on Phelps Dodge. This is not to say that if they leave and get an education, they can't come back and work for the company. But they will be able to offer something to the employer other than brawn. And to have some choice about what they do. We don't just want to raise people to feed to this machine."

Fina said that if there had been any doubts before, most women felt they *couldn't* move away now—on principle. "This is where our rights are being violated, so if this is where we want to live, we have to defend our rights here, where we make our living and our homes. It's obvious that the enemies of the labor movement thought the Arizona copper strikers would be easy to whip into line, that they didn't have allies to come to their defense. We are proving daily that this just isn't so.

"Our cause, this violation of our human and civil rights, is the gravest issue in the state of Arizona. If we don't fight it, what comes next for every man, woman, and child in this state? Now we know what Mr. Paine meant when he said, 'Tyranny, like hell, is not easily conquered.' Ask any of the homeless or the unemployed. Ask any miner in Arizona."

# 5

# Ask Any Miner

aby Doll Schwartz was the seventh of nine children, and her father, who was in charge of naming her, had run out of ideas. Fortunately, she has preserved a sense of humor about her name. "It was kind of rough growing up with it," she admits, "but sometimes it breaks the ice. Like when I get pulled over by the cops."

She has dropped the "Baby" now and goes by Doll. It suits her, after a fashion: she is small and fine-featured, with wavy blond hair and blue eyes. But this woman is no china doll. If she were, she would be in pieces by now.

Doll is a miner. The strike of 1983 was her second, so she already knew about life without a paycheck. It wasn't a hard decision. "Not that striking was going to be easy—I'd been laid off and had just been back nine months. I needed that job. But there was no doubt in my mind that I would walk out." First of all, she said, going into work without a union contract would be stupid, like doing a dangerous job without safety gear. And second, the hardships of a strike couldn't be worse than what she had already suffered in the Phelps Dodge mine.

She was one of two women hired at the Morenci pit in 1975, the first since World War II. Doll was twenty-one. "My husband and I had just moved here from Bisbee—he transferred from the mine down there. I didn't know anybody in town, didn't have a job, and was really bored. I cleaned the house three times a day, you know, but there's only so much you can do. . . . I decided it was either divorce or go to work. I put in my application, and then I would go up to the office every day just to let them know I was still here. I think the secretaries in the office are actually the ones that hired me—they got so used to seeing me.

"I was hired as a lubrication helper. That means you're an assistant to a lubrication mechanic and go around with him in the pit, servicing all the big equipment. I got a lot of harassment. My foreman just didn't want a woman there. He would hassle me, say things like I couldn't talk to my partner. Can you believe that? The two of us would be working under a machine together for eight hours, and we weren't supposed to talk?

"As a helper, I would have to ride around the pit with some guy in the service truck. They would make a pass, and when I pushed them off they'd get mad. Sometimes they wouldn't bring me back to the women's change room when I had to go to the bathroom—they'd tell me just to go out there in the pit, behind a rock or something. The first time a guy made a pass, it made me feel awful; I went home crying. My husband wasn't much help. He said that wasn't a good enough reason to leave work. I could never come home and talk about work. He would talk all about how hard he worked, what happened on his job, but not me—my job wasn't important. And I was actually making more money than he was!

"It was mostly my foreman that made trouble, more than the guys on the job. I got so discouraged at one point I actually quit. I went into the office and tried to explain to Olsen [her supervisor] what was going on. I was crying, but I told him, 'Don't hold crying against me. Sometimes this is what women do—we cry.' Later they told me that after I left he threw my resignation in the trash. They just figured I'd had a bad day."

Around that time she bid into a position in the locomotive shop. Because of her seniority, the union guaranteed that she would be given at least a trial period on the job. "The foreman didn't want me in there. But the repairman I worked with was a young guy, and he was going to give me a chance. The work was really heavy. The first thing we had to do was turn the engine over to see if it needed a valve job. Sometimes you had to change a brake shoe, or we'd change out the drawbars, the knuckles, the gear boxes. Everybody said I couldn't do it. I'd say, 'How do you know I can't do it? *I* don't even know that I can't do it.' But the foreman always said I couldn't do the same work as a man.

"But he was just wrong. For instance, there was one guy who couldn't lift the air wrench. He was always complaining that it was too heavy. But I was able to lift it. That made me feel great! It's true the work was hard, but usually if I watched the men I could figure out some easier way to do something.

"They used to tease me because I got so dirty. There was this one guy they called Mr. Clean—his job was to take off the big metal screens that serve as the air filters for the engine. They would be black with gunk—oil and crater— and he'd take them off, steam-clean them, and oil them up again, and he wouldn't have a speck of crater on him. I watched him to see how he did it. He told me, 'You just have to be careful, pay attention to where things are.' I got pretty good at it.

"There was a twenty-eight-day probation period to see if you could do a new job, and if you wanted the job. One day, right before the end of the twenty-eight days, my foreman told me I was going to have to use the air wrench for eight hours straight. He actually told the other guys not to help me. They told me about this. They knew I pulled my own weight, and they didn't think it was fair. So they showed me how to do certain things easier, and I came through it all right. At the end, the foreman told me if I really wanted the job I could stay. I told him I'd earned that job."

Less than a year after she started work in the locomotive shop, Doll became pregnant. When her foreman found out, he tried once again to make her give up, this time by sending her to the service yard to do work that involved constant squatting and heavy lifting in awkward positions. She pulled an abdominal muscle.

"They sent me to see a company doctor, and I was lucky, I got the good one, Dr. O'Leary. He was really mad when he found out what they had done to me. He wrote a letter telling them I was capable of working but that the squatting was dangerous for me and that I should go back to my old job in repairs. So I got to go back. The company got the idea I wasn't leaving.

"I had to use the men's bathroom, of course. I would kick the door and say, 'Whoever's in there, get out, because I gotta go!' One day one of the head guys was in there, and when he came out, what a look he gave me! Right after that they gave me my own bathroom. The guys built it, fixed it all up for me, and asked me what color I wanted it painted; I said yellow. They would have painted 'Doll' over the door, but they had to just put 'Women.' "

Her co-workers were not just being solicitous because she was pregnant. She had their honest respect. By this time she was a first-class helper making fifty-six dollars a day and had earned the nickname "Fifty-six dollars worth of a-lotta-help."

Doll's weight went from 94 pounds to 154. By her seventh month, she said, she looked pretty much like a barrel on legs. She had to leave for work a half-hour early each morning, because it took her that long to walk to the pit from the parking lot. "By that time I'd just about had it. One day while I was working, an air hose came loose. They're really heavy and fly all around—it's compressed air—and if they hit you they can really hurt you. The way I stopped it finally was I jumped on it, just stood on it. So there I was, down in this little servicing pit with about two feet of room on each side, pregnant out to here, with that air hose whipping around. I thought to myself, 'I have proven my point.' I stopped working the next day."

At that time there was no maternity leave, and Doll says her union co-workers ridiculed her for even suggesting it. "They would say, 'Why should you get paid leave for being pregnant? You sure had fun getting that way.' I asked them, 'What about a guy that breaks his leg when he's out playing baseball? He had fun doing that, and he gets medical leave!' " Doll's logic, if offbeat, was convincing; she won six weeks' paid leave.

After her son was born she decided to quit, since her family wasn't desperate for the money. But circumstances changed. Within a year she was divorced and in need of a job. She went to work as a secretary for the city. "It was okay for a while, but after working in the mine, $3.10 an hour just didn't make it. I knew I could be making those bucks. So I put in my application. I'd had it in for three weeks when they hired me as a cleanup laborer. They were creating a new department, the leach plant. I started back as a laborer making around $10 an hour.

"I was a novelty out there. They had me work as the janitor, which was usually a job for the older guys. They treated me really well. I guess you could say I took advantage of a good situation, but I figured after all the harassment I'd been through, I could use a break. Then we got laid off for a few months, in December of 1980. When I came back there was a new foreman at the plant who really wanted to get rid of women. The superintendent was even worse; he made it real obvious. Whenever I was alone he would yell and cuss at me. He would always make sure the foreman was around, too. Finally something clicked—I realized he was trying to provoke me to the point where I would cuss back, and then they could fire me. He was using the foreman as a witness, to be his stoolie.

"Plus he really pushed me. He expected me to do the eight hours' work I had done and then do all three offices. They brought in this brand-new big old buffer. It was too big. I know how to handle a buffer—you have to hold it low, below your hips. I told him I couldn't operate that big thing. So the super told me *he* would show me how to operate the buffer. Well, it only took him about two seconds to get that thing out of control and up on the carpet. He had me and a chair all tied up in the cord. He said, 'Well, I guess you were right, it is kind of hard to operate. We'll have to get something different.'

"He expected me to do more work than anybody could do in eight hours. I told him that I couldn't do that much in one shift, so he turned my statement around and tried to use it to get me fired—said I'd admitted I couldn't do the job. I was down at Cole's Pizza that night talking about it, and one of the guys there happened to be a grievance man for the Steelworkers. He heard me, and asked me about my situation. The next day I went in and everything was taken care of just like that. I didn't even have to file a grievance. My super wasn't too happy about it. He said, 'I didn't think you would go to the union. We could have worked something out.' Sure! I was impressed when I saw what the union could do for me."

But every victory led to new harassment; life in the mine was never going to be pleasant for Doll. "Finally it was too much, what with a divorce in the last year and all the hassle on the job. When I went in to work I felt like a caged animal. Someone would just say 'hi' and I would start crying. My doctor gave me a medical release for sexual harassment. When I went in with my release, my super yelled and cussed, said I was worthless, all kinds of stuff. Then the foreman walked in, and the super just turned, like Dr. Jekyll and Mr. Hyde. He said, really sweetly, 'Doll here needs to go to the hospital.' "

She was sent to a hospital in Tucson and placed in the care of a psychiatrist. She began to improve immediately. At the end of her medical leave she was hired back as a laborer in the Morenci mill. There she had bad luck again: her foreman was one of her ex-husband's buddies. For fun, he assigned Doll to work with her ex and his girlfriend. Doll stuck it out.

"It was hard work in the mill, too, shoveling that ore off the belts. It was hot and humid and smelled like ammonia. They always made the new people do the dirtiest jobs, clear out the stuff under the belts that hadn't been cleaned up in twenty years. They would make us crawl down into these tunnels that were full of black soot and concentrate. It would get all over you, in your eyes. That was a savage job."

By 1983, Doll had finally reached a bright spot in her career. She stated with pride, "I'm an operating engineer." Her favorite job was operating the moly plant, in which molybdenum is extracted from the mill waste. She described it as "a whole little miniature mill."

"In the moly plant the operator has control over everything. You have to get the reagents just right, and you have to be careful—you're working with sulfuric acid and sodium cyanide, the chemicals they use in a gas chamber. I am a good operator. I get a high percentage of moly out of the ore. It was always hard for me to get these jobs, but I'd convince them to let me try. 'Teach me,' I'd say. 'I can learn it. I'm not stupid.' Once he gave me a chance, my foreman would be saying, 'Well, let's see what else she can do.' He told the other guys I was a good operator.

"I went through a lot of awful stuff, but because of it, things are better for women now. I think I changed some of the men's ideas about women. At least I can feel good about that. Pat and I, the first two women that came in, sort of laid the groundwork for other women. The company learned, and the unions learned. The unions brought in maternity leave, for instance, after both of us got pregnant. I guess they realized this was something they had to consider—that women get pregnant.

"Women have been good for the unions, and the unions are good for the women. They've done a lot for us. And now I know I can go out and get another job, preferably a union job. I don't worry about supporting myself. I know I can do that."

In 1984, the second year of the strike, women made up 15 percent of all workers in the mining industry (Bureau of Labor Statistics). They are, of necessity, a rough, tough 15 percent. Doll Schwartz said that, more than anything, working in the mine had changed the way she felt about herself. "Really, I feel like there isn't too much I couldn't do. It's built up my confidence to where I know if I set my mind to something, I'll do it."

Years ago, when she was a lubricator assistant, Doll occasionally caught sight of a much older woman who'd been working in the mine since World War II. Her name was Opal. They were in different departments and never really had a chance to talk. Now it's too late. But Doll still wonders about Opal's life: Was it even tougher for women back then? Was the work harder? When the men came home from the war and wanted their jobs back, was the harassment unbearable?

Flossie Navarro says "yes" to all of the above, and she should know. Before getting her medical retirement in 1967, she shoveled rock in the Morenci mine for twenty-three years. She didn't stay there all that time because of any fondness for shoveling, she told me flatly. "I didn't really like the work at all. But we was raising kids, and we needed the money. We raised eleven—Ed had ten already, and then me and him had one. So it wasn't a matter of liking it, it was a matter of having to.

"I don't really have no understanding about the women's movement because I've always drawed the same pay as a man. You got in there and done your part because you was getting paid just as much as he was. I always felt like if he had to do an hour's work I should do it too. The only difference in the paychecks was for the extra day. Back then there was a state law that women could only work six days a week. Then we'd get two days off. After I went to shift work I'd work six days and the seventh you was off. The men, see, could work twenty-eight days straight through and then get their time off.

"I really didn't want to work more than six days, but it would have been better when you was on graveyard shift. You'd work six nights and kind of get your eatin' and sleepin' straightened up, and then you'd be off and have to be up early with the kids. Then you'd have to go back and work six more nights. That was kind of aggravating. You'd rather go ahead and work that one night, not for the money-wise but for the rest you'd get."

Flossie is a union maid, through and through. She began with the CIO, during the war, then joined Mine-Mill, then the United Steelworkers of America. "Twenty-three years I was union. The union made sure everything was fair. The dues I paid every month wasn't that high—it was worth it. Each time the union fought and got us a paid holiday or sick leave or whatever, we just got that right along with the men. When I first went to work we only got two or three holidays a year. In '44 I got sixty-four cents an hour to push that wheelbarrow. It was the unions that got us better pay." Flossie was emphatic on this point. "P.D. wasn't going to give us nothing. They don't say, 'Here it is, come get it.' No, they don't!"

Bringing up the strike proved to be a reliable way to rouse her ire. "I think that's a damn dirty deal, is what I think about that! What's involved in the strike is what we fought for all those years—the unions. And it makes you mad and gets you hot under the collar to see them try to take it away. But what can you do? You'd just like to give someone a rap across the mouth."

Flossie, like so many others, felt that racial equality was especially at stake in the current strike. She had seen the bad old days. "Now, I never wanted a promotion myself. I was just satisfied to go and do my job if they'd leave me alone. But Ed, he tried to go up. Every time he'd come up in line for seniority somebody'd whack him down again to the bottom. Because he was a Mexican."

Ed Navarro, one of Carmina Garcia's two surviving brothers and the man Flossie married, had grown up among the peach and quince orchards at Eagle Creek. His family had been driven from their farm, and he was working as a laborer in the mine when Flossie came in. Because of poor health, he wasn't drafted, and he remained in Morenci through the war. Not surprisingly, this was when he was finally promoted to repairman—when the only alternative would have been to promote a woman.

Ed still had vivid forty-year-old memories of working with women in the mine—including the one who became his bride. "Oh, I saw them push those wheelbarrows. They would get a good load on them and haul it about fifty yards over there and dump it. It kind of hurt you to see women doing that."

I asked Ed if he respected Flossie for doing such hard work. His eyes sparkled, and he answered without hesitation, "Yes. That's how come she married me."

Marriages between Anglos and Hispanics were extremely uncommon in those days, but Flossie insists this wasn't a problem for her. "Oh, people didn't think much of it; they would say things. Now, my family always treated him good—they couldn't believe he was a Mexican. They didn't see too many back in Arkansas. When we went back there people would stare at us. But I'll tell you one thing. If you ate in a restaurant, they would take your money.

If you stayed in a motel, they'd take your money. They didn't ask if it was 'mixed' money.

"There was another thing I could never understand. If a Mexican woman married a white man, people around here didn't think that was so bad. The woman would change her name, you know, and all. But if a white woman married a Mexican man, that was different; they didn't like that. To me, I never could see the difference. The kids are going to come out mixed, ever which way they manage it!"

Regardless of popular opinion, she and Ed consider their union successful. "We'll soon be married thirty-four years, and we never fought over money. Right, Ed? I brought home that paycheck, too, so I felt like I could always do what I wanted with the money, and we agreed on things. I always figured what was his was mine, and if what I had wasn't his, that was his fault!"

Flossie sometimes thinks she might have liked to stay home with the children, but with eleven, that simply was never an option. There wasn't enough money. She sighed, remembering the year they had two graduating from high school and two from eighth grade, all at once. "Kids have to have an awful lot," she said.

"We never told our kids what to do. We just raised them to go to school and behave theirselves and not get in trouble, and thank God we never did have one get locked up, I don't think. Well, really that's something to be thankful for, isn't it?" She leaned back, clapped her hands down on the arms of her overstuffed chair, and looked across the room at Ed. And laughed. "We raised eleven kids, and now here we are looking at each other."

Halfway up the hill between Clifton and Morenci is a bar called the Refrigerated Cave. That's what the sign says. It is cool inside, and dark enough to make you think about going pale and blind, like those cave fish. It's a relief to get away from the heat and sun, though, and the Cave is also touted for its corkscrew french fries. It was a favorite haunt of Arlene Moreno, Mary Lou Gonzales, and Margaret Skidmore, a threesome who became rather notorious during the strike. All three stand somewhere under five feet five. Margaret is fair, with wavy hair; Mary Lou is dark-eyed, talkative, and feisty; Arlene is the quiet one, with long black hair and the air of physical stillness often possessed by Papago women.

The sight of three women drinking beer together is nothing remarkable until you remember that in Clifton, from the beginning of time until 1983, women didn't go into bars unless they were accompanied by a husband. But Mary Lou, Arlene, and Margaret went where they pleased, and had for some time. They were miners. After breaking that monstrous taboo, all the little ones seemed hardly worth bothering with. The Refrigerated Cave is where they wanted to go for the afternoon, and there we sat, while they told me about their jobs.

In a copper mine, they said, there are three ways to do things: the right way, the wrong way, and the Phelps Dodge way. I asked for an example. "Okay," Arlene said. "Sometimes we have to use jackhammers while we hang by a rope. You have to jackhammer your way down this incline. If you go over the edge, you could fall into the crucible, where the molten metal is. Think about that for a minute."

I did. I thought about the one and only time I'd used a jackhammer, and then I thought about the laws of physics. "It's crazy to be using a jackhammer while you're hanging on a rope, isn't it?" I asked.

"Right. The hammer throws you back."

They were happy to provide other examples. One of the worst jobs, they agreed, is cleaning the stacks. Each smokestack has a door that opens at the bottom so a worker can go inside and clean it out. "That flu ash is really hot," Margaret said. "They're supposed to wait to send you in there until it's cool— below 120 degrees. But sometimes they don't, and that dust falls down on you. It's got arsenic and stuff in it, and it is *hot*. One guy got buried in it up to his waist."

For protective clothing, they get paper coveralls. "You have to try and tape it around the wrists and wherever—you have to improvise. Then, once you get all taped up, you just hope you don't have to go to the bathroom. If you do, you just get that darn hole cleaned out as fast as you can."

Both Margaret and Arlene have worked in the "arsenic holes." "You wear a respirator," Margaret said, "but even with the respirator I'd go home feeling sick every day. It doesn't protect you. I felt like vomiting all the time." (Lung damage from sulfur dioxide and arsenic fumes in the smelter and silica in the pit is the worst slow killer of miners in this type of operation.) "My skin was green where the arsenic got on me, because sometimes the paper would tear."

When inspectors from the Occupational Safety and Health Administration (OSHA) were coming around to monitor hazards, everyone knew it. The foremen always made sure everything was clean that day, and certain workers would actually be told to stay out of sight.

Of the three, Arlene had worked in the mines the longest. She was hired in the mid-1970s, after the unions won a sex discrimination suit in 1969. But most of her co-workers were not thrilled about her being there and complained that having a woman on the job made it look as if their work was easy or trivial. "There were times I thought about quitting, but I just couldn't. The women in the general office, the secretaries, were saying I would stay, and the men were saying I wouldn't—they had a bet going.

"I worked in the smelter, in the reverb furnaces, where the slag comes out. From there, they send the ore over to the converters, and then it goes into the anodes and they make the copper molds. Usually I had to jackhammer around the reverbs to clean them out. It was dirty and dusty and hot. I also cleaned out ash pits, right around the furnaces. At first the job was scary. They would just tell you to do something and then leave you. More or less you'd have to figure it out by yourself. I was always wondering if I was going to get blown up or something."

Mary Lou pointed out that Arlene had good reason to be worried—the job was dangerous.

"Yeah," Arlene conceded. "There were guys that got burned by calcine. That's concentrate that's been baked at a real high temperature in the furnace. It looks like powder. If it's on the ground and you don't know it and you step in it, you get real bad burns. Through your shoes. At first I really was afraid of getting burned, but as time went by I was less afraid. I felt good about doing my job."

Mary Lou interrupted to relate an incident. "One time after I'd started working in the mine, this foreman said to me, 'We got a girl in there that puts those men to shame.' He says, 'Man, she sure knows how to use that jackhammer!' And he's not the only one that told me about this girl, that she was a damn good worker." Mary Lou paused, with obvious pride in her friend. "They were talking about Arlene. I didn't even know her then."

After ordering another round of beers and exchanging supportive small talk with some male strikers who had walked into the bar, Mary Lou told me she had started in the Morenci mine in 1978. For nearly a year after she put in her application, she heard nothing. When she was finally called, she was flabbergasted by the assignment they gave her: powerhouse pumpman. She didn't even know what a powerhouse was.

"It's an operator's job, I found out, with a lot of responsibilities. You work downstairs in the powerhouse taking care of the air compressors, the floor converters, the blowers and pumps that come off the turbines, and all this. The first day I was scared to death. They start by telling you that if anything goes wrong it can blow up the powerhouse, or it can make the water back up into the smelter and blow the furnaces up, because they're all connected. All I was thinking was, 'God, I hope I get it right!'

Anyone who thinks that being a miner calls for nothing more than good biceps and a twenty-pound hammer should talk to Mary Lou. "Some of the guys that tried to break me in, I just don't think they had real sufficient training. Not enough to explain things very well. They just said, 'This is it, and what you do is put it on this and this and that's it. And this is another one, and when this goes wrong you go like this and this and that's it.' Whew! And then I was down there by myself.

"But on my own I learned the job real good. I read the book—they have a big old manual that explains everything. I would read a little in the book, then I'd go look at the pump and mark it in my head what it was and how it ran. I learned."

Mary Lou was on the job a few months before she ran into the familiar snag. "I was told that the general foreman did not want a woman in this power plant because it's a lot of responsibility. There had never been a woman in the powerhouse before. I just decided, hell, they're not going to tell me I can't do this. I would just have to do an extra good job.

"There's a lot of split-minute decisions you have to make, and a lot of valves that are hard to turn. Even a man has a hard time. Some of them I had to put a lot of elbow grease into. But I've always thought if you give a woman a chance at a job, she can probably do it. Sure, some things a woman might not be able to handle physically, but not all men can handle it either. Sometimes it took two or three of us to turn those valves. Basically, I could turn them as easily as anybody else.

"The general foreman was one of these that's prejudiced against women and Mexicans, so I had two strikes against me when I walked in. I tried not to let it bother me. I just wanted to do my job and not kiss somebody's ass, that's the way I look at it. I knew some guys were just waiting for me to screw up, but I never gave them the opportunity. I just had to be better than them. That's the way I felt."

As the years went by, Mary Lou never moved from that position. It was her choice. "I had the opportunity to move up the ladder, but I didn't want to go on to another job, even though it was higher paying, until I really knew the first one. After I learned to handle all that equipment and do my job well, I felt good. The last year I was there, I was breaking in a new guy as an operator. The general foreman said to him, 'You listen to her, because she's one of the best operators we have.' I thought that was great. I knew myself it was true. It took me five years to get to that point, but now I know it."

Mary Lou, Arlene, and Margaret all said the union was essential to their safety and peace of mind on the job. "Without the union, I could go and complain about something to the foreman, sure, and he'd probably say, 'You don't like it? *Pa'fuera!'* [Get lost.] So I joined the union, because I felt they could fight for my rights better than I could go it alone."

Arlene reminded Mary Lou that she tried to sign her up for the union when she was first hired, and Mary Lou refused. Mary Lou defended herself. "I didn't think things could be as bad as they are at the mines. But I found out. In less than a year, I joined."

The first grievance she filed, and won, was for a better schedule. "When I first started working they would run me twenty-four, twenty-eight days straight. Over the Christmas holidays the senior operators wanted off, and since I was the bottom man, bottom person, I had to fill in. That was all during Christmas and New Year's. I never got to do anything with my family. And I was so tired—too tired to be doing that job. They would take me from shift to shift. I'd come off P.M.s one day, and they'd call me up that night to come in days. Come in days and try to go to sleep and come in graveyard that night. They had me bouncing like a ball. I finally got fed up and filed a grievance on it, so they would put me on a regular schedule.

"They'd get by with that kind of thing until the union would put a stop to it. There was a two-month strike, a while back, where one of the demands was not to have to work over fourteen days straight. It was just a side issue, but we won it. Before that they could work you any days they wanted to. They didn't care about a person, you know, that you have to sleep, that you want to have a weekend. You really need a union at this place. This corporation's past history speaks for itself. I don't have to sit here and tell you, because it's past history and they're not going to change unless they're forced to.

"The guys I work with now say, 'Yeah, when I started, all the track gang was Mexicans, and the white boys got into the machine shop.' The only reason P.D. started hiring women, Mexican women especially, was because of the union and federal law. Without that, you can believe there wouldn't be any Mexican women in there right now. Maybe white women, but no Mexicans or blacks or Indians or what-have-you. That corporation is very biased."

It's hard to imagine why anyone would endure so much harassment, hardship, and danger to life and limb, for any amount of money—if they had a choice. And that is the point, they don't. Not in this town. Before she became a miner, Arlene was a babysitter. She also supported herself for a while at the Morenci dry-cleaning shop. At twenty-three she had still been earning minimum wage at jobs most people consider the territory of high school kids padding their allowance.

"I didn't really know whether I wanted to work up at the mine or not," she admitted. "When I first got the application, I filled it out and then rode around with it in the car for three weeks. But I knew that unless I worked for the mine there really wasn't a chance of ever getting a good-paying job."

Mary Lou, who grew up in nearby Safford, worked at a manufacturing plant there for seven years before she was hired by Phelps Dodge. She sewed tents and backpacks; it was a nonunion shop, mainly women. "Tell me what the minimum wage was in '71 and I'll tell you what I was making when I started there. After seven years I was making $3.50." As a powerhouse pumpman, she started at $8.07 an hour.

If not for the decent wage, these women wouldn't have considered going into arsenic holes or cleaning furnaces or dangling from ropes to run a jackhammer. It's wasn't their idea of a good time. So they were baffled that anyone would be willing to cross the picket line. They claimed the work wasn't safe. With many untrained people operating the equipment, the likelihood of accidents was enormous. The mine was now being run not by miners, they said, but by people who only weeks before had been secretaries, ranchers, or short-order cooks. Clifton's weekly newspaper, the *Copper Era,* reported on September 12, 1983, that in their haste to replace strikers, Phelps Dodge had even hired a convicted felon. (The FBI came into the mine and removed him.)

"There have been accidents," Mary Lou said, her dark eyes intensely serious. "A lot more since the strike started. They've been shipping the people out to hospitals in Wilcox or Tucson—they don't want them here in the company hospital, because they don't want anybody to know about it. But we find out, from salaried people we know. There was even a guy killed."

Phelps Dodge had not released an official report on the death of the worker, but obviously this wasn't something that could be concealed in a town the size of Clifton. "We know the family," Mary Lou said, "and we know they buried somebody."

"For this kind of work," Margaret said, "you have to have a union. What the scabs are getting now is really ridiculous. They don't have any rights, and they're getting six dollars an hour. That's not a paycheck to risk your neck for."

The most recent contract Phelps Dodge had offered the strikers was a joke, they said: they could return to work, but the scabs would have seniority. The strikers would go on waiting lists to be called in and would give up their benefits, and they would be working under scabs. "The contract we went on strike for was just to keep the same things we had," Mary Lou said. "We weren't asking for an increase in pay, let's be real clear on that. The newspapers are calling us greedy, but all we want is to keep our same medical and wages. The company wants to take away half the medical benefits, half the retirement, half our vacation. We just want to keep what we've earned."

They were angry at the way the newspapers tended to make their requests seem either outrageous or trivial. One report they read said miners went on strike "for nothing more significant than hairnets and water." They suggested that the reporter ought to go into the mine for a day to see what it's like. They had some other suggestions for him too.

Shirley Randall worked with Arlene in the ash pits. When they were caught in a furnace explosion, Arlene helped Shirley to safety, possibly saving her from losing her hands. Shirley is grateful. As for the rest of her co-workers, the men, she doesn't have a lot of happy memories.

"That work nearly killed me the first thirty days, it was so hard. I didn't know if I would make it. But my husband said I couldn't do it, so I stuck it out, and after the first thirty days I didn't hurt anymore.

"On my second day they sent me to the bedding plant. At lunch break I was sitting there by myself—I didn't know where everybody disappeared to at lunchtime—so I got my lunch and sat there, dirty hands and all, and ate. I saw a spill start, but nobody's life was in danger, so I just sat there and watched it. The foreman had told me over and over again that morning, never pull the emergency ropes for a false alarm.

"It spilled until it shut the conveyor down. There were some machinists working there, and they had a five-gallon bucket of tools sitting there. When it got close to bellying that bucket I asked them if they wanted me to move it. They said sure. And I just kept watching that spill. Pretty soon it got bad enough that bells started ringing everywhere, and here comes the foreman. He yelled at me, 'Why the hell didn't you pull the rope?' I said, 'You told me, only if it's an emergency.' He said, 'Well, what the hell do you CALL this?'

"So he made me clean up all that spill, my second day on the job. I was really mad. I got up on that pile of muck and I cussed, and I put just as much as would fit on a shovel. Everybody came and told me I should file a grievance, but I couldn't, only if I wanted to lose my job—I was still on probation. So I just got mad.

"I went home crying sometimes. Lots of days I cried there. I didn't want them to see me cry, but I was more concerned with letting them see that I was afraid. Jack Lone also started the same time I did, and he was working there with me. The third day, they sent us back to the bedding plant, and he worked from about 7:30 till about 9:00, and then he put his shovel down and quit. So I used him as an example of what not to be. I was proud because I could take it, even though he couldn't. In those early days I would think about that to make myself feel better.

"Now Jack's a scab."

When Shirley first went to work for P.D. her family was far from supportive. Her mother simply said that women "didn't do that." Her brother Bobby, a welder, knew what the smelter was like and didn't want Shirley in there for her own sake. Her husband didn't dissuade her from applying, though he told her he doubted she'd get hired. "I said, 'Maybe not, but without an application in they're not going to come looking for me.' Really, my husband wanted me to work there. His father drowned in this river, and his mother had worked so hard and raised her family on nothing. So my husband pushed me to get my GED [General Equivalency Diploma], and to do this. He wanted me to have confidence that if something ever happened to him I could support the kids.

"I put up with a lot of hassle from the men because they thought the wife should be at home. But I told them, 'It could be your sister, it could be your daughter having to support family.' It's true! A lot of women end up having to do it alone. Why should one woman's family do without the necessary things when another woman has a husband who can earn a decent wage? It's not the kids' fault, and it's not the woman's fault. Why can't a woman make as much as men, if they do the same job?

"Now, oh, boy! Who knows what those men are thinking—their wives are out on the picket lines. Some of their wives have been arrested. I think those guys have probably changed their minds. But then, I was pretty convincing, too."

Shirley says she endured relentless sexual harassment on the job. "My foreman would use his position to try and force me to do things. With him it was every day, *every day*, that I worked. Even after I had seniority, so that I should have been driving a truck, he kept me cleaning ash pits all the time. So he could go up and see me forty times a day. I asked him, 'Why do you send me to the ash pits every day?' And he said, 'So I can have you right under my thumb, Shirley.'

"I think it's happened to a lot of women who've worked up here—probably all of them. But we still did our jobs. And I am proud that I could lift the heavy doors, turn up a wheelbarrow and dump it the right way, instead of tipping it over the side like girls do, you know. I worked hard at my job. I built up physically, developed muscles. It didn't help my femininity any, but it sure helped my self-confidence."

In January 1979, Shirley was badly burned when a furnace blew up. It had snowed during the night, a rare event in Morenci, and people had trouble getting up the icy hill to the mine. Everyone was late and in a hurry. The concentrate being fed into the furnace was damp. When moisture enters a smelter furnace, where the normal temperature is 2,800 degrees Fahrenheit, it vaporizes instantly. The result is an explosion.

Shirley and Arlene were cleaning the ash pit—an area just above the furnace where the ash is collected from the air uptake. Shirley was watching while Arlene used a pressurized air hose to blow the ash to one side, where they could rake it out. "It was really cold in there that day," Shirley recalled. "You'd think the furnaces would be real hot, but you have to stand right next to them to feel any heat because there's a suction; they suck in cold air. I was standing right next to the furnace with my hands almost against it, to warm them up.

"I'd always been told that a furnace gets real quiet when it's about to blow. I never understood that, until that day. All of a sudden I knew it was going to blow. And Arlene was out there.

"I ran out to get Arlene, but as soon as I ran off the platform, she already knew there was going to be an explosion, and she was running back to get me. If I had stayed where I was I would have been okay. But I was out there right in the middle of the fire. Those furnaces are under pressure, so when they blow up it's just a big fireball that comes out.

"By that time it was black—Arlene had gone into the smoke, looking for me, and she burned one ear and breathed in all this black yuck. Neither one of us could see anything, and I couldn't get out of the fire. It seems like I was in it for a long time, but it couldn't have been more than a few seconds or I'd have been gone. I have a hard time putting it together, because I guess I went into shock. I put my hands up like this in front of my face and kept turning them. When I finally got out of it, I didn't realize I was hurt.

"Arlene got me down to the office somehow. By that time my ears hurt, and when I pulled my glasses off I saw that my hands were just blistering, the skin hanging. I still didn't realize I was hurt so bad. I thought they were going to fix me up and send me back to work. While I was sitting in the foreman's office waiting, I remember being embarrassed because people saw me. Anything that went on up there, people just flocked.

"I was in the hospital for six weeks. The doctor told me that if I hadn't had callouses on my hands, I would have lost my hands. The veins would have perforated. If I'd been in that fire any longer, I surely would have."

Shirley laid her hands on the table and turned them over to show me. They didn't look bad, unless you looked closely. The sides of her fingers were heavily scarred and still tender, five years after the accident. At the time, she said, they looked like barbecued ribs. The skin under her fingernails peeled off like potato chips.

"While I was in the hospital P.D. went in and completely redid the second floor, because it was real hazardous. It was their fault that this accident took place. Then, on the day I went back to work, I went to the safety office to get my equipment, and they told me that I had not been wearing any safety equipment. The bosses had told everybody I was going to be fired for ignoring safety procedures. Which was an outright lie."

Three months after the accident Shirley finally quit her job because of continued sexual harassment. She was just too tired to file another grievance. But she was still in for one more surprise—she received a letter informing her that when she left Phelps Dodge, it would be with the understanding that she had completely recovered from the accident and had no permanent scars.

"I got real mad. I called the union, and Angel Rodriguez told me they would handle the case. I did get money, I won, but I wasn't really interested in the money. I wanted to get up on the stand and say what they had done to me."

Health and safety issues are a common battleground between Phelps Dodge employees and the company. Especially in dispute is the question of how well a worker must be to return to the job. Eddie Marquez, for instance, was proclaimed healthy by a company doctor and sent back to work a few months after he had open-heart surgery at the age of fifty-six. "Seven other guys had had that same operation," Ed says, "and they were all given medical retirement. But the chief surgeon for P.D. said, 'I'm going to make an example out of Eddie Marquez.' That was his mistake."

With the help of the union, Eddie fought for and won his medical retirement. An independent physician stated that it would be dangerous for Eddie to lift more than twenty pounds.

Monopolization of medical care can be one of the most frightening aspects of a company town. Getting a second opinion from a doctor who's not on the company payroll involves not only a considerable expense for the miner, but also a very long drive. From Ajo, the nearest hospital that isn't owned by Phelps Dodge is well over a hundred miles away. Gloria Blase came up against this problem when she was injured on the job. She was working on a crew building tracks for the rail cars that carry ore out of the pit. Her right hand began to bother her after she and eight other people carried a thirty-foot steel rail over a hill.

"I told my boss it was hurting," she recalled, "and he said, 'Oh, it'll get better, it's just sore.' So I worked Saturday and all day Sunday. I kept telling him it was hurting me a lot, and he kept saying it would go away. He said he couldn't let me go home because we were short-handed. So I stayed.

"On Monday morning when I woke up, I couldn't move my arm. My husband had to lift it and move it around, because I had no feeling in it. It was completely cold. I went to the company hospital, and they gave me one Tylenol with codeine, for the pain, and said I was fit to go back to work the next day. I went back that night, and the doctor wouldn't even come in to check it. He just told the nurse to give me another pill.

"This went on for a long time. I have a medical background, and I knew enough to be worried about my arm. I also knew they weren't going to listen. Three years ago the same thing had happened to my other hand, and they just gave me 50 milligrams of Demerol and sent me into work. That's what they give you for surgery. I was taking that, and still working!

"Finally I told them, 'If you don't give me a referral out to see a noncompany doctor, I'll go on my own, and then I'll sue this damn company!' They gave me a referral. I went to Tucson, and the doctor there told me my hand was grossly abnormal. They did surgery the next week."

Gloria was still on disability, recovering from surgery on the tendons in her hand, when the strike began. Because she was still unable to work, the company had to continue her disability pay; the minute she was declared "well," she would be considered a striker and the checks would stop. Gloria continued making the long trip to see her physician in Tucson. "One day when I went in for my appointment the doctor said, 'I got a phone call from somebody in Phelps Dodge who said he was a doctor. He told me you were well enough to work. I just want to let you know about this phone call. I don't work for P.D., I work for myself, and I call the shots as I see them.' He told me that I couldn't possibly go back to work yet, that my hand wasn't healed."

Soon afterward, Gloria was terminated for allegedly breaking the windows of a company car with a sledgehammer. There were no witnesses, and no such incident appeared in the company's films, but her disability pay stopped coming. Shaking her head in amazement, Gloria said she couldn't have picked up a sledgehammer if her life depended on it.

The termination hardened Gloria's resolve to stay on the line and fight the strike to the end. "I decided we have to win this for the sake of everything. Not only for the union, but for the self-respect of this town. The scabs are already the losers. If they get hurt or fired, they don't have anybody fighting for them."

Gloria's belief in the union was based on tangible things—protection from hazard and discrimination. Born and raised in Ajo, the daughter of a Mexican father and a Papago mother, she had known just about every kind of prejudice in her twenty-nine years. But even more than her own experience, her father's life had taught her the necessity of the union. "My dad has always been a union man," she said, "an operating engineer. He worked as a locomotive operator for thirty-four years.

"For more than twenty of those years he was a groundman on the crane. The other operators were all white. My dad never got the benefits of being an operator like they did—the bonus, or the extra vacation weeks. For only the last four months he worked with an operator's time card and an operator's wages. It took him that many years to get it. That's why he decided to retire, so he could go out with an operator card.

"I remember the hard times we had for the strike of 1964. I was young then, but I knew what the strike was for, and I knew where my dad would be without it. As soon as I was hired, I joined the union."

Respect for their fathers was a common denominator among the women who worked for, and then fought against, Phelps Dodge. For Janie Ramon, the first woman in the Ajo mine, the word "union" is synonymous with her memories of her father. "My dad would go to union meetings and bring home stickers and stuff. He always had a union sticker on his hard hat. Before he was killed, in a car wreck, when I was going to school in Flagstaff studying to be a teacher, I was going to be in the teachers' union."

Doll Schwartz also looked to her father as a role model. "Dad was a miner in Bisbee, a Teamster. We were a union family. I learned a lot from him. He would bring home Teamster stickers, and I'd put them on my bike. There were strikes and hard times and a lot of mouths to feed—there were nine of us kids, five girls and four boys—but the thought of going in never crossed his mind. He was a man with morals. Once he found a purse with six hundred dollars in it—in those days six hundred dollars was like six thousand dollars—but he didn't touch it. He made sure the purse was returned to the lady.

"My dad was everything to me; he could do anything. When my shoes broke, he fixed them. Whenever he was working on something I would be there handing him his tools. I've been a repairman's helper since I was this high!"

Arlene's father and grandfather were miners, and strikers. Her friend Mary Lou, who didn't come from a mining family, looked to these and the other old-timers when it came to making a decision about the strike. "They've been in there thirty-five, thirty-seven years," she pointed out. "What can I tell them after just five years? They know what a union is, and if they weren't going to work without one, I wasn't either."

Lydia Gonzalez Knott followed the same line of reasoning. Her father, who was president of the Boilermakers at the Morenci mine for more than twenty-five years before he died, left a substantial moral legacy to his children. "My brother and I are both miners," Lydia said. "Before the strike we sat down and we talked. A lot of people were saying they were going to go in without a contract. I told my brother, 'You know, it's something we can't do because of our dad.' We never had a second thought about the decision we made.

"This whole business started with those air traffic controllers, and now us, and it's got to stop somewhere. We were raised to feel this way. You follow your unions and you respect them, and you respect the company if you can. But really, how the hell can I respect this company? We're fighting for our jobs, our future, for food on the table for our kids. If we don't get a contract we'll look for work someplace else."

Lydia felt that working without a contract would be something akin to slavery. For evidence, she pointed to current conditions in the mine. "The scabs in there now are working twelve-hour days for twenty-six days in a row. I've worked that twenty-six days on and two days off, and that's hell. After twenty-six days I was grouchy!"

Lydia's children, who were gathered around her kitchen table, solemnly attested to the truth of this last statement.

"I wouldn't do it," Lydia declared. "I've seen some people cross the picket line, go into work, and then change their minds because of the way they're working them. People write to the papers and say P.D. had us spoiled. That makes me mad, because we gave those people a good eight-hour day, and we worked hard. I really enjoyed my job. If I had a contract I would still enjoy it. I was always learning new things, working with jackhammers, air wrenches. I learned to operate all kinds of cranes. I had my doubts at first, but I told them if I couldn't handle a job, I'd be the first to admit it. So far I've never had to."

Lydia has a letter she treasures, written by her foreman several years ago at a time when she was about to be laid off. It reads, in part: "I may have had some personal reservations concerning a woman's ability to handle this type of heavy industrial equipment, but Lydia has consistently proven me wrong."

Lydia's children were eleven, ten, and five. She was supporting them on forty dollars a week from the union—her picket pay—and a very occasional child-support payment from her ex-husband. That was it. As a striker, she couldn't even qualify for food stamps.

I wondered if her two older children, who were approaching the age when the "right" clothes and possessions attain such universal importance, might resent their mother's decision. I never had to ask. As we sat around the kitchen table talking about air wrenches and 360-ton cranes, her children's eyes followed Lydia's gestures with frank admiration. When she talked about the union they were quieter than most children in church.

"The kids are real supportive," Lydia said. "It surprises me. I was fooling around with them one day and said I might as well go to work, because you kids ask me for money all the time. They said, 'Forget it, Mom, we'll go live with Uncle Larry. We don't want you to be a scab for us.' The three of them told me that!"

A little while later, Lydia's oldest son, Travis, brought out two caps. With the reverence that many boys his age reserve for baseball teams, he explained that the insignias were those of his grandfather's union—the Boilermakers— and his mother's, the International Association of Machinists. He wore the two caps faithfully on alternating days, and insisted on wearing the IAM cap when he had his school picture taken. In a decade in which parental values seem to grow obsolete as fast as hairstyles and hemlines, the lessons Lydia learned from her father were safely passing on.

I met Vicki Murillo between sets—she was singing with a mariachi band for a strike benefit. She had on a bright flowered dress with a tight bodice and a flowing skirt and was wearing a scarlet carnation in her shoulder-length black hair. She didn't look like a typical mother of six or a typical copper miner, if either of such things exists. But she is both.

She was hired as a laborer in 1978. Her husband, now retired, was also a miner at the time. In their household, Vicki said, a second paycheck was a matter of necessity. "We were paying for a home, a car, and we had the six kids. At first my husband didn't much like the idea of me working there, that I wasn't going to be home. Or he thought I might leave him—sometimes marriages broke up once the wife started earning her own money. But I asked him, 'How in the world do you think we're going to pay the bills? Do you really want me to quit?' A lot of times I earned more than he did.

"I was in the reverberatory furnaces—my job was to charge the furnaces with concentrate. You're dealing with tons of material, so you don't shovel it, you drop it down from boxes. Each box has a door that you open with a chain, to unload it. It's important not to overload the furnace or plug it up, because it could blow up. But you have to keep enough in there to keep the fire going.

"It was hot work, over a hundred degrees. We had to wear these humongous heavy coveralls, and gloves, safety glasses, everything. All you could see of a person would be their eyes." Vicki shook her hair and laughed, peering between her fingers to demonstrate. "When I was dressed for work, I just looked like one of the guys. The only way you could tell it was a woman was maybe by the walk.

"It was very dangerous work, and it was hard for me at first. I tend to be a very feminine person. I was a singer—all I had done before that was sing with different bands. It was a tremendous change. When I went in, I had to compete with the men. They would say I had just gone in to take some man's job. I had to prove myself, that I wasn't in there to take anyone's job, but just to *do* a job.

"It's hard for women. If we don't have the muscles, you know, we have to use our brains, to outsmart them. To find shortcuts to get the work done. You'd be surprised, but sometimes I'd end up helping them. They might have thought I just got in on my looks, but I showed them. I felt proud of myself.

"I got really mad at my foreman because he would always give me a not-so-good worker for a partner. One day I asked him why, and he said he was trying to push the guys. He would tell them, 'See all those tons of concentrate? A WOMAN did that! Are you gonna let a woman beat you?' He told me he was trying to make good workers out of them, but he was using me, really. He gave me three guys like that. And I earned their respect. Sometimes the wives of men working up there would tell me, 'So you work with so-and-so. They say you are a real good worker.'

"My husband told the other miners he was really proud of me and that he understood why I was tired sometimes. I never heard it from him—I had to hear it from the other guys. But as time went by he understood that my job was important. And it reassured him to know that if something happened to him, I could provide. He knew I wouldn't be fooled by someone talking sweet.

"Obviously it changed my relationship with my husband, in so many ways. It was hard. We could never go anywhere—I worked days and graveyards and was either too tired or had a shift change. Sometimes I would come off graveyard, get three hours of sleep, get up and fix dinner, make tortillas or whatever, and go back in on the second shift. I was always sad on holidays, knowing I would have to leave. I would fix up the picnic stuff, and then their father would take them on the picnic while I went in to work.

"The kids were afraid for me sometimes, especially the older ones—my oldest is nineteen—because they knew the danger. My hands were constantly blistered and scaled from handling those forty-pound bars. And when the sparks from the furnace would fly, anywhere they would hit you they would burn right through the protective clothing, they're so hot. I handled eighty-pound jackhammers—if those hit you there would be a big bruise. And the acid fumes from the smelter would burn your hair. The kids worried, especially when I was tired.

"When I had a short shift the kids would sometimes fix sandwiches. They helped, and my husband helped. I did the major household things, the important things. But they knew they would have to help. It was good for the family—it made them grow up. Even my husband! Men will try to get you to baby them, you know, act like they can't even find a shirt in the damn closet. I told him, 'You can find your shirt. You can throw clothes in the dryer. For heaven's sake, you can learn to do this stuff!'

"One day I asked him to put our daughter's hair in a ponytail. He said, 'How do you do that?' I told him, 'You brush it, and you put the pins in, and you put the rubber band around it.' Well, he was complaining and saying he couldn't do it, but I'll be darned if I didn't come back and she had a ponytail.

"We all learned a lot. For me, it made me realize you can do almost anything you want to, that you can build your body up. I feel now that I could do anything.

"I've learned a lot from the strike, too. It was a hard decision. It had taken me forever to get to that job level—I had worked my way up. But I wouldn't want to go in there without a union. For one thing, it would be dangerous. I'm sure of it. Look at all the accidents they've had. Whatever the foremen tell them to do, they have to do."

A woman, especially, should think long and hard about working without a union, Vicki said. "The foreman could abuse and harass you, and what could you do? I think it must be the same for any woman in an industrial job. Things are changing in this country—women are getting into these jobs. I feel that if a woman doesn't have a union behind her, she isn't safe. And it works the other way around too. Women have helped to improve the unions, and the consciousness of the men in this kind of work. Very definitely.

"The decision to be a striker was very important to me. It took guts to stay out, and it showed I was as good as a man, as *moral* as a man. They respect us for that. I think the men expected the women to go in, because they thought we were weak-minded and couldn't make an important decision. The men around here thought of women as being like that—that we would bend to authority and do whatever the company told us to do. I've taught my kids not to give in easily. I guess I'm a good example for my daughters, because I showed them that a woman doesn't have to rely on a man. A woman can stand on her own feet, and she can have an important life. They know if their mom could do it, so could they.

"Another thing we've all learned from the strike is that you don't need a lot of money to stay together and make your life work. A lot of times it's better just to have good friends. The kids have learned that they can't just ask and get—they have to wait their turn, or make do. They don't need all that stuff to survive.

"We don't know what the company will do next, but we know for sure that the strike hasn't broken us, or our lives. I think it's shattered the scabs' lives more. We can go anywhere with our heads up, but where they go, they go in fear."

Within the first week after the Phelps Dodge strike began on July 1, 1983, the company secured injunctions to prevent striking miners from assembling at the plant gates in Morenci, Ajo, and Douglas, Arizona (shown here). Strikers' wives immediately took their places on the picket lines. Photo by *Arizona Daily Star*.

When Phelps Dodge began hiring replacement workers in August, thousands of strike supporters blocked the mine gates in Ajo and Morenci. Governor Bruce Babbitt ordered a cooling-off period; strikers cooperated. When Phelps Dodge reopened its gates to replacement workers ten days later, Morenci and nearby Clifton were occupied by four hundred state troopers and seven units of the National Guard. Photo by *Arizona Daily Star*.

The Morenci Miners Women's Auxiliary organized daily picket lines to greet strikebreakers as they passed by the People's Clinic on their way to work. At right is Anna O'Leary; at rear left, Eduardo Marquez. Other picketers are, from left: Vera Campbell, Josefina Ruiz, Jenny Castañeda, Sylvia Jaquez, and Alice Castañeda. Photo by *Arizona Daily Star*.

Clifton and Morenci strike supporters assembled in the American Legion Hall to hear visiting representatives of their national unions. Front row, from left: Fina Roman (in striped shirt), Beverly Cole, Nancy Hicks, Vicky Sharp (in cap), unidentified, and Clifford Hicks. The hall was later destroyed by the flood. Photo by Ron Chaff.

On October 1, 1983, the San Francisco River swelled out of its banks and took much of Clifton downstream. The town was left without running water, electricity, natural gas, or sewer service, and more than a third of Clifton's 1,800 homes were damaged beyond repair. Most of the losses were suffered by striking families. Photo by Ron Chaff.

Members of the Morenci Miners Women's Auxiliary (and friends) in the Senior Citizens Center, preparing sandwiches for the Cinco de Mayo rally, May 1984. From left: Sally Gonzalez, "Sister" Bonilla, Dada Saiz, Ginny Aguilar, Raymond Najar, Barbara Estrada, and Clara Moreno. The auxiliary regularly organized from the Machinists' Hall kitchen, but after disagreements over strategy between the women and union officials, they could not use union facilities for Cinco de Mayo. Photo by Ron Chaff.

At the June 30 rally in Clifton, strike supporters were tear-gassed by Department of Public Safety troops. Several fled into Alice Miller's liquor store (far right) and were trapped when a tear-gas canister was fired into the store. Miller, who was eight and a half months pregnant, and nineteen others were arrested; many more were injured. They later won civil rights suits for discriminatory law enforcement, false arrest, and unjustifiable tear-gassing. Photo by Ron Chaff.

"The mile-high, mile-long, all-woman picket line" at the Morenci mine. Phelps Dodge attempted to discourage the women from picketing by dumping piles of dirt on the shoulder of the road, but picketers simply stood on top of the dirt. The DPS officer is pointing at Berta Chavez (to immediate left of cameraman). Photo by Ron Chaff.

# 6

# *We Go with Our Heads Up*

essie Tellez served tea and cookies in her living room. Her home is not especially large, but it's noticeably graceful. Dark green ivy trails up the white clapboard exterior, and the interior is airy and bright. "Looking beyond the immediate" is a motif that runs through the floor plan: the kitchen, in the center of the house, is open on every side to the surrounding rooms; one interior wall is built of glass blocks. At the front of the house three walls, each with a picture window, angle together to form a large Victorian bay. If Clifton were situated on top of a mountain, instead of at the bottom of a gorge, the windows would have commanded a spectacular view. As it was, we looked out at the opposite side of the canyon.

As the morning sun climbed behind us, the red-orange wall of rock was embroidered with deep maroon shadows that alternately grew and receded. Several hours into the conversation I decided that this view, though unconventional, had its merits.

Jessie has always done her best with what life has given her. She designed this house. She bought a book and took a correspondence course, then took every measurement and drew the blueprints. She and her family tore down the old cottage they were living in, room by room, and replaced it with a new home on the same foundations.

"It was a beautiful cottage, with ivy all around and zinnias I had planted, but we were flooded out twice, the second time when my daughter was born. I had just come home from the hospital. The water came in the back and out the front, and I decided I'd had enough. I was the one that started tearing down the porch. My husband was furious, but it was an old wooden house and my kids were catching colds. My dad and mom helped me, and my son helped my husband beat up the cement. It only cost us seven thousand dollars to build, but it was my castle."

Jessie's maiden name is Morales, but she looks northern European: she is tall, fair, and blue-eyed—like her father, she says. She speaks often and lovingly of her father, who is still an important presence in her life. If he were alive he would be nearly a hundred now. Jessie is well into middle age herself, with roots that run deep in Clifton. Her mother's great-grandfather brought his family into the area while fighting alongside Pancho Villa. Her father's people—like Carmina Garcia's—were living on this land long before its name was changed from "Mexico" to "Arizona Territory."

"So this has been our land. We didn't migrate from the south; we have been here for generations. When my father was fourteen he helped build the first road from Safford to here. He tells me the story of when they were digging the road through what we call Needle Mountain. At that time needles were very precious, and any man who had one would carry it stuck through his hat. While they were digging the road a man tore his pants, and he took another man's needle without asking permission. He started sewing and broke the needle, and this guy he had stolen it from got so angry, he shot him. Almost killed him."

Jessie's family history is rich and varied: her paternal grandmother came over from Spain to marry her betrothed sight unseen; her maternal grandfather, "Guadalupe de la O," had a bellowing voice and a red beard that terrified Jessie as a child and convinced her that he was one of the Vikings she had read about in school. But her strong consciousness of history is not to be confused with nostalgia. Jessie told me pointedly, "There are ladies I know—Anglos—who say, 'I wish we could return to the old times, they used to be so nice.' I tell them, 'Well, it was probably nice for you, but you have no idea of how it was for us.' When you grow up here, you just know that people are prejudiced. Chase Creek was the business district, so there were Spanish, Anglos, Italians, even a black family there, but all the rest of Clifton was segregated. My mother used to clean houses for the Anglos. And the schools! Our teacher was a little old lady that wanted us to sing all the time. They just thought we should be happy and play the guitar. They weren't that interested in having us learn. When we'd drop out of school, they didn't care."

But Jessie cared. For as long as she can remember she has felt a burning impatience to better herself. After graduating from Clifton High School at seventeen, she went to Los Angeles and enrolled in a school of clothing and makeup design. Her destination: Hollywood.

"I never told anyone about wanting to work at a movie studio because I thought they might laugh at me, but I really wanted to go. I learned all the different periods of clothing and hair design. I knew all the bones. I even thought of going into medicine. But after I graduated from there my parents pulled me home to marry the only boy they had ever allowed me to date. I told my mother, 'You channeled me into marriage because you were afraid I would get pregnant and dishonor the family.' And she said yes, that was true. They didn't trust me. If only they had known how moral I was! I wanted to do so many other things. But this is how it was. It was a very frustrating time to grow up."

More than thirty years have passed, and Jessie is still trying to get the education she was denied as a young woman. When the strike began, she was routinely making the hundred-mile round trip to Safford to attend art and psychology classes at Eastern Arizona University. Her friends told her she ought to go to the Women's Auxiliary meetings too.

"I had never joined the auxiliary during other strikes. I spent the time sewing for my children—from one strike to the next I'd store up a trunkful of material so when the next one came around my children could still have nice clothes. But this time I did go. I went to my first meeting toward the end of September. I was elected treasurer, and I froze the funds because there was so much disorder. We needed to see what we had.

"I've always been organized—I've had to be. Women are organized at home, raising the children and keeping everything going, but the transition from that to organizing for the strike can be a little difficult. We were having problems with the leadership, it was a very fast turnover. These women had never done anything like this before.

"But everyone learned together. I was treasurer for about two months and got the books straightened out, and then turned it over to someone else. I kept encouraging the younger women to take leadership roles. I've encouraged them to take classes at Eastern Arizona too. I think there are so many intelligent women here. I haven't really known them—I'm of a different generation, a different background, and I'm not a gregarious person, so even though it's a small town, we mix with different circles. I'd rather be home painting or writing poetry than going to a dance. So I knew these women, but I never knew them as I do now."

Women like Jessie found two important resources in their lives that became crucial during the next phase of the strike: one was an enormous, untapped creative potential; the other was a profound attachment to home, specifically to the houses in which they lived. During the late fall and early winter, the strike escalated into what became known as the "eviction war."

"Everybody I know is getting eviction notices," Lydia Knott lamented. She, like Jessie, lived in a home her family owned, but most strikers were in company housing. "P.D. is offering them five hundred dollars to turn over their houses in good condition and get out now. But people are saying they won't leave, not even for a thousand dollars. They've lived in these houses all their lives."

One of Lydia's friends, Nancy Hicks, had been given a September deadline, now months past. "I haven't moved," Nancy said, "and I don't intend to move because of some kind of bribery from P.D. Let me tell you something about this money they're supposedly offering us to get out. They are going through your house with a fine-tooth comb, and if there's marks on your wall, nail holes where people have hung pictures, they deduct so much for this, that, and the other. By the time they're through, you don't get anything. But I'll tell you what: I don't care if they offered me the moon, no scab is going to move into my house. Until this strike is over I'm not going to budge."

In Ajo, too, where virtually all housing was company-owned, striking families dug in their heels. Gloria Blase said the notices came rapid-fire: first a suspension, then termination of her job, then the eviction. She and her four kids, ranging in age from two to seven, couldn't even think about moving out.

They hated the idea of leaving their homes, but even more, the strikers resented the thought of being displaced by people who, in their opinion, didn't belong there. Viola Davis told of seeing "traveling scabs" come into Ajo bearing license plates from Ohio, New York, Florida, Tennessee, Montana, even Alaska. She also pointed out that P.D.'s long-standing rule against groups of men living together in company housing had been suspended. "And they've let them have unlimited credit for their furniture, all their needs," she said. "They're trying to attract scabs whatever way they can."

One of the most infuriating turns of events was brought on by the presence of an organization called WOW, the Wives of Workers (nonstriking, that is) in Clifton. Strikers reported that WOWs were being driven around town to choose homes they would like to move into; the occupants would then be evicted.

The company's policy, stated in a letter from Vice-President Pat Scanlon, was that it would evict anyone who had been fired for strike misconduct, fallen behind in rent payments, or become "an undesirable tenant." The letter conceded, however, that the company would evict others "if the housing was needed." Company officials denied that the WOW organization or its members had any role in the evictions, and this notion may have been based more on rumor than fact. Nonetheless, the scenario was absolutely real to Clifton women. And more than anything else that had yet passed before their eyes— including tanks, SWAT teams, and floodwaters—it made them see red.

The strike supporters held the universal conviction that WOW was a Phelps Dodge product, with company backing. Many of its members were female relatives of company personnel, but Scanlon denies that the company founded the organization. "I was surprised to hear of it, though I thought it was a pretty clever idea. My understanding was that it was a self-help group. These were wives of men who were working, and also women who were working themselves; they were, as you can imagine, taking a lot of guff. As far as I know, it originated spontaneously out of the need these women perceived to have somebody to talk to." He was not surprised to learn that many of the original members were wives of management personnel. "They took as many threatening phone calls, the same kind of abuse that the rank-and-file wives did," he said, "so it's only natural that they joined too." In letters to the local newspaper, WOW members made much of their law-abiding and ladylike approach to their town's problems (as opposed to the women on the line, who definitely had crossed over into the domain of unladylike behavior). As it turned out, WOW was not especially effective. The group's biggest project, a get-acquainted dinner for nonstrikers new to town, was canceled. Most important, the formation of WOW was an open acknowledgment from the Phelps Dodge side of the fence that the strike had to be fought on female turf.

Meanwhile, women squared off for the eviction battle. Carmina Garcia explained in no uncertain terms the strategic importance of this conflict. "Don't you see? They're trying to get rid of us. If people leave their homes, there's no place to go but out of town, so the strike is over."

The evictions struck a nerve in Carmina, whose family had been forced out of Eagle Creek so long ago. "P.D., oh, they have always moved people around and around, and this time I guess they just thought everybody would leave. They sent them letters, and sent them letters, but the union told them not to get out as long as they were paying their rent. Then P.D. said they were going to try and send the DPS to get them out. We told people just to stay in there.

"The Ladies' Auxiliary is ready to go. We keep waiting to see what's going to happen. If we all go up there and sit down in the house, what can they do?" The issue was deadly serious, but Carmina couldn't help laughing, imagining the scene. "If the lady threw a tea party, let's say, and all the women would just sit there on the floor, what in the world could they do?"

A little bit of success is a powerful thing. For the first time in their lives, the women of Clifton began to see themselves as a force to be reckoned with. Before they knew it, they were keeping the whole town running. But it didn't happen overnight. "You have to remember," Jessie Tellez explained, "how people around here feel about women. Oh, we have responsibility, all right. When you're bringing up your children, anything that goes wrong in the house, the husband blames the wife for that. In the beginning I was very submissive, while I was raising my children. My son who lives in California says, 'When I see on TV that lady that comes out with the Kool-Aid, that reminds me so much of you.'

"But I guess I have always been strong-minded, and things bothered me. When people started going to the picket line there were ten Anglo women to one Hispanic. I started asking around, and the Mexican-American women told me their husbands didn't allow them to go. Their husbands thought it was a disgrace for women to be on the picket line."

Jessie said the turning point was when picketers began getting arrested without just cause. "That made people very angry, and they wanted to stand up. When the man was arrested, the wife would show up the next day. And seeing more women show up, other women got encouraged.

"It was the same with the auxiliary. Many of the ladies, their husbands wouldn't allow them to go to the meetings at first. Then they would let them go, but the men would drop them off and pick them up. I used to ask them, 'Don't you know how to drive?' and they'd say, 'Well, yes.' And I'd say, 'Do you have to go and drop your husband off if he has a meeting?' 'Well, no,' they'd say. I didn't want to cause problems at home, but then I could see that they were so frustrated."

At first, a number of men who dropped off their wives at auxiliary meetings actually sat outside the hall and waited during the meetings—to protect the women, they said, in case of a scab attack. The women tolerated this heavy-handed chaperoning but increasingly resented it. When the "guards" eventually dwindled to just one man who persisted in coming to meetings with his wife, they asked him to knock it off. "He just couldn't let her out of his sight, is what it was," one of the members said. After that, he stayed home. So did his wife.

Most others cut the apron strings. "Now the women have gotten the car," Jessie said. "They come by themselves, and they stay as long as they want, and after the meeting they gather and have coffee or something, and they go home when they feel like it. That doesn't mean our husbands like it, but this is a right we take for ourselves. I told them, 'Don't you feel great?' "

They did. Around this time, some of the auxiliary women created an uproar by going to the bar "alone"—meaning in a group, without husbands. The gesture itself was substantially more intoxicating than the beer.

Jessie didn't go to the bar, but she made her stand on other turf. "Our husbands try to be strong, try to rule the roost, and every once in a while we have to tell them, excuse the word, but this is bullshit. What makes them think they're better than we are? We are very intelligent in a lot of areas, give us some credit! We take their seed and nurture it—look at the beautiful children I've given my husband; day and night I was with them. I don't know how men are in other places, but around here, the most important thing to a man is his children, so that other people can see that he's a man. I feel sorry for them. We make their meals, everything. They're helpless.

"We have started to realize they're not any better than we are. In fact, today I told my husband, 'Why don't you wash the dishes? Why is it that I have to wash your towels, your sheets, change your bed? You're not able to do these simple things? Nobody waits on me!' "

This attitude did not sit well with many husbands. Suddenly the picket line wasn't the only dividing line in town. Men of every stripe and creed were perturbed by the new breed of female that seemed to have emerged. The women took advantage, especially when they perceived sexism from the strikebreakers. "Now we have really found how to get the scabs' goat," Shirley Randall said. "It definitely bothers them to see women out there on the line. They've started doing anything they can think of. We've had scabs pull their pants down and show us what they have—which is not a lot."

"No balls," her friend Trudy explained for my benefit.

"They do this because we're women," Shirley continued. "They think it will shock us. I think it's pathetic."

The antagonism didn't stop at indecent exposure. The strike was heating up to a new level of violence. Evelyn Caswell, who had become a regular on the picket line, was hit by a car. "A scab was traveling south," she recounted a long time afterward, "and made an illegal turn, cut across in front of us, and got me. My hand was messed up. I still can't close it."

On the line that morning were six DPS officers and thirteen picketers. The DPS reported that Evelyn was hit by a car; some other witnesses say the car hit a traffic sign, which then hit Evelyn. She doesn't know what hit her but estimates that she was knocked about ten feet into the road. "Somebody said I was lucky I wasn't killed, and I said, yeah, but then, if I was really lucky, I'd still have a good right hand."

The DPS officers told her their job was not traffic control, but strike control. To Evelyn the difference seemed academic. "Those people up there drove any which way they damn well pleased. I never realized the seriousness, the extent that the company could control things. There was an injunction against fire-arms, and if they had enforced it on both sides, it would be fair. But you can stand here any day and watch the scabs go into work with rifles in their pickups."

Evelyn was absolutely correct about what could be seen from the street. Nonstrikers were allowed to carry guns, and did. Occasionally they brandished them. The unions began to collect documentation for a lawsuit alleging discriminatory law enforcement; by the time these cases went to court, they would have accumulated enough file cabinets of evidence to sink a small ship.

Undaunted by threats, the Morenci Miners Women's Auxiliary organized a support system to meet the basic needs of the striking families, who comprised virtually the whole town of Clifton and much of Morenci. The most urgent project was a food bank. Berta Chavez, whose five children made her plainly aware of the need, was one of the food bank's founding mothers.

"In the beginning of the strike," she said, "I just didn't have anything to feed the kids. Talk about learning not to take things for granted! So I went to some of the other ladies in the auxiliary, and they were really nice. They gave me a bag of macaroni and cheese, beans, and rice. I was so happy.

"We realized this was something a lot of people needed, so I started getting food from everywhere I could, and donations, and we threw it all in together down at the back of the Steelworkers' Hall. We were asking all the merchants. Some were generous, some didn't want to get involved, and I got some donations that were anonymous. I tried to get food from the federal government too, but then you have to give it to everybody, and I was just working for the strikers. Finally we raised enough money and got a little bit of food and started helping people out. It was real nice."

The unions, which had more resources than the auxiliary and at this point a far greater infrastructure, helped to acquire donations to the food bank. Through their connections with a federally funded agency, they enabled the auxiliary to distribute free turkeys for Thanksgiving. Shirley Randall said she felt humiliated when she had to line up for free food at Thanksgiving. "I don't even like to go to yard sales—I'm afraid of what Mrs. Jones is going to think. I stood in that line, though. Otherwise we wouldn't have had a turkey."

Reservations faded fast when it dawned on Shirley and everyone else that Mrs. Jones had hungry kids of her own to think about. These were extraordinary times, and they would have to rely on one another as they never had before. Shirley headed up a day-care cooperative in which women took turns watching the kids while others held picket duty or did organizing. When Jessie Tellez's roof began to leak, she decided she would just have to think of a skill she and her husband could exchange with another striker who could fix it. Barter became central to their lives, and in some way—however direct or convoluted—every essential need was met.

Dr. Jorge O'Leary, a physician employed in the Phelps Dodge hospital at Morenci, had been fired for supporting the strike. A Phelps Dodge spokesperson explained: "He's been expressing sympathy with the union cause, and he's been very critical of the company's hospitalization, medical, and surgical plan." But after serving the communities of Morenci and Clifton for twelve years and delivering some 2,500 of their citizens, the Mexican-born doctor was not about to close up shop. He opened what was christened the "People's Clinic" in an old feed market beside the highway above Chase Creek and vowed that no striker would go without medical care. The free clinic was supported by donations from unions and physicians in Tucson, Phoenix, and Chicago—and eventually by Bruce Springsteen, who donated ten thousand dollars in November 1984 from the proceeds of his Phoenix concert. The clinic was inspected by Arizona public health authorities and rated "excellent." Not bad for a former feed store.

The day after O'Leary was fired, representatives of the Women's Auxiliary showed up on his family's doorstep with covered dishes and a warm welcome to the brotherhood and sisterhood of strikers. Within a few days Anna, the doctor's energetic, articulate wife, had joined the auxiliary and was helping to organize a clothing exchange. "This comes and goes," she explained. "There's no permanent place for it yet, which is unfortunate, because we have to put things in the Steelworkers' Hall and they're always yelling at us, 'When are you girls going to get this junk out of here?' We really need our own place.

"The way it works is, everybody brings in their clothes that their kids have outgrown, and we stack them according to size and gender, and then you come shopping. You might have all these size 6s that you can't use, and you're looking for 8s." Any parent who has watched a child go through three jeans sizes in a school year can appreciate the simplicity of this idea—and the fact that it could be a godsend. Clifton mothers wondered why they hadn't thought of it before. They vowed to continue the practice forever.

Not every need was met so smoothly. They had shortages in some areas and a surplus in others—mainly clothing, which was donated literally by the ton from outside communities. "We've had to stack them in the church, everywhere," Anna said. "We even ended up taking clothes down to Mexico. You don't want to discourage a charitable act, you know, but . . . If only we could eat them!"

Members of the auxiliary wrote letters to national teachers' unions and associations to solicit money for their children's schoolbooks. They also sent mailings to international unions and to every women's auxiliary they could think of. In answer to their letters and their prayers, support groups for the copper strikers sprang up all over the country.

Resourcefulness was the one precious commodity the women had in abundance. When tension grew in the high school—where strikers' kids had to wear someone else's last-year's clothes, and everybody knew it—Berta hit on the idea of forming a break-dancing group called the Small Town Breakers. It was a stroke of genius that defused the bomb of adolescent anger and channeled it into an all-absorbing project. They had car washes to raise money for uniforms, and Berta found places for the group to perform. She was characteristically optimistic. "Now that people have seen what they can do, I think they'll get more involved with the kids. After the mayor saw them dance he called and asked if I could use a couple thousand dollars for the kids to have breaker of the month or something like that. This is getting us places. I tell the kids, next time, maybe Hollywood."

Far from being overwhelmed, Berta and Jessie and their friends enjoyed organizing their town. They looked forward to their "Wednesday night out" for the auxiliary meeting. "I can't wait to get a babysitter and go," Trudy Morgan said. "I haven't missed a meeting since I don't know when."

The enthusiasm grew on them. At one time the auxiliary meetings were as efficient as possible, but now they spilled over into prolonged, friendly potlucks. The women looked for reasons to meet more often than once a week. When the union organized a stress workshop and brought in a therapist from out of town, only women attended. "Wouldn't you know it," commented Jessie Tellez. "But when she found out about our meetings, the therapist said, 'You're giving each other therapy and you don't even know it. You ought to meet twice a week.' " It was the only way they were going to last, and they knew it.

Men got together too, not in an organized way, but informally, for example, once a week when their strike benefit checks came in. "I think the men talk about different things than we do, though," Jessie said. "We talk about the children—how our kids don't want to go to school for fear of the scabs' children, all the tension they have to live with. When the DPS follow us around, it's our children we're worrying about. When we bring out these things at the general meetings, the women make the men cry."

Jessie clucked her tongue and shook her head. "When they don't have work, they don't know what to do with themselves, really. The men are feeling very vulnerable because they're not bringing in any income. That's very important to men; I never realized how important. One man told me,

'You know, I feel like shit. I always felt so good to know my household was being kept up because of me. Now I have to go over to the union and have them hand me a measly little check. I'm glad to be getting it, but you don't know how I feel.'

"For us it's different. The women are used to stretching the budget to feed their children, and they know how to stay busy all day long. There's a lot to do, but the men just don't seem to be able to get themselves going, without a job to go to. It's very abnormal for them. I guess it's our experience as housewives—it's just our nature to keep going through it all. We can take any blow that comes. What I think this strike really shows is that if men wouldn't put so many walls in front of us all the time, they'd be surprised how much better life would be!"

Women like Jessie at first saw their auxiliary work as an extension of their years as housewives, but by the time they were telling their husbands to iron their own shirts, it had become something else—among other things, a blessed escape from domestic labor. For the duration of the strike and after, contradictions persisted around the question of whether the auxiliary work ran with, or against, the grain of traditional female roles. Plainly, it involved a new level of economic consciousness for many women.

For Berta Chavez, for instance. "You know," she said, "two years ago we would *never* have thought we could be doing these things. Running things this way. I'd probably still be charging at that stupid store. I used to go into the P.D. store every day, look around, and charge. It's so easy. All this time, all the money we were making we were giving straight back to them. Now I see how they get you coming and going. I never go in there at all. It's hard to believe we were so dumb. Now we're doing everything for ourselves—how did we wise up so fast?"

It's a good question. Berta felt that the hardships of the strike forced her and her friends to look beyond the superficial concerns that can preoccupy life in a small town (any town, for that matter) and see what mattered when push came to shove—things like friendship, family, and community. Berta had never read Karl Marx or the doctrine of "from each according to his capabilities," but she had a clear notion of what it means to give what you can, accept what you need, and be part of a community that cares for all its members. It was an expansive notion for a group who, as one of them put it, had always thought of themselves as "just a bunch of little old measly housewives."

Admittedly, some aspects of this new job very nearly got the better of them.

Finances, in particular, seemed intimidating when ledgers expanded to more and more columns and budgets grew to six figures. Jessie had told me that the Women's Auxiliary sometimes had problems managing its money, and sure enough, while we chatted in her living room, Shirley came in with the treasury books and a severely worried expression. Our conversation was suspended while the two of them put their heads together and straightened out the books. They were reviewing requests for help with kids' school expenses.

"I looked at every application," Jessie explained to Shirley, "and for every item I tried to find an average cost, like for gym shoes some had put $10, some $40, so I put down $20. We have to find a happy medium. If they go down to Safford they can find tennis shoes for $19.95. We have to help each family equally. . . . "

Afterward, Jessie told me her peers in the auxiliary lacked confidence in some areas because of their limited experience. "The men are always out there in the world, exposed to organizations and finances. We're just barely starting to learn. But give us a little confidence and we can be brilliant. Like Berta, who organized those Breakers—she's a very bright woman. She should go to school." Jessie stopped herself, and sighed. "But right now the strike is eating up all our time, all our energy. We have to try not to scatter our forces.

"When I feel this way, overwhelmed, I try to work on things one at a time. Like I always told my kids, if you don't feel like you can clean the whole house, start with one room. If the whole room looks like too much, then start by just vacuuming. These are the little things we have to do to get some control over our lives in this terrible situation."

Possibly this was the secret of their success. A housewife is thoroughly acquainted with enormous, endless tasks. When your job is to feed a child who will be hungry for the next eighteen years, and do laundry that will never stay clean, you develop a philosophy. Men, Jessie observed, are used to having more structured work that has clear beginnings and endings.

Anna O'Leary also had insights into this question. "In our culture, in Mexican society, the one who *really* rules is the mother," she explained. "Or the grandmother, or the mother-in-law. She's the one that holds the family together and keeps them there. The men might not think they listen to what she says, but because they want to please her they behave as if they're paying attention. They say, 'Yes, we'll take that under advisement.' And maybe you don't do what she says at that particular time, maybe it will take several years for you to come to her and say, 'I don't booze anymore,' or whatever, but you do. She's the conscience.

"When I was married the first time and my mother-in-law died, seems like that family just fell apart. The oldest son and his wife of fifteen years got divorced; then we got divorced. My brother-in-law, who had been to Vietnam, sort of went off the deep end. Before, maybe we only held things together to keep a front for her, but maybe it becomes a self-fulfilling prophecy, that if you act united, you are united. Sometimes it works that way.

"People tend to think that what a woman does or says is not very important, but she does have this important role in the family. And it's been the same with the strike. You know, each family is a little union. You might have your squabbles, but the minute somebody comes along wanting to beat up your brother, your nails come out. How can men say we don't know anything about unions when the first type of union is the family?"

Anna felt that even though their strike-related work became much larger than a domestic role—even a contradiction of it—the women came to it naturally in the beginning. "There has to be some transfer of skills from running a family to all these things we're doing for the strike, setting up the food bank and so forth. One woman I can think of, Berta, has five kids, and she's always on the move thinking of ways to provide for those kids. I admire her a lot. She's not going to sit still and watch her kids starve. Because she's got one objective, and that's to get food on the table, she's got to develop these different skills.

"And there's political training. The mother is a buffer, a negotiator. The father says one thing, the kid wants another, so the mother will go to the father and say, 'You ought to give her a break. Let her go to the dance if she'll be in early.' You learn about concessions, negotiating. And you're also the moral force, the teacher. It's the mother who teaches the child not to steal, not to be dishonest.

"Social skills, political skills, logistics—how are you going to get the supply from the source to the function and so forth—all of these things transfer. The social advocate, the moral advocate, just about everything you encounter in a workplace, a woman has also developed the skills to handle within her own family. So it's not surprising at all that housewives have pulled all this together."

Anna has always felt pulled in two different directions. For two years, she said, her husband, Jorge, allowed her to go to school in Tucson. She was excited about getting a college degree, but she missed being home, baking cookies and doing things for the kids. "I felt like the more I was gone, the more they started to forget where home is. So after I finished school I stayed home, and I kind of enjoyed it that way. I felt I was more necessary at home than out in the business world or whatever, so that was my choice." Now she was busy again, up to her elbows in organizing work and missing the old household routine. But on reflection, she said that in many ways it was all the same work.

"You know how when you're cooking, you put in an egg and it holds the rice and everything together? That's what we are. We're the egg of the family. Just trying to hold together all these falling-apart things."

# 7

# *Falling-Apart Things*

velyn Caswell woke up one morning to find a dead chicken on her roof. "I'm probably the only person *that's* happened to," she surmised. Her husband was in Texas at the time, looking for work, so Evelyn was on her own when it came to dealing with dead-poultry problems. "I found myself pretty strung out," she said. "I mean, that thing wasn't just dead, it was gross. It had been dead for a while.

"I tried to get P.D. security—I live in a P.D. home. Then I tried to get the deputies, anybody, to come out and make a report, but nobody would come. They all laughed like frigging hyenas; thought it was the funniest thing they'd ever heard of. Finally they came when the neighbor, my dear darling scab neighbor that had thrown it up there, complained to the deputy that there was a dead chicken on my roof, stinking like crazy. Now, I had gone up there with a ladder and looked, and I could tell from about five feet away that it was a chicken, but just barely. So when the deputy came over from next door I asked him, 'How did that fellow next door know that was a chicken on my roof, from thirty feet away?' He said, 'Oh, he could tell.' But I hadn't seen him with the chicken in his hand, so what could I do about it?"

The next day Evelyn encountered the neighbor's wife while she was shopping. "I was so hurt, all I could think of was that I wanted to hurt her the same way. Well, she has a double chin and whiskers, so the first thing that came out of my mouth was, 'Do you want me to buy you some razor blades?' She went berserk, tore my shirt, tore my glasses off, and tried to step on them. We just got in a great big old fight. I ended up with a charge of disorderly conduct.

"The deputies came and broke it up, and I was already thinking of filing charges against her, but the one that had hold of her looked at me and said, 'You get out of here, Mrs. Caswell, and don't come back.' He tapped his temple and said, 'It's all in your mind, Mrs. Caswell. You didn't see anything, and you didn't hear anything. You get out of here.' Of all the things that have happened, that scared me the most."

Evelyn did file charges against her neighbor, but the county attorney dismissed them because of insufficient evidence. The neighbor was allowed to file a countersuit against Evelyn, which was still pending at the time we spoke. Evelyn didn't see much humor in her situation. She seemed to be in a state of dull shock. Before the strike, she said, she didn't get into fights in the five-and-dime; but then she didn't find dead chickens on her roof, either.

"You're damned if you don't, and you're damned if you do," said Michelle in a quiet voice, casting a nervous eye toward the door of the Circle K. We stood near her Chevy in the parking lot while she kept an eye on her toddler in the back seat and waited for her mother-in-law to come out of the store. Michelle was small and blonde and had a look about her of chronic fearfulness. It was plain that she would rather not be talking to me about this.

"I'm supposed to be a Mormon. I mean, my husband's family, we're Mormons. And they all tell my husband that the Lord says he should go in and provide for his family. So he's working." She glanced over at the door again. "I don't much care for it," she confessed. "But you can't go against that, can you?"

After six months of growing pressure in the Phelps Dodge towns, no fences were high enough to contain the hostility. "And we're not just talking about neighbors," Vicky Sharp said, "we're talking brothers, sisters, best friends. I have a cousin who has always been like a sister to me. Now I can't talk to her. There have been many separations and divorces."

Vicky's friend Nancy added pointedly, "I told my husband that if he went in, which he wasn't even thinking about, but I said if he did I wouldn't put my children through that, I would divorce him. I couldn't trust a scab husband—it's breaking a contract, just like cheating on a marriage. They're low-lifes."

That was exactly how just about everyone felt, old or young, on either side of the fence. Nancy's teenaged daughter said her social life was a wreck, since she couldn't think of going out with guys from scab families. Carmina Garcia quit driving the school bus because it broke her heart to see childhood friendships torn apart. Gloria Blase said her seven-year-old no longer spoke to her best pals, now that their fathers had crossed the line. Gloria lost her own best friend too, who crossed over even after Gloria offered to make a car payment for her.

Diane McCormick stopped doing her laundry at the only laundromat in town because it was "scab owned"; she said she would sooner do wash in the river. Berta Chavez said she spent most of the time looking down at people's feet, checking to see if they were wearing P.D.-issued metatarsal shoes—"the sign of a scab." Stella and Mike Baray had a son-in-law on each side of the line, so birthdays and other family occasions now required extra-careful planning. A pair of identical twins stopped talking to each other. Maggie Castañeda said she had to quit going to church because she couldn't stand singing in the choir next to a scab. Every ritual of daily life, even funerals and weddings, became segregated down the union line.

It happened that the line also ran, with relatively few deviations, right down the community's century-old ethnic division between Anglos and Hispanics. In their analysis of the strike published in *Feminist Studies*, Judy Aulette and Trudy Mills pointed out that the racial character of the hostility was illustrated in the graffiti that appeared on the walls: "One graffiti writer, responding to the word 'SCAB' painted on a building, [wrote], 'I'd rather be rich than an ignorant fucking Mexican union-loving son of a bitch.' "

But if loyalties were lost, loyalties were also gained. Wars make strange bedfellows, and strikes can make for even stranger best friends.

Trudy Morgan's house was in Verde Lee, a tiny settlement about five miles outside Clifton. Trudy, Shirley Randall, and I sat drinking coffee in her kitchen. Trudy and her husband had begun building this house before the strike, and when his checks stopped coming from Phelps Dodge, the construction came to a standstill. Trudy had learned to live with the situation: throw rugs were neatly arranged on the concrete floor, and pictures hung on the sheetrock walls flanking her husband's eight-point buck trophy.

As we talked about the strike, the neighbors, families, and life in general, I was struck by the contrasts between these two women. Trudy is blond and ruffled, a latter-day Debbie Reynolds. She loves to talk, and her telephone rang constantly. She frequently admonished her two young children, "Be nice. Don't be rude." Since her father was a car dealer, not a miner, Trudy grew up in one of the few Clifton families that was not strictly working class. She knew little about unions until she married a miner.

In contrast, Shirley was raised in a union family and has strong memories of when her father was fired in the strike of 1959. She is a tall, no-nonsense woman who wears jeans and T-shirts and often a baseball cap. She speaks quietly and deliberately. She has four children, two of them in college at Eastern Arizona, and like everyone else, she has a lot of bills to pay. But she and her husband never had any question about which side of the strike they would be on.

These women came from different worlds—or as different as one is likely to find within the confines of Clifton—and I was fascinated to watch them weave the sort of conversation that an outsider could instantly recognize as close, relaxed, and loyal: the language of intimate friends.

Trudy acknowledged that the strike—and nothing but the strike—had brought them together. "Any other time, I don't think I would have known Shirley. I mean, I knew her growing up, but I wouldn't have hung around with her." Shirley gasped with mock indignation. "Well, we wouldn't have, would we?" Trudy insisted. "Until the strike? Think about it."

"Was I nice to you first, or were you nice to me?" Shirley asked.

Trudy thought this over. "I can't remember how we started."

"Over that damn flood! I came over and washed a whole bunch of your clothes."

"No," Trudy said, "that was Boo Phillips's clothes."

"That's right."

"Then it must have been at the auxiliary meetings, wasn't it?"

"It was when I came and got your clothes for the exchange," Shirley said. "I didn't know you from Adam. I came and took some of those clothes."

"Oh, yeah," Trudy laughed, and turned to me. "We definitely have more women friends now. It used to be just a lot of gossip around here, but now people have more important things to think about. Oh, I know the other still goes on, but we can tolerate it a little better if it's one of us that does it. It's just not so bad."

She poured more coffee and invited Shirley and me to tolerate a little gossip. "With the scabs there's been split-ups and all kinds of headaches because husbands went in and their wives didn't want them to. There was Deborah; she was out to here pregnant and already had two other kids. Her family is union, and she was going to auxiliary meetings. Well, her husband kicked her out and then went scabbing. She's remarried now, to a striker. At least I *think* he's a striker . . . "

Shirley spoke up. "There's a lot of people I could not stand before, that I've reevaluated. They were interested in things I wasn't interested in. But . . . "

"They ain't so bad, now, are they?" Trudy said, laughing.

"They're good people. Even the men."

"And the ones that have been put in jail," Trudy said, "I think those are our heroes. If we ever do win this strike, they're the ones that have won it for us. The ones sitting at home and not doing a damn thing, not even going to the picket lines, they're the ones that are like my parents: 'We'll sit back and let them do the fighting for us so we won't get a bad name.'

"My dad owned Mullins Motors, and you see, when you're in business you can't make any money giving your help twelve dollars an hour. You have to give them five and six dollars and then you get more money. I didn't grow up with unions and this kind of thing. My parents always told me, 'If there's problems, you let somebody else fight for you. You can go ahead and reap the benefits from it, but don't stick your neck out on a limb.' It's very strained now, with my parents. Oh, my mom. 'You shouldn't go to that picket line,' she says. 'Ladies don't flip people the finger.' I know that, and it's not easy to do, but, by God, what do they want us to do? All we have to fight with is our mouths and our fingers. Mother asked me, 'Do you do those things when you go? DO YOU?' 'Nooo,' I used to say. But then they saw me on TV. Oh, my God!"

"You ought to see Trudy's little boy," Shirley said. "He's union all the way. He loves going down to the Machinists' Hall, the Boilermakers' Hall, and he knows all the union officials by name."

"It's true," Trudy said. "Jennifer, my little girl, is not really strike-oriented. But my four-year-old, oh-ho-ho! We see a scab, and out that window goes the finger. I've finally got him so he won't do it, but for how long, I don't know. Until I do it, I guess," she laughed. "My mother is totally mortified, of course. She'll take him in the car, and oh, Lord." Both Trudy and Shirley were overcome with laughter.

"No," Trudy went on, wiping her eyes, "my mom's not thrilled with me at all. They think it's my husband's job. He ought to fight it, not me. In fact, they begged us to go up to Alpine with them, to get me away from the picket line. They wanted us to spend some time in their cabin that they had just redone. They don't hurt for money.

"When the strike first started we almost went in—I can't say that we didn't—but after we made our decision, we never questioned it. That was it. Now I'm secretary of the Women's Auxiliary, and Shirley's treasurer."

I was curious about how someone with a nonunion, or anti-union, background could become so thoroughly involved. I asked Trudy what made up her mind.

"They've stolen from us, that's what! This scab neighbor across the street gets her daughter all the Cabbage Patch dolls, and me? Here I am with my sheetrock and my cement floors. I would like to see my house finished. She's ready to rip up her carpet and start on her second batch, and her house is six months younger than mine! And there's the little things that hurt the kids. The neighbor kids go and get the $5.99 GI Joes, three and four at a time, and you have to tell your little boy, no, sir. And my daughter won't have $400 worth of school clothes like the neighbors do. Jennifer will go and ask her grandma for odd jobs, and they'll pay her, so she can save up her money and go and buy a little something. It hurts to have to say no to your kids, but I guess they're better off this way." She seemed a little doubtful. "We've survived. You learn to do without. And we do give them hell, don't we, Shirley? That's where you relieve a lot of your pressure, at that picket line."

Shirley and Trudy discussed their upcoming court date; they had been accused of, according to Shirley, "driving past a scab's house and yelling pretty bad stuff." "They did take pictures of us, yelling and gesturing, but I have never thrown a rock," she said. "And the lady had thrown rocks at me. I called the sheriff's office and told him I had five witnesses, but the county attorney said there was no evidence, that I had to be able to show some damage. The rocks she threw at my car were so small they didn't do any damage. At first I thought it was funny. I mean, who would throw a little rock like that, the size of a pea? If you're going to throw a rock, make it count."

"These things that we do," Trudy said, "I *never* would have done before. Somebody wrote to the paper that the Women's Auxiliary was a cult and that there are women and children in this town that only know how to talk with their middle fingers. It was the Waggles of Wain, I'm sure—the WOWs. But we have been forced into this. Forced even to violence. It's wrong, it's sad, but that's the only way we have left to fight. And the scabs are afraid of us! Many's the time I've seen them turn and go the other direction, and all I had was a mouth on me! They feel guilty. They live in fear. The women in this town have a lot of power."

Shirley agreed, but said that the scabs have power in a way the strikers don't—they're allowed to carry weapons and make threats while the law turns a blind eye. "We live in fear too," she said. "That's what's brought us to this."

"Oh, yes," Trudy said. "I did fear for my life one time, at the Circle K. We were all down there on the line—this was early in the strike—and rocks were going over, and the DPS were everywhere. Oh, God, it was awful. My husband was there, and I told him, 'Let's get out of here,' but Larry said no, he wasn't leaving. So I went and parked at Circle K. A scab came in there to get some gas, and I got up my nerve and yelled, 'Hey, scab!' And he showed me his gun. He lifted it up and said, 'You'd better watch it, lady.'

"Then somebody started screaming, 'A gun!' and then Fred, who used to be sheriff, came and asked if I wanted to be put on some kind of a list of witnesses. Well, the man had showed the gun to me—it was for my benefit— but I said, 'No, I don't want to get involved.' Larry said, 'By God, you *are* involved, and you're going to do it.' So I put my name on the list.

"That's what I mean about my parents, you know. Don't get involved—I hear that in my head all the time. It's very hard for me when someone tells me, 'I wish you'd stay away from those ladies on the picket line.' But now I say, 'You leave my ladies on the picket line alone. They're wonderful ladies.' And they are—every damn one of them that gets up there and yells and screams. I know it doesn't look nice to somebody who doesn't understand, but if that's all you have to fight with, then you give it your best shot. My ideas of what's good and bad have been turned upside-down."

Trudy's ambivalence is especially evident when it comes to her children. Just as often as she shows them how to call a scab a scab, she instructs them to say "please" and "thank you" and "excuse me."

"I just hope my kids will not end up in this situation," she said. "I hope they'll marry doctors and lawyers, or be one, so they won't . . . but I guess it's good for them to struggle too. If they have it easy all their life . . . I never had to work, and if I'd wanted to go to college, it would have been paid for. I wouldn't have had to work for it. But I didn't want to go. I went with Larry since I was a sophomore in high school, and I just wanted to stay here and get married. My life was all planned out. Now, though, I look at my kids, and I know I'd rather see them get an education, get out. Or, I don't know, if they stay, at least I want them to be union."

Shirley said that many families were feeling this upheaval, but she believed strikers' families were faring better than the others. "People might fight over the bills that can't be paid or something. But I think they're a lot closer. My family is. Me and my husband work real good together. We just put a new roof on our house, and we did it together. When we go get firewood we go get it together. I think we ought to be in business together."

Such harmony is unimaginable for Trudy. "Without my mother-in-law," she said, "I would have just plain gone crazy. The last six months have been hell with my side of the family. Dad gets all this information from the sheriff's office, and then comes and tells Larry he'd better go in because they're going to replace you, and all this. Larry would just sit down and cry because my dad had upset him so bad, and he didn't know what he needed to do."

Trudy said she had gained better friends than she'd lost. "I still don't know if I'm really confident—when I'm by myself, forget it. But I'm really outspoken when I'm with somebody else. Then I'm tough. Me and Shirley make a hell of a team. Shirley and I are blessed with voices that carry."

Shirley stirred her coffee and nodded. "Yes, we are. There have been times when I was on the line up by the People's Clinic, and my kids were all the way down by the church in Chase Creek, and they would tell me, 'Mom, we heard you yelling *pigfucker!*' "

Fillmore Tellez, Jessie's husband, came over to talk as I was parking my truck in a vacant lot down in Chase Creek. A modest man, he stopped himself several times during the conversation because he was on the verge of using a word he didn't want to say "in front of a lady."

I asked him if he'd heard other "ladies" use swear words lately. He looked pained.

"I understand why they do it. They have the right because they're cornered. What else can they do? Their husbands' jobs have been taken away, and they can't buy food and clothes for their children, so I understand. But I respect women, so when this happens—when they yell those things—I don't see them. I don't hear them."

He also hates to see children getting involved. "They're trying to accuse the kids of being troublemakers," he said, "but it's not their fault. They're good kids. I was the Boy Scout leader for many years. I've watched them all grow up, and this whole thing makes me mad." One of the DPS officers assigned to Clifton had once been in his Scout troop, and Fillmore was now of the opinion that this young man was a traitor, rising through the ranks by identifying and turning in his boyhood companions.

While we talked, a scrawny, black-speckled bird walked up the alley toward us. Fillmore identified it as a dove and explained that people once raised them here. Some of the birds still make their nests in the empty attics of old brick buildings in Chase Creek. Fillmore gave a weak laugh and said, "You'd never expect to see a bird of peace in Clifton."

"On the bright side," Berta Chavez intoned with her usual enthusiasm, "there was Christmas. That was one of the best things. As a matter of fact, I can hardly wait for Christmas to come around again." It was a typical January day in Clifton, sunny but cool, and Berta and her sister Diane had joined me for a cup of coffee in the Wagon Wheel to warm up after the picket line.

Diane said, "We always went to the Christmas celebration that P.D. had for us. Why did we do that? P.D. this, P.D. that, P.D. theater, P.D. Christmas tree. Even a P.D. Santa Claus. We finally snapped out of it!"

"Oh, yeah," Berta said, "this time we had it our own way. It all started one night when I was lying in bed thinking about the kids, wondering, 'How are they going to be taken care of at Christmas? I don't want them up there at any scab tree.' Then I said to myself, I'm going to get a tree."

A permit to cut a large tree in the Coronado National Forest cost thirty dollars, and tags for small trees were a dollar apiece. Berta and her friends drummed up some donations, borrowed a truck, and headed up the Coronado Trail. "We got about sixty trees to give away. We piled the tagged ones on the truck, and in between we stuck little ones without tags, so we could have enough for everybody.

"Then we had to look for the main tree. Man, we looked all over the forest. The one we finally picked was *huge*. That sucker must have been eighty feet tall. In the forest it looked so little, but it ended up so big! Poor truck." Berta covered her eyes. "We dented Jimmy's truck."

When they returned to Clifton, the tree looked lopsided. David Martinez drilled holes in the trunk and stuck in extra branches.

"It was nice, though," Diane said. "We set it up right down here in the plaza at Chase Creek, and decorated it so pretty."

"Just beautiful," Berta said. "I wish you could have seen it. And we had hot chocolate and cookies and food galore, tamales and all, on Christmas Eve. The Communication Workers from Tucson brought up a few gifts—coloring books and things. It wasn't anything big, but there was enough to give everybody something."

Diane said, "It was a little sad, in a way, but they learned to feel lucky for what they got. Other Christmases they had gotten, oh, so many presents. Jeez!"

"That's true," Berta said. "Two Christmases ago I gave my little boy a three-wheeler. And this year they got little homemade cars somebody had donated. But the main thing was that everybody was down there together in Chase Creek."

"You just felt like crying," Diane said. "Everybody was so content."

"Yeah, but God, was I tired. It was only just a few ladies all this time doing everything, and trying to get more donations. One day the ladies had filled about a thousand bags with that hard, sticky candy. It was all stuck together and looked awful. I looked at it and said, 'We can't give this to the kids. We're strikers, but *still* . . . ' So we took it *all* apart again, wrapped them up individually in paper and put it in the bags, and it came out nice. Our Santa was Ernie Robledo, Cleo's husband. And get this, he came in a Corvette! Our Santa came in style!

"I felt really good—it was one of the best experiences of my life. What made me feel so good is the fact that our kids didn't have to go without. We showed P.D. we didn't need them. Now we realize this. We can rely on ourselves, and on the community of Clifton. Everybody said it was the best

Christmas ever, and even some of the scab kids came down to our tree! They still had the one up at Morenci, but not many people went to it, less than a hundred I heard. And they had to *pay* their Santa Claus."

Christmas was a successful occasion for the strikers and their families, but it was also symbolic of a divided community. In past years the celebration had revolved around a single tree in Morenci; now there were two—one of which was decorated joylessly under the guard of Phelps Dodge nightwatchmen.

Berta acknowledged that the division was something nobody could really be happy about. "Halloween, for instance, was always nice here," she said sadly. "We'd hear about the terrible things that could happen in big cities, but here you knew your kids were safe. Everyone would get dressed up and go and trick or treat. This last year nobody went. We gave the kids a party 'cause we didn't want them going to scab homes. We were afraid they'd give them poison or something—and, of course," she laughed, "they were saying the same thing about us."

Cleo Robledo has seen strikes before, but none like this one. "We can't ever be the same Clifton and Morenci that we were," she said. "It will be years and years and years, people will remember this. If only the scabs hadn't gone in, this whole damn thing would be over now. I don't know why they did it, either. They aren't making anything now. They're hurting for money— all their dogs come over to my house to get fed."

The strike was six months old and nerves were raw. Every few days someone lost control—sometimes wreaking serious havoc, sometimes not. A major food fight broke out one night in Cole's Pizza Parlor in Clifton. ("She let him have it, pepperoni and all!" was how Berta described it). Several strikers reported having guns pulled on them outside the Circle K; the daytime cashier there, an exhausted-looking woman, verified that these reports were true. Berta, Gloria Armijo, and a troop of others chased a scab out of Chase Creek ("He *knows* this is a union street," they said), brandishing beer bottles and pool sticks.

"They have their way of looking at it, and I've got mine," said a woman named Vivian who had decided, against her husband's wishes, to work through the strike. "I wasn't going to put my kids through another strike, after being laid off and doing without for I don't know how long. I made my choice and I'll stand by it. I don't care what they do to me." She said some strikers had repeatedly broken the floodlights she'd put up for safety—after her husband left—on the outside of her mobile home. She looked thoroughly tired of the whole affair.

A typical sheriff's report in Clifton's newspaper, the *Copper Era*, gives an idea of the week's activities: José Vega reported that a window on the driver's side of his Ford pickup was broken with a BB or pellet gun; Renaldo Roman reported broken windows and a car pushed into the wall of a house; Deni Arvant reported BB shots through the rear window of her camper shell; Laura Wright reported that an acidic substance had been poured on her Chevrolet Impala (her arm blistered when she brushed against it); Placido Chavez reported that "some type of chemical" had been poured on the top of his 1974 Chevrolet and the two rear tires punctured; Stan Thurgeson reported that his windshield was broken by rocks while he was driving it; and finally, Deputy Matt Szady reported that his patrol car was struck with rocks while at a traffic stop (no serious damage was sustained).

Meanwhile, the WOWs were still striving to boost the morale of those crossing the line, and Morenci's organization of business and professional women inducted into its ranks a small group of women miners who had opted to work through the strike. They were given the honorary title of "Hardhats." The organization had never before considered miners to be "professionals," but then, times were hard.

Pat Scanlon reflected, long after the strike, that the ill will and division in the company towns ultimately worked to P.D.'s advantage. "In the days before the strike," he mused, "there was a 'them' and 'us' mentality between the company and the employees—a dichotomy of interests. But once you have these guys out there throwing rocks at you and kicking your car doors and making phone calls and so forth, that sort of changes. Everyone who's inside that plant is in the same boat: managers, foremen, workers, everybody. So the 'us' becomes everybody who's working, and the 'them' is those guys on the picket line. The best way the workers could get back at them was to thumb their noses at them and say, 'We'll get even with them by producing a lot of copper at a low cost.' And we have made a concentrated attempt to preserve that attitude in the work force. I certainly feel that P.D. is better off because of it."

Terri Martinez, a striker's wife from Clifton, was arrested twice for getting into fights. The second one occurred in the five-and-dime, after her nine-year-old daughter correctly and loudly identified a scab. "From there the fight started," Terri recalled. "She swung a magazine at me, and I bashed her against the shelves. There were some saints' up on the top shelf—they were trembling—and Pampers all over the floor. These two other ladies in the store, a striker and a neutral, plus another young boy tried breaking it up, but we already had each other by the hair. The cops caught up with me later. I guess my daughter was proud. She said, 'Ah, my mama beat up a scab!' "

Some let their anger out, some kept it in. Doll Schwartz cried every night, she said. "I had close friends that went in, and it tore me apart, worrying what might happen to them. To all of us. I don't like hating people, but you can't help it here."

Jessie Tellez wrote poems. One was entitled "Childhood Friend." Her voice broke when she read it to me.

> *You're angry at me, my childhood friend*
> *because beside the highway I stand.*
> *The union line I did not cross.*
> *Respect of friends I have not lost.*
> *I watch you as you pass the line,*
> *you do not look my way.*
> *My heart hurts each time you pass.*
> *I'm the friend betrayed . . .*
> *All I know is my heart aches*
> *as you hurriedly drive by.*
> *You can't escape the wrong you did*
> *the day our friendship died. . . .*
> *With dignity I stand beside*
> *my union and my friends.*
> *And you, poor soul, how do you feel,*
> *with blemished conscience real?*

# 8

# My Union and My Friends

After two months of monumental silence, negotiations between Phelps Dodge and the thirteen striking unions resumed on January 23, 1984. After ninety minutes, the negotiations broke down again. There had been no progress in reaching an agreement.

It was the worst of times for the strikers. Over the following days, which grew into weeks and then months, a pall fell over the dinner tables of striking families while everyone waited hard for the talks to begin again. They didn't. Phelps Dodge officials said the strike was over. Union negotiators said this was just a ploy to intimidate the strikers, but by this time it was easier to believe in Santa Claus than in that settlement just around the corner. Sentiments swayed wildly between certainty of victory and utter, black despair.

The 1980s were starting to look like a turning point in America's labor history, in which unions would be doing all the turning—into dust. PATCO, the national air traffic controllers' union, had been obliterated with a stroke of President Reagan's pen. Continental Airlines was now adopting a similar attitude toward its striking employees, attempting to conduct business as usual with replacement pilots and machinists. In November, Greyhound Bus employees had accepted a contract that cut back their wages and benefits at an average rate of 14 percent annually over the next three years. The National Labor Relations Board ruled in January, in a case involving United Auto Workers in Milwaukee, that a company could legally move from a unionized to a nonunionized plant to cut labor costs. A state Senate committee in Arizona proposed a constitutional referendum outlawing strikes by public employees. Collective bargaining, it seemed, would soon be a relic of a bygone age.

But the copper strikers refused to believe there was no power in their numbers. The questions they asked most frequently to cheer themselves were, How long can Phelps Dodge keep operating without skilled labor? And how long will the scabs work for peanuts without a union to protect them from long shifts and dangerous conditions?

The first question was becoming a moot point; those short-order cooks and grocery baggers hired by Phelps Dodge since the strike began were, by now, seasoned miners with seven months' experience. Bob Johnson, the company man in charge of recording each day's productivity, said things looked good.

The second question had more bite to it. Reports of accidents rolled out of the mines with the regularity of freight cars. Sometimes rumor embroidered them into horrific tragedies, but at other times no embroidery was necessary. The day before the negotiations, sixty-seven-year-old Wesley Bromley had died in the Ajo mine. He had fallen under the wheels of a train he was guiding toward the loading dock to be filled with ore, and he perished instantly. Bromley was an experienced miner who had come out of retirement to work during the strike. Phelps Dodge officials said the accident was not strike-related; strikers pointed out that retirement is a union-won privilege and a safety measure. While that might seem to be stretching the point, it is true that if P.D. had not kept operating during the strike, Bromley would have been enjoying his retirement instead of working in the mine.

No one could claim that it was exactly business as usual in the smelters and mines. The shifts were still shorthanded. Old-timers claimed they could tell from their front porches—by watching the color of the smelter smoke—how much ore was being processed, and how well. In their opinion it looked pretty bad. Whether or not this was true, times were hard in the industry. Eleven U.S. copper firms, including Phelps Dodge, were now asking the U.S. trade agency to limit copper imports, so troubled were domestic producers by low prices and profit losses.

To make matters worse for Phelps Dodge, the company's request for its 1984 permit to operate the Morenci smelter had been denied because of continuing violations of an EPA agreement. Federal studies had linked emissions from copper smelters to the growing acid rain problem in the Rockies, and the EPA had called for an $81 million construction program to reduce sulfur dioxide emissions at Morenci by December 1985. As an interim measure, the company had been asked to curtail smelter operations during certain weather conditions. By April 1984, the EPA was still not satisfied with the company's efforts.

Financially, if not strategically, the strike seemed to be costing Phelps Dodge more than it gained. The new workers may have accepted low wages, but they also required fringe benefits such as helicopter rides and security guard escorts, not to mention replacement of many hundreds of broken windows. For months, the company paid for buses to bring workers from Safford and other communities into the Morenci mine. Families of nonstrikers at the Ajo mine were occasionally put up in hotels in Phoenix. It seemed a high price to pay, especially for mainly unskilled labor. It wasn't hard for

strikers to put two and two together. "The way I see it, the plan is n
reduce costs but to get rid of the unions," said Gloria Armijo. "It *has* to be,
because they've been spending so much and making so little. With us, they
were at least breaking even."

An outpouring of national and international support gave the strikers the
courage to hold on. Their struggle had faded from the front pages of state
newspapers, and from here on in would be considered newsworthy only if
there were a blood-and-guts angle. But abroad there was more interest than
ever. A German film crew came to Clifton to make a documentary. It was an
interesting sight: the German director sitting atop his camera truck told the
picket line, "Now you must imagine we are the scabs," and forty women
hooted and gestured obscenely into the camera lens as it slowly drove by.
After take three it was a wrap, and everyone applauded.

Members of the Women's Auxiliary were surprised when letters began
trickling in from Europe—in English, no less. "You know, this country is so
egocentrical we can only think of one language to write in," remarked Anna
O'Leary (whose first language, of course, was Spanish), "but these people can
write in English or French or German or Spanish—depending on who they
want to talk to!" The letters were extremely supportive and showed a sophisticated understanding of the strike—the average Belgian now probably knew
more about it than the average Arizonan. "But the one thing many of them
say," Anna pointed out, "is that they can't understand how something like
this could happen in America. They think things are fair in America."

The Morenci Miners Women's Auxiliary heard from nations and people
they had never even thought about, on subjects that surprised them. A letter
from the auxiliary of the National Union of Mineworkers in England—then
engaged in a coal strike—informed them that women were instrumental in
holding that strike together too. They heard from a representative of the Irish
Republican Army and from revolutionaries in Central America.

Fina Roman, still the auxiliary's president, said these letters were not only
inspirational but also eye-opening. There was a world out there. "I think these
other political groups support us not only because we're copper strikers, but
because we are human beings whose rights are being violated. They recognize
that a threat to one person's rights jeopardizes the rights of all.

"But unfortunately," Fina went on, "there are others who don't share the
active participation that's necessary for the defense of this strike. People who
should be, and could be, on our side."

Foremost among those who "should be and could be" were the national
leaders of the striking unions. At the local level the unions were working

hard to help those in greatest need with house payments, utility bills, and legal support. At the end of January the unions filed lawsuits in U.S. District Court questioning the legality of the evictions. All across the country there was a groundswell of support coming in from the rank-and-file. It was the "guys at the top," many strikers agreed, who should have been doing more.

This vague concern was made concrete when Ron Weisen came to town in January. Weisen, at that time president of his United Steelworkers of America (USWA) local in Homestead, Pennsylvania, was campaigning for the presidency of his international union. He was an underdog candidate, running against USWA officers Lynn Williams and Frank McKee, who at that time had direct responsibility for the strike. Weisen was not elected, as it turned out, but it wasn't for lack of support from the Morenci Miners Women's Auxiliary, who greeted his ideas with thunderous approval.

"We need fighters in this union," he told the Clifton audience in a special meeting organized by the auxiliary. "We need to do what we did in the 1930s. We have to get out in the streets, take our gloves off, and start fighting." He denounced USWA leadership for its role in imposing a concession contract on the basic steel industry the year before and for their lackluster response to U.S. Steel Corporation's plant shutdowns and layoffs of more than fifteen thousand steelworkers.

"It is a shame and a betrayal," he said, "that while our international leadership talks a lot about solidarity, they have done very little to mobilize the ranks of the USWA to directly support the Phelps Dodge strike."

If he were in a position to do so, he said, he would organize the kind of fight that Phelps Dodge was asking for: "Every single resource of our union— financial, political, publicity, and the transport of thousands of USWA members to stop the strikebreakers and support you at the gates—would have been yours a long time ago." Weisen felt that the USWA needed to be more aggressive. He proposed the establishment of an international union headquarters in Clifton for the duration of the strike.

Many of the strikers had begun to feel that their international organization was treating them like poor relations. But because of Weisen's radical position within the USWA (that is, his dim view of the leadership and his faith in the rank-and-file), his visit was opposed by local USWA officials in Clifton, who suggested that the Women's Auxiliary stay out of union politics. When they ignored this advice and brought Weisen anyway, the union men were affronted, and most boycotted the event on principle. Afterward, the women were firmly warned that their business was to toe the line of their union's philosophy and strategy. It might just as well have been suggested that the starving masses go home and eat cake. Weisen's words still rang in their ears like a war cry.

Picket lines grew larger and more spirited than they had been for months. Official negotiations were deadlocked, however, and it was hard to know what direction they were moving in, if they were moving at all. The women recall this time as a season of restlessness.

"Okay, we were taking care of the food and clothes and everything, and we were taking care of the picket lines, but it still wasn't enough," Berta Chavez said. "I remember one time when we went all the way to Safford in a caravan just because we were so mad, we had to do something. Just on the spur of the moment, we took off in our cars. We thought if we went all the way to Safford we could at least get away from the DPS. But we couldn't; they were already there. There was always a leak. To this day I feel there was somebody strong in the union that was working for P.D. Every time we wanted to do something, the cops would know."

The response to this growing restlessness was an increased police presence. Earlier in January the state police had proposed a curfew for the city of Clifton, but this was rejected by the town council. Nevertheless, DPS director Ralph Milstead told the state legislature that he expected to keep a "special force" in Clifton and Morenci for up to three years. According to a report in the *Arizona Daily Star* on February 7, this project would cost Arizona taxpayers approximately $1 million, over and above the $1.5 million the DPS had already spent on the strike.

More than a few Arizonans were irritated by this hefty price tag on what by now seemed like a tempest in a teacup. But to the strikers, the presence of the DPS special force was a stress far beyond irritation. It was a symbol of their second-class status in what had once been their home. "We don't even have highway patrolmen watching out for speeders anymore, trying to keep our town safe," Vicky Sharp complained. "Their full-time job now is to take care of scab workers. If they stop somebody, nine times out of ten it's a striker and they are run through the mill. They are stopped, asked to get out of their vehicle, the vehicle is checked thoroughly to see that it's in good working condition. Then, if you have a bad attitude or if you say anything that they don't care to hear, they treat you like a DWI. They make you walk the center line. They draw a circle on the pavement and make you stick your nose in it. Check your equilibrium, the whole works. This has happened to people we know."

What sounded like wild exaggeration turned out, time and again, to be true. Police records substantiate, for example, that a striker in Ajo was stopped in his vehicle, arrested, and jailed for not having his driver's license in his pocket. (It was at his home, a few blocks away.)

This one-sided law enforcement bred visible arrogance among the protected. One morning before dawn, several shots were fired into the home of Angel Rodriguez, president of the local Steelworkers. (The man who fired the shots was eventually sentenced to one and a half years in prison; his accomplice was placed on a release program that allowed him to work for Phelps Dodge during the day and return to jail at night.) On the picket lines, women complained of being spat upon, swerved at, and threatened with bodily harm while the police looked on but did nothing. The officers contend that they were under direct orders to watch strikers and prevent them from causing trouble, which is exactly what the officers did—and not one iota more. Anna and Jorge O'Leary told of an incident in which a woman in labor had come to the People's Clinic, parked her car in front where a picket line was being held for the shift change, and commenced to give birth in the front seat. The picketers called for Dr. O'Leary, and when he ran out of the clinic he was shocked to see a DPS officer standing beside the woman's car, ignoring her screams.

The memory caused Anna to go pale. "That guy didn't even move," she said, shuddering. "He had his arms crossed liked this, looking around with his nose in the air, while everyone was screaming for help. The baby's *head* was coming out. He just looked away. I couldn't believe it. This is—I don't know how you could describe such a thing—just unreal."

The baby was born in good health and was named Jorge, after Dr. O'Leary. The excited picketers on the line waved a new sign that said, "It's A Boy!" He was the first of several young Jorges in Clifton, and it was a good bet that not one of them would grow up to be a police officer.

"Obviously we have less respect for the law now," Diane McCormick said. "We were raised traditionally—act like a lady, Catholic, catechism when we were little, and all that. You always respected authority. Now here we are yelling at the DPS while our kids are standing right by us. When they come into this town, it's 'Eeew, the DPS! Scab lovers!' and all this stuff. One time Berta and I watched this DPS go into the mine, and she called him a scab lover. He turned back and said, 'What did you call me, ma'am?' She said, in this real sweet voice, 'A scab lover, sir!'

"It's because they've treated us badly, and how much can we take? It makes you feel like you're going to go crazy after awhile—they're always harassing us. They follow my sister and me home from the picket line. Or we'll pull in at the Circle K, and they pull in and just sit there and watch us."

Berta Chavez kept a journal of these days. She wrote it on anything she could find—scraps of her kids' school papers or the backs of auxiliary meeting minutes that say things like "Gloria reported there are enough beans" and "Linda received a letter about her picture being in the paper." Her journal is basically more of the same, except that among entries such as "Quiet day, went to make tortillas at Paul's house with Stella, Candy, Martha, and Terry . . . ," there are also entries such as "We heard that scabs from Safford are making homemade bombs. They have DPS officers in there now on the weekend to protect them."

A sampling of other entries, from several different days:

"Mrs. Shupe was at the line and a scab threw a piece of slag rock, broke the skin. . . . "

"A scab pulled out a gun on Mary Lou at the Circle K. I was a witness. So were the cashiers. We put in a report, but they say they can't do anything about it. . . . "

"A scab swerved into a stop sign where we were picketing and it fell on a friend of mine, Evelyn, and knocked her down. The DPS went to see if the scab was hurt, instead of Evelyn. . . . "

One especially difficult day ended with this poignant lament: "I just can't believe what's happening to us. I sure wish I had some way of getting this thing over with."

As the strike wore on, Berta's journal revealed clearly the fearful sense of being watched that many women in Clifton were beginning to feel. For example:

"Some scabs came down the road and I yelled at them. Also had a small conversation with one of the News Media men. Felt the pressure of somebody or several people staring at me. I felt uneasy. I looked across the highway, saw the DPS was pointing at me with a very angry look on his face. The other officer told him something and he put his finger down. I had the kids so I just left. I didn't want to get arrested with my kids in the truck. I went home and forgot the incident."

A few days later:

"Went down to the union hall to see what was happening. Wanted to see the lawyer to tell him about how the DPS was keeping an eye on me since they came in. Later decided to all go up and picket on top of the Hill, plus in front of the Clinic. As soon as I took off, the DPS followed me up. They were looking through binoculars at me again. . . . "

The next day:

"DPS is still watching me. I left Clifton about 4:45, and they were by the Western Auto. As soon as I got in the car and went to put gas in, they left."

And three days later:

"Scab neighbors having a party—started calling us names. Threatened us, also threatened to burn my house down. I called the cops. Pat was a witness, she heard the gun shots. They had guns out, told me 'DPS is on our side,' and said they were watching me. How did she know they were watching me all this time?

"I just happened to look up on top of the hill, and I saw the DPS. I could see the sun reflected off that gold shield they have on the side of the DPS cars. They must have been watching me for some time."

Berta's life became hell when she felt she was under constant surveillance. To escape for a while, she tried spending the night at her sister Diane's house. "I was so tired," she recalled. "I was sitting outside on her porch drinking a beer. The porch is high up, overlooking the town. Well, I just happened to look over and the DPS were sitting in their cars right across the way, on the other side of the river. Staring right up at the porch. I got scared, but I said, 'I'm not going to show them I'm scared.' I just sat there for a while. I thought I saw somebody get out—I wasn't sure, because there was a tree—but they stayed there for a long time. Later on that night I looked out the window and he was still watching.

"I kept thinking, where am I going to go? If they come, I'm going straight up the hill—they don't know the hills like I do. But at night we would see them shining those big spotlights all over the hills. Why? At home I was always asking Candy, 'Have you got the pistol?' I would check over and over again to make sure the house was locked."

Berta had already been arrested once in October for allegedly throwing rocks at the picket line on a day when Berta says she was not in town. The charges were dropped. In January she was arrested again.

"There was a big, big picket line up in front of the People's Clinic that day, both men and women," she recounted. "We'd started having the main picket line there every day instead of at the mine gate. This one DPS officer, Larry, had been eyeing me for a long time, and he kept on looking at me that day. I could see something coming.

"The scabs were coming out, and somebody on the other side of the road threw a rock, pretty far away from where we were. When this rock came they started arresting people—Paul what's-his-name, and Richard, they were just grabbing people, whoever. We were getting really mad. I was especially mad when they grabbed Paul, because he had his little boy right beside him, and they knocked Paul down.

"When that happened I started getting excited. I was up at the front of the group, and I started yelling, 'Union! Union!' and jumping up and down. They all started yelling, and everything just seemed to go berserk. I saw the DPS guy, Larry, but I figured nothing was going to happen because he was looking away from me. He was walking closer and closer to me, but still looking away, and then suddenly he grabbed me and said, 'You're under arrest.'

"The crowd started going nuts. I saw Lydia Knott taking pictures. My brother was coming to help me—he's nineteen—but they shoved him and hit him with a club in the stomach. Luckily my husband was way on the other side—he didn't know it was me they were arresting until it was all over. I always kind of sneak away from Candy when we're on the line, because he doesn't like me to be yelling so much. So when they yelled at him, 'Your wife is arrested!' he said, '*What??*' "

Berta was handcuffed and pushed into a patrol car. "They had my hands way up high behind my back, and I told them they were hurting me—they had about five guys on me. I said, 'I'll cooperate, just don't hurt me,' but the more I'd say that, the more they would bend my arm. Then Cleo jumped in. That's when she got arrested too. There must have been ten of them on her.

"People were getting mad, banging on the sheriff's car. When they took me down to the station there were people all around the car, everybody walking down there with the car. And I was yelling, 'Union!' right in his ear. The police officer was trying to cover his ears, shaking his head.

"When we got to the station, Cleo and I were really pissed off. At one point there was nobody in the office but us and Larry, and he said they needed somebody to make an example of because they couldn't arrest everybody. So they picked us out. When it came out in court, of course he said he couldn't remember having told us that. At the hearing I just stared at him. I was calm, because I knew I was innocent. And he was shaking, switching his story. He said he never told Cleo and me anything about making an example of us. But he most definitely did."

Cleo Robledo corroborated this story. She said she and Berta were never read their rights and were held without charges for most of the day. Eventually, she said, the justice of the peace felt that there had been plenty of time to file charges against them and ordered that the two women be released. Cleo never heard another word about the incident, although two days later she was served with eviction papers from Phelps Dodge. She made plans to file charges against the arresting officers, who she claimed had punched her, pulled her hair, and cut her arm through her sweatshirt with the handcuffs. Her eviction notice was later rescinded.

Berta did not get off so easily. "When they booked me," she said, "they said I was arrested for inciting a riot or something like that, but they didn't file any charges, and finally I was let out on my OR [own recognizance]. Then later, several days after I was released, I found out I was charged with inciting a riot and also a felony—assault with a deadly weapon. And get this: the weapon was my fingernails."

Berta learned of the felony charge when she read about it in the local newspaper, the following Wednesday. She had never been told.

"I don't know why they didn't tell me in person—probably they were afraid I would have bitten their heads off! So the kids at school found out about it before I did. They were asking my kids, Is your mom really a jailbird?"

Berta's charge of inciting a riot was dropped, but the felony charge—assault with deadly fingernails—was not. To Berta this was no laughing matter; if found guilty, she could face five years in prison. Soon afterward she was offered a plea bargain.

"I had a letter stating that I could take two years' probation, a little bit of time in jail, and they'd drop the felony. Probation would mean staying off the picket line, I guess. My husband said it was up to me to decide what to do. We would make jokes. He'd say, 'Maybe I can get a job as a security guard, where they put you.' It's hard to think about five years in prison, you know. It was tempting to take the bargain. But I refused it. I'm going to go before a jury. I'm innocent, so I'm going to go through it all the way."

Berta still managed to hold on to her miraculously upbeat outlook on life. Immediately, she was back out on the line. She told me that during her arrest, despite DPS claims that she was "handled like a lady," she was so badly roughed up that her brassiere was torn beyond repair. Months later she would still shout at the top of her lungs, whenever her arresting officer passed by the picket line, "Hey, Larry, you owe me a bra!"

One evening in late spring the Morenci Miners Women's Auxiliary was assembled in Chase Creek, planning a rally. The meeting was interrupted by a man who came in shouting that the police were arresting kids on the street.

Jean Lopez, the auxiliary treasurer, knew her teenaged daughter had gone up the street for a soda. She dropped her pencil and ran. "I thought, Oh, gosh, they've got her. And sure enough, I got down there and this DPS officer had her by the arm, about to arrest her. She and these three girlfriends had been having an argument about their boyfriends or something—no hitting, just arguing—so this cop parked across the street at the Circle K and called for a backup. For four teenaged girls. The paddy wagon was there, and about fifty DPS officers, and National Guards. The whole area was packed. Lights flashing and the whole bit.

"They wanted to take my daughter. They tried to question her, and she kept telling them, 'I can't answer your questions—I'm a minor and you can't question me.' She knows her rights. I've told her and I've told her what they can and can't do to you. She just said if they would give her a chance she would go get me, that I was at the auxiliary meeting.

"I had got down there by that time, and the DPS told me that my daughter was being very rude. I said, 'Rude according to what? What were you trying to do to her?' He told me that she refused to give her name. And she told the other girls, 'And *you* don't have to give them your names either! Don't tell them anything.' So they were very upset with her. They had her by the arm and told her, 'If you won't talk to us now, we'll take you down to juvenile and take care of it.' She was so angry, I had to put her in a car and have a lady drive her home. She was furious that they had handled her that way. There were no charges named at any time. I thought it was one of the stupidest things I'd ever seen."

Jessie Tellez saw the incident as a territorial showdown—the sort of response you'd expect if you tried to nab a bear cub while its mother was browsing nearby. The officers had formed a circle around the girls, Jessie said, but when they saw the faces of the women who moved toward them down the street, they backed off. One by one, the children ran out of the circle of police officers and stood behind the women.

"Then," Jessie said, "I called out to the DPS, 'Go away from our area! *We don't want you here!* GET OUT OF HERE!' We chanted and chanted, and the officers finally got in their cars and drove away. But there was one officer still up at the Circle K, probably waiting for others to come around so they could arrest us.

"The women said, 'What do we do now, Jessie?' And I said, 'Let's go shopping.' So we all went into the Circle K. Some of us had money, and some of us didn't, but we all went in there and slowly walked up and down the aisles, buying a soft drink or whatever. We took our time. But he was still there. So we went to the door and started chanting again, 'Go away! Go away!' And finally he took off. I said, 'Well, women, it looks like we've secured the area. Let's go.'

"We'd never practiced that, it just came naturally. It's an animal instinct for a woman to protect her young and defend her territory. I didn't think about it until afterward, but it was just very natural for us to do that. It's all part of women's work."

# 9

# Women's Work

Fina Roman had never been farther east than the downhill end of Clifton. Now she was flying over an endless landscape of dazzling lights, coming in for a landing in New York City. To Fina, it looked like another planet.

"There was this young man sitting by the window and I kept trying to lean around him, and finally I said, 'Well, look, I've never been here. I've just got to look out this window!' The next fifteen minutes I spent practically in the poor guy's lap. Looking down at the lights, the Empire State Building, and everything. He was very nice about it. For days I walked around with my head up in the air, looking at those tall buildings."

But Fina hadn't come as a tourist. She was scheduled to speak at a rally in New York and at another one a few days later in Boston. As a way of keeping up morale and getting outside support, the Women's Auxiliary had launched a program of speaking tours.

Anyone might get weak knees and a cottony throat speaking to a milling throng on the streets of New York. But for women who had never in their lives strayed far from Clifton and Morenci, the courage required was nigh unto incomprehensible. These were women raised under the dictum of "speak when spoken to," and it had taken months for some of them to gather the nerve to express their opinions in their own auxiliary meetings. Some were still uncomfortable expressing their opinions at the family dinner table. Now they were venturing into the great wide world and standing up before the multitudes.

In New York City, Fina spoke on Wall Street. The rally tied up traffic for ten blocks. With Fina and the other speakers leading the way, a thousand people had marched from the South African embassy to Phelps Dodge headquarters to make a public statement about the company's ties with apartheid.

In Boston she also shared the podium with anti-apartheid activists. One of them was a man she liked very much by the name of Jesse Jackson. He had just announced his intention to run for the presidency and was on his way to South Africa, but he pledged that when he returned he would throw his energy behind the Arizona copper strikers.

Fina remembers the trip with enormous excitement. "When you see fifteen hundred people looking up at you, expecting you to say something intelligent, what a feeling! I think it meant something to the people back east that a handful of people in this little mining town had held off a corporate giant for all these months. Those unions whose membership numbers in the thousands, even half a million, were looking to us."

Fina said she spoke mostly about the women's role, what the striking families were going through, and left the nuts and bolts of the strike for the union leaders to discuss. She is modest. Fina had a thorough grasp of logistics and strategy and had no problem articulating these ideas when I heard her speak to a strike-support rally in Tucson. The following is a portion of that speech:

"I represent the Morenci Miners Women's Auxiliary, who do me the honor of serving as president of the most courageous organization in the world. Women who do not hesitate to pick up and proudly carry the union banner— from walking the picket line, organizing rallies, going to jail, to walking into the governor's office. Women who a few months ago had never made speeches now address conventions in major cities in strong, firm voices that do not waver even though tears run down their faces. Phelps Dodge must wonder, What kind of women are these? Did they even think of women as worthy opponents when they lodged their attack on the unions? Probably not. I know the DPS didn't.

"I have not heard those who swore to uphold our rights through elected office speak out in defense of them now. Will the politicians—who this election year call for our votes and our trust—turn out to be summer soldiers? Will they really make a firm commitment to change the common destiny of those of us whose dollars and pennies fill the coffers of the IRS? We who made industries like Phelps Dodge great with our sweat and blood? We who defend this country's greatness when called upon? Whom should we approve, by our voting power, to be the representatives and guardians of our constitutional rights? Will the politicians who promise justice deliver? Will the politicians who propose, produce? Once elected, will they find it politically expedient to forget the working masses? But why do we question? Why are we cautious? What has all this to do with copper strikers?

"It is 'we the people'—the old, the poor, the average—who have become scapegoats for the greed of the industrial giants. As the American worker will not be a slave, neither do we want to be masters. But taxation without representation is a principle which is not negotiable! Not in Arizona, nor in Nevada, nor in California, nor in Washington, D.C.!"

Four other auxiliary members made a whirlwind tour of fifteen Colorado and California cities in eighteen days. They raised thousands of dollars and thousands of consciousnesses—including their own. Jean Lopez came back a changed woman.

"I just never thought I could *do* anything like that," she said with a sparkle in her eye. "I had never done it before, that's for sure. I'm not really shy, but to speak up there all by myself, to try to get a point across—that was something I could never do. In Denver, the first day of the tour, I got up on stage and looked at all those people, and my heart was beating bam! bam! and my legs were shaking, and I just asked God not to let me fall off the stage. And, by George, I did pretty well."

How did she have the nerve to agree to this tour in the first place? Jean laughed. "To start with, I kind of backed myself into a corner. Some people from California were up here for a rally, and they said I should go on tour. 'Yeah, yeah, sure, I'll do it,' I said. I never thought anything would come of it. And then it actually came through.

"First I asked my husband, and he said, 'You go for it, because later on in life you're going to be kicking yourself if you don't.' My kids said, 'Just think, Mom, you're going to talk to all these people, and you're going to be really important.'

"But that wasn't what decided me. I was motivated by what I had seen here. I knew there was more or less a media blockout where they don't want our side to get out, and the company was showing themselves as the good guys. From that I got the courage. I felt very strongly about the wrong that was being done here, against Governor Babbitt sending in the National Guard. I felt angry about the police brutality I had seen. I saw my own friends chained and beaten. Just *being here* made me so angry, I could find the courage to do anything. I knew it was very, very necessary."

So she did it. Denver was the first stop, then Sacramento, Modesto, San Jose, San Francisco, Oxnard. "I think we hit just about every California town there was," Jean said. They spoke to Teamsters, hotel workers, and even the Steelworkers' national convention in San Francisco. When I asked her about that, Jean closed her eyes for a few seconds and smiled. "Now, *that* was scary. Because it was just men. A whole convention hall full of men, thousands of *men*. The place was packed.

"When we first got there we talked to one of their officials. He wasn't too crazy about the idea of women talking to their convention—he said it's never been done. So we were a little upset. But I said, 'Why not?' Well, he hemmed and hawed, and finally said, 'Okay, I'll give you five minutes.'

"So we got up there and the guys were kind of shifting in their chairs, like they didn't really want to hear what we were going to say. Making faces like, 'Women, what are they doing in our hall?' you know the type of thing. That's the feeling I got.

"But then we gave our speech, and it was fantastic. We got a standing ovation, and they started donating from the floor. I think we got about three thousand dollars. I couldn't believe it, just couldn't believe it. Then they invited us to be their special guests for the banquet that night—a hundred-dollars-a-plate dinner! We were kind of like celebrities, the four of us little women sitting at this table with everybody looking at us. People would come over and introduce us to their wives or girlfriends or whatever. They kept telling us we were doing a fantastic job."

Jean's partners on the trip were Carmina Garcia, Beverly Cole, and Jessie Tellez. The Steelworkers' convention, where they'd turned around a hall full of doubting Thomases, was a memory they all carried close to their hearts. It wasn't the only one, either. "These men are being challenged, let me tell you," Jessie said. "After we went on this tour, [local USWA president] Angel Rodriguez got up one time and said that he had always felt that the woman's place was in the kitchen, but these ladies have a different idea, and they've shown that they're pretty effective. He said, 'Now whatever they want to do, we'll back them up!'

This backing was more rhetorical than actual. When one woman went to speak to a convention in Chicago, her husband was not waiting for her when she came home. "The problem started when I was up there," Alicia said. "There was this guy Daniel, with the Workers' League, who had also come to Chicago. He had given us these pamphlets on the strike to distribute, which I thought were very helpful, you know, but at this convention they had strict rules about distributing literature, and it would have impaired our efforts to get on the floor. We had to deal with the higher echelons of these women that were organizing the thing, and I was thinking, well, heck, my first objective is to get up and speak, so if this literature is going to bother them, I'll just put it under the table for now.

"Well, Daniel got real mad and he called my husband, who was very involved in the strike, and told him I had no idea what I was doing, that I was being influenced by the bourgeoisie and everything else. It was man with man, talking about how they know so much more and everything. I tried to explain to my husband, 'Look, I know what I'm doing here. I've got to play by their rules for a little while if I want to get to speak, and that's what the people back home have sent me here to do.'

"But he said, 'You don't know what you're doing.' Of course, he was taking Daniel's word for it. Why? Because Daniel's a man. He said, 'I want you to come home right this minute!' And I said, 'You're crazy! I've just been here one day. Hopefully by Sunday we'll be on the floor.' 'Well, that's not good enough,' he said, 'I want you home by Sunday.' I took a deep breath and said, 'Well, I'm not coming! I have a mission. I want to accomplish it!' And I did, too."

Alicia says it was the first time she'd ever said "flat out no" to her husband. "I was so far away, that may have made it easier. But then, on the other hand, to be so far away, not knowing if someone would be there if you needed them . . . I had never been in that situation before. I was in a rush to get back because I knew he was mad at me, but also I was so scared, all the way home."

Dead tired at 2:30 A.M., Alicia came home to an empty house. True to his word, her husband had packed up the kids and gone to Tucson.

"When he finally came back he just said, 'I want you to know from this moment on you're not to have anything to do with the strike.' I told him I had already kind of put my foot in it and that I couldn't back out now, because there were people depending on me. He said, 'Well, you do things in your name then. Don't use my name, because from this moment on we're through.' "

Alicia told him to go ahead and file divorce papers, if that's what he wanted to do. Then she reminded him that he had gotten her into this strike business in the first place. "I told him, 'I've had a good teacher—you! You stuck up for your rights, and P.D. fired you for it. Well, I'm sticking up for my rights now, and you're firing me as your wife!

"So we left it at that, and it took him about two or three days to get over it. I guess he wasn't that anxious to fire me, because in the meantime he ate my cooking."

Some of the women had the full support of their families, while others, like Alicia, were fighting in several war zones at once, but they all kept going. They spoke to labor unions, political conventions, teachers' associations, lawyers' associations, human rights groups, and the National Organization for Women. In cities from California to New York, the women from that dusty little town in Arizona kept turning up and talking or pleading or insisting themselves on to the agenda, and kept getting standing ovations.

Anna O'Leary went to the national convention of the Coalition of Labor Union Women (CLUW). "There were over a thousand people, and we'd been talking to everybody we could about getting to speak, but the higher-ups had already had the agenda set up way ahead of time, so we weren't going to be allowed. Still, we'd talked to so many people and there was so much enthusiasm in the rank-and-file, we figured there was no way they could ignore us. It would have been political suicide. Finally we got through to this one lady pretty far up the ladder who said, 'Maybe.'

"So we were standing in the doorway forever while these ladies complimented each other and nominated each other and said how marvelous they all were, putting feathers in each other's hats. By that time people were starting to yell, 'We want to hear about the copper strikers!' They kind of ignored it. Then finally they asked if there was any new business, and one of the ladies stood up and said the words 'copper strike' and there was just this roar from the floor. We'd done our job, *everybody* knew about us. A lady with big hair and this kind of nasal voice grabbed the gavel and said, 'Now, ladies, ladies, all right, let's give them a chance.' And it kind of settled down, but by that time there was no getting around us, so then they said, 'Now, as we promised . . . '

"I'll never forget it: as we were walking up to the podium everybody in the whole place stood up. It gave me chills. Ten minutes before they were all yawning and falling asleep, and now they were shouting their heads off. I swear I saw one person standing on her chair. I said everything I could think of to say—they had only given us five minutes for our presentation, but it ended up going on for half an hour or so. When we stepped off the podium people were chanting 'Union! Union!' It went on and on. Finally the woman in charge got back up there behind the microphone and was saying in that nasal voice, 'Now, ladies, ladies!'

"Then we asked, Could we do something that has never been done at a CLUW convention, and that is pass the hat? So someone shouted, 'I move that we make an exception just this once and pass the hat,' and they did. Everybody was so excited, it was contagious. They opened up the floor for comments, and people stood up to resolve that they all support the strike, send so much money per month, and all this. The grand finale was that this one little woman stood up and just started screaming and hollering, 'We ought to be out there like these women; we ought to be out there on the picket line!' She was hysterical! The woman on the stage was saying, 'Sister, sister!' And that kind of ended the thing. Oh, what a day that was."

Every one of the women who went on speaking tours had her own memory of a perfect moment. But between those moments came hours and days of exhausting travel, disorientation, and homesickness, and sometimes grave threats to their domestic tranquility. They were not in it for the glory. Jean

Lopez stated this well. "I wasn't there to be famous or anything," she said, "I was just an ordinary person going out to give a message: that this fight is going on, and that it's a matter of human dignity—people being arrested for merely saying they support the copper strike, human issues like that. We wanted the national unions to acknowledge that this strike was still going on, not to give up on us. To tell us how we can win this thing."

The truth of the matter, though, is that by this time they were not really waiting around for anyone's advice. The Morenci Miners Women's Auxiliary was auxiliary to nothing—it was captain of its own ship. If these women had once thought of their work as sneakers and schoolbooks and sacks of beans— a series of stopgap measures—they now understood the full significance of the weight they were carrying. The minute they put it down, the strike would be over.

And the burden was getting heavier daily. There had been a temporary cease fire in the eviction war while the unions challenged Phelps Dodge's right to evict the strikers, but on April 20, 1984, a federal ruling upheld the evictions, and the battle raged again. The company set new deadlines, and many families stood firm, with backing from the auxiliary.

The worst of their worries was an insidious rumor, now growing into an assumption in the outside world, that the strike was dead. The women decided they could prove their detractors wrong only if they could get people out on the streets and keep them there.

Cinco de Mayo (May 5), which was just around the corner, is an important holiday in southern Arizona. It commemorates a somewhat arcane event— the battle of Puebla, fought in 1862, in which Mexican troops turned back the invading army of Napoleon III—but more important, it's a celebration of the strong Mexican-American heritage of the region. Clifton always had a fiesta then anyway, so the auxiliary hit upon the idea of organizing this year's celebration into a strike-support rally. The strikers could spend an enjoyable day picnicking with friends and family, have a few speakers and a march up the hill, and show the world that they had not given up.

It was at this point that open conflict flared between the women and the men.

A rift between the local union leadership and the Women's Auxiliary had been rumbling under the surface for quite a while, and occasionally—as when the auxiliary brought in USWA renegade Ron Weisen—it had surfaced as a warning tremor. Now it opened into a chasm.

First, union leaders tried to talk down the rally idea, saying that negotiations were coming up and it would be wiser to take a quiet, nonconfrontational "wait-and-see" approach. The women thought "wait and see" sounded a lot like "roll over and play dead." When the union said it wouldn't sanction their rally, the women voted to have it anyway. The union then *forbade* them from having the rally and said that if they did, union members would call for a boycott and even leave town to demonstrate their lack of support for the endeavor. The women of Clifton smiled and hummed and made tortillas by the bushel. A lot of other people, both inside and outside the community, said they wouldn't miss this rally for the world. It looked to have all the makings of an unforgettable day.

During this period I had a chance to hear the men air their complaints about the Women's Auxiliary. Four local union leaders had come to Tucson to show a documentary, *High Stakes in Morenci*, about a 1955 strike against Phelps Dodge. Because I was unable to attend the public showing, I was invited to watch it the next day at a small gathering in a friend's living room. I was the only woman present.

The strike that was documented in the film bore little resemblance to the one I'd been witnessing over the last ten months. The setting and the company and probably even the contract disputes were the same, right down to the same roadside ditches along Highway 666, but the players were all different. In this film, only men walked the picket line, and men did all the talking. At the "Ladies' Auxiliary" meeting, women listened attentively to a male speaker; they leaned forward in their chairs with hands folded in their laps, dressed in prim shirtwaists, pumps, and earrings. The auxiliary meeting of 1955 could have vied with church as a place for displaying one's fashion consciousness. Granted, these women probably knew that a movie crew was coming to their meeting, but still . . . In recent months I'd seen women gleefully giving the finger to TV photographers. No amount of camera equipment could have altered the agenda of the auxiliary meetings of 1984 or coaxed many auxiliary members out of their jeans and union T-shirts. The film was a documentary of a good deal more than a strike. I settled back to watch.

The film is overdubbed with the voice of a male narrator who explains in a cheerfully condescending tone that the women are voting on whether to have a party for the children. "Good idea!" they all exclaim. A good-natured, grumbling husband is "drafted"—in the tradition of Blondie and Dagwood—to make the piñata.

At the party, little girls wear billowing dresses with lots of petticoats, and the boys wear ties and have slicked-down hair (a far cry from the fatigues and combat boots and painted-on black eyes of Berta's break-dancers). One woman at the party, giggling at her own outrageousness, sports a pair of rhinestone dangle earrings to which 'Mine-Mill' buttons have been attached. I couldn't help thinking of the plastic earrings the Women's Auxiliary had recently special-ordered as a fund raiser: one of each pair said "Screw the Scabs," and the other, "Screw the DPS."

Later in the film the women are shown on a makeshift assembly line in the kitchen, merrily slapping out tortillas. One woman bashfully waves a hand in front of her face as the narrator pronounces her "the champion tortilla maker of the strike." Later the women show up on the picket line to dish out chili and tortillas for the picketers. The men are so proud of their wives, they go back for seconds.

In one of the final scenes, the whole town is assembled to hear the latest word on negotiations. The men speak of rejecting the latest offer and staying out on strike. A woman stands up and declares, "If the men want to go on with this strike, the Ladies' Auxiliary will gladly continue in the kitchen!"

The film wound to its conclusion, and the lights came on. Vince, a union man in his sixties, joked that they ought to show it to the Women's Auxiliary in Morenci.

One of the younger men, John, said, "Are you kidding? They'd throw rocks at you!" All the men laughed, and then shook their heads sadly. For the life of them, they could not understand what had gone wrong with the goddamned women of this world in the thirty years since the strike of 1955.

I kept my mouth shut.

A third union official, a man in his early thirties nicknamed "Babe," leaned back in his chair and crossed his arms. His biceps bulged impressively. The one on the right bore a tattoo of a naked woman with remarkable breasts. "These ladies in the auxiliary are on the wrong road," he said. "A *bad* road. I've been trying to tell them for a year now, they're on the wrong track. They should be making food, having parties for the kids, not out there trying to tell *us* what to do!"

John nodded. "That's right. They're supposed to be moral support for us, not the other way around."

Babe explained to no one in particular that the women just didn't know the ropes. "I've been doing this for sixteen years, and I still don't know everything about it. How can somebody just come up off the street and think they know what to do? There's *rules*, there's authority you have to be responsible to." He uncrossed his arms, and crossed them again, giving his tattoo lady a workout. "You have to listen to the higher-ups. You just have to."

The other men agreed. This was obviously an extremely serious matter. And understandably so—at a time when the world economic structure had stripped them of their paychecks, their jobs, and virtually all control over their lives, strike business was the one show they had always been able to run, without question. Now the rules were changing.

And much of the rancor just came down to gut response. In her book *Sisterhood and Solidarity: Feminism and Labor in Modern Times*, Diane Balser points out that if wage earning has traditionally been considered unfeminine, organizing and striking are thought to be even more so. In 1824, she writes, the *Boston Transcript* described the U.S.'s first woman-run strike as "an instance of woman's clamorous and unfeminine declaration of personal rights which it is obvious a wise providence never destined her to exercise." The march of women out of the Lowell mills was described as an "Amazonian display."

Clearly such displays can be unsettling to men even within the union ranks—especially if those men feel they ought to be providing for the erstwhile Amazons themselves. An alliance between unionism and feminism should never be assumed; these two have been uneasy fellow travelers for the entirety of their journey.

After an uncomfortable silence, Babe said, "I think they're getting on the right track now. I heard they were having a tortilla sale to raise money for the school kids."

"Make *tortillas?*" Berta asked incredulously. "Hey, I'm microwave material!"

She knew all about the idea that women ought to stay out of the business end of the strike, and she had no patience with it. "Right from the beginning the union guys didn't want us to get real involved. They said you can help, but we don't want to be *together,* really. They wanted us to make tortillas and bring food. . . . But really, where would we all be now? Women have been so involved in this, and more women are working in the mine too, so the whole idea's got to change. And it is. I think there's going to be a woman in the next union election. I hope so, anyway."

Fina Roman agreed that the role of the auxiliary had been bent into a new shape, and it was bent by historical necessity, she said, not merely by collective female whim. "In the past, women didn't participate in union meetings, didn't become involved in negotiating or fund-raising issues; their main purpose was morale boosting. But today we're facing a unique situation. Men have had to leave the area to find work elsewhere, due to the length of the strike, and that leaves the wives not only with the job of maintaining the household, but also of maintaining the strike. I don't think there's any question that that's what we've been doing. Look out on the picket line any day—it's women. We're forever in the news. Also, there are more women employees and union members than there were in the past. We are now a more vocal, active part of the union movement.

"We've experienced frustration because we had so many questions and had no answers from the men. Why isn't the union leadership here? Have you spoken to them? What do they say? What is in your contract that has been turned down? These are questions that women, in the past, had not asked. Now we're asking. We've received quite a bit of static from the men, because it's a new role for us, and one that they don't quite agree with.

"We try to work closely with the unions, to relate to each other the needs of the strikers. And we have tried to become very informed about issues that relate to the strike. Women now watch the stock market, they read newspapers, they address groups, they join organizations that are sympathetic to our cause. In the past this wasn't the case. I think this has been a learning experience that is going to be beneficial long after the strike is settled.

"I think the men respect us more than they would like to admit. And that's fine. We respect them too. We may fight with them, complain about them, but we're proud of them. Otherwise we wouldn't support them as avidly as we are."

Anna O'Leary said the women's changing role in the strike had begun to unravel some of the deepest threads in the fabric of Hispanic family life. "Many of us have started seeing a connection between the company abusing authority over strikers and men abusing authority over women," she said. "But it's not simple. You can't always just tell him to go jump in a lake. We've still got to conserve part of our tradition.

"Our culture has been in existence for a thousand years, whereas the authority we now live under has been in existence only two hundred years. When the Europeans came, they were able to pick out the best of different cultures and use it. Anglo-American culture is very mixed, when you think about it—they adopted the Christmas tree from the Germans, the stockings from the Dutch. They were able to use whatever symbols and beliefs that were convenient to them. Like the Protestant work ethic. They figured women could work too, I guess.

"For us it's not that easy to pick out what we want from Hispanic culture and say this serves us, this does not. Because we are the culture, there's no one else to adopt from. When you're a minority group living in the shadow of someone else, you have to be very careful about this. Hispanic culture is ours, and we are it; it gives us our identity. And in that culture it's traditional that the man has worn the pants.

"So I'm not going to say women unite and throw off the yoke of your husband's domination. I think a woman should respect her husband, and he should respect her, and if he wants to wear the pants and make the decisions, that's up to the two of them to work it out. Just because some men at the top are making laws that affect us badly, we can't all go blaming our own husband for that—he's probably just some little bastard there watching TV with a beer can. We have to work toward political empowerment for *all* of us, and we're not going to do that by kicking our husbands out."

Anna conceded with a smile that while men in Clifton were officially the bosses of their households, this was mostly an honorary title. "Oh, sure, my husband was one of those. He didn't want me going up to the picket lines. But I didn't wait for him to say, 'Today you are allowed to go to the picket line.' I just started going, and he didn't say anything, so that was it. One day he came home and said, 'I don't know what this world is coming to, this strike is really taking its toll. The bar is full of *women!*'

"I'm not saying it's good that women are at the bar. But if they're there, maybe overstepping the bounds a little bit, maybe it's in the logical course of things—the dynamics. Who's to say what's to come of it?"

Cinco de Mayo dawned hot and bright, a perfect day for a fiesta. The auxiliary set up booths for selling tamales and lemonade and beer and "Screw the Scabs" earrings. Chase Creek Plaza was decorated with blue and red ribbons, the mariachis tuned their guitars, and families began to arrive. The local union leaders had left town to demonstrate their nonparticipation in the rally, but thousands of people still showed up, and the town was in the mood for a good day. As they mingled with friends and ate and danced in the plaza, they noticed the mountaintop above them was dotted with Phelps Dodge "watchmen" looking down on them. The strikers consoled themselves by thinking about how hot it must be up there.

Supporters rolled into town from Phoenix, Tucson, and even California. The auxiliary women, Dr. O'Leary, and some of the out-of-town guests gave speeches of inspiration and solidarity. (When it came to a choice between the union boycott and the auxiliary's strategy, Jorge O'Leary had come in clearly on the side of the women.) At two in the afternoon, the auxiliary organized a contingent of exactly one hundred people (still the maximum number allowed at the mine gate) to march up the hill to picket the three o'clock shift change. The women had devised a simple way of making sure the number was correct—they cut one hundred ribbons for armbands and handed them out to the first takers as their "passports to the line." The remaining crowd marched up the hill behind them but went only as far as the People's Clinic, where they lined Highway 666 and waited to shout at the workers and DPS officers who would soon be coming down the road.

Berta Chavez was one of the "ribbon gang" up at the main gate. "We'd left all our kids down below," she said, "because we thought there might be trouble up at the gate. We've had guns pointed at us on the line before, and I'd always been scared that some scab might pass by and open fire, and if the kids were there . . . We thought it was better to leave them down at the fiesta.

"So there we were waiting for the shift change. But not too many scabs had gone through, just a few, and it was quiet—too quiet. Then, before I knew it, I saw four DPS officers take off like a bat out of hell and someone said, 'Look down the mountain!' They were sending all the scab cars back *up* the hill. My friends and I looked at each other and said, 'Oh, my God, the kids!' So I said let's go. We went down the road. When we got down to the bottom we met some other friends, and they said they wouldn't let them go through because a riot had broken out. That's how the DPS put it."

Berta's and Diane's kids and several others who were there described the scene this way: "It was mostly kids, it really was," said James, who was twelve. "Just kids against the cops. All the grown-ups thought that if there was going to be any violence it would be in Morenci, so they said all the kids stay down here, so we all went to the picket line in Clifton. So what happened was that _____ Epperson's dad, who's a scab, pulled out a gun on the line, and that's when everything happened. It was a pistol, and he pointed it at us, just like that." James demonstrated with his finger. "Like he was shooting at us, kids and everybody. There was about 150 kids."

"I got scared," said Elaine, who is several years older than James. "I was ready to run, but everybody just went toward him, not away from him. I didn't know what was going to happen. We told the DPS, 'Well, aren't you going to do anything? He has a gun!' And everybody got upset because they wouldn't do anything."

"That's when all the trouble started," James said.

A little girl, about eight, said, "We were going to walk to that gas station, but then everybody started throwing rocks at the cops."

"We all got in a line and were just waiting," Elaine said. "Everyone kept saying, 'Don't do nothing, don't do nothing.' The cops stopped and nobody said nothing, and then the cops got out their riot gear. And the kids got sort of mad, and somebody threw a rock and broke the cop's back windshield, and he got back in and left and everybody got excited. They said, 'Hey, man, this is pretty good.' But then no more scabs came down, and more DPS came and started blocking everybody off. They wouldn't let anybody leave; they wanted us there. We said, 'What do you want us here for? How come you're not letting us go home?' And they wouldn't say nothing, they were just staring up at Shannon Hill. So everybody started fighting back."

"All the scabs were going from Morenci down through Shannon Hill," James explained. "There's a road. So, since the DPS wouldn't let us go *up* the hill, we all went down toward the Shannon Hill road. There was a whole big group of us on the bridge, blocking off the road so no scabs could come through, and the DPS came and kept yelling at us that they were going to shoot kids off the bridge."

"But they wouldn't let us leave," Elaine said. "Where could we go? Up the cliff, like Spiderman? We couldn't go home, the cars were on the other side [of the police blockade]. They had us completely blocked off, but then they kept saying to leave."

Diane interjected, "The police say things like that so that later on they can say, 'We told the crowd to disperse before any arrests were made . . . ' "

"It turned into just a big war," Elaine said. "They started with the whistles, started arresting the grown-ups, people who were just standing there. They would arrest them and throw them into the bus. Everybody started fighting back because they were arresting people who weren't even doing anything. It was mostly the kids that were fighting. The grown-ups showed up afterward, when it was almost over. The kids stand behind their parents a lot. People are tired of DPS pushing them around."

Meanwhile, Berta and her friends were frantic. "My friend Roy was driving, and he said we should just run the roadblock through, he was so worried about his kids. But instead we went down through the cemetery, but that turned out to be where the cops were. They stopped us and said we couldn't go through.

"So then we tried to go through Shannon Hill, and got all the way down. As soon as we could see Clifton I saw all the people. The DPS were all over the place. There were people up at the clinic, and people on one side of the gas station, and the DPS had a blockade right down the middle. People were yelling; kids were throwing rocks. DPS had their riot gear on, and it was hotter than hell. By the time I got there they had already arrested eleven people, thrown them in that paddy wagon with no windows. We were all yelling, 'Give them air!' Finally, after about thirty minutes, they gave them air, and then they took off. People threw rocks, cursed at them.

"Then all hell broke loose. The DPS started throwing tear-gas bombs. The mayor tried to stop it, but it didn't help. Then the Catholic priest tried to stop them, but that didn't help either. And why? All because of a stupid scab that pulled a gun on a bunch of kids for nothing. If he hadn't done that, nothing would have happened. And the police didn't even go after him!"

By evening the crowd had dispersed and the fiesta had resumed in Chase Creek, but the mood had definitely soured. The police—some of them requiring a few stitches—had retreated to the fringes of town. Phelps Dodge, in consultation with the DPS, decided to cancel the 11:30 shift change and opted instead for the now-familiar plan B: flying cots and TV dinners into the plant.

Joe Epperson, the man with the gun, was eventually taken into custody—probably for his own protection—but was then released. Although hundreds of witnesses had seen him aim the pistol, county attorney Bill Coffeen said he would not press charges because Epperson had acted in self-defense.

The next day the National Guard returned to Clifton. Berta's journal entry for that day reads:

"Here they are, back again. When will it be over?

"Tonight we took off for the picket about 9:30, after the news, then went up to see Nancy Hicks. Came up to Morenci and, sure enough, there were DPS swarming all around up there, especially on Iris Street, where Nancy lives. I couldn't for the world remember where she lives, so I went down the street looking and the cops stopped me. Asked me for my license. The other cop was asking Petra questions on the other side. He was very rude, put the flashlight right on her face. He asked what we were doing, which to me didn't seem like any of his business.

"Found Nancy's and knocked on her door but she was gone. Just her boys were there. The little one told me he heard over the scanner that the ones in that beat-up old truck are going down Iris. I resent that remark. We have a nice, fixed-up '56 truck.

"Went down to Morales's, found everybody down there. Of course the DPS were there. Nancy was trying to collect money for her husband, because she had written out a check for his bail but the people at the Sheriff's office wanted cash, which to me is dumb. She got her money and went to go get him out.

"The DPS also arrested, without knowing it, one of our lawyers. He heard things he couldn't believe. After they found out he was a lawyer they released him.

"Later we also heard a warrant was out for Bev Cole. She got a ticket for littering on the picket line, and when the DPS went to write out her ticket he said, 'What is your name, Bev?' And she said _____ which is a scab's name, so now she has a felony charge too. We just wonder what's next. You can tell P.D. is up to no good.

"That's about all that happened that day."

# 10

# Up to No Good

On June 8, the unions made an offer they hoped would end the strike. They would accept paycheck deductions for their medical insurance, a freeze on the cost-of-living allowance, and a two-dollar-per-hour cut in pay for six months. The concessions were offered with the understanding that they met or exceeded all of the company's original demands.

Phelps Dodge turned down the offer, now adding one more demand to its list: strikers would have to return to work without seniority. Phelps Dodge had, after all, issued a guarantee to the replacement workers that had since been determined by the Supreme Court to be an enforceable contract; thus, the company had encumbered itself with a legal and financial obligation to the new hires. "One of the things the unions asked for time and again was that the replacements had to go," said P.D. Vice-President Pat Scanlon (who was called into negotiations early in the strike after labor relations director Jack Ladd fell from a windmill and broke his back). "And we said to them, as one of my friends used to say, N.F.W! No way. If we were to do that, we might be liable to each one of those replacement workers for something like a million dollars. I said, we're not gonna undertake a $300 million potential obligation; forget it. Even when they finally capitulated on the contract terms we wanted, they still wanted to put all the strikers back, but we had to keep the new hires in there." This would have meant that a miner who had twenty years with P.D., on returning after the strike, could be working under a miner who, eleven months earlier, had crossed the picket line for his very first look at the inside of a mine.

Not surprisingly, the strikers took the demand as an insult to their integrity and their craft; furthermore, the company claimed it now had all the workers it needed, so that even if the strikers agreed to give up their seniority, most of them would be placed on layoff status anyway. They were prepared to swallow just about any bitter pill to end the strike, but this was too much.

And so, it seemed, there was nothing left to be done. The women at the auxiliary meeting that night felt cheated and angry. They had been running full-speed-ahead and now, suddenly, the carpet had been yanked from under their heels. It was natural to look for someone to blame—even the union officials, who had tried but ultimately failed to negotiate a settlement. The women felt that it had become *their* strike in many ways, and yet the making of strategy and negotiations had been kept out of their hands. It was as though they were expected to fight a duel but weren't allowed to use firearms. They had their own ideas about strategy, and some even had a rising interest in providing a new generation of union leadership. They had acquired useful skills and strong opinions.

"Now, Cesar Chavez had a good idea," said Viola Davis, of Ajo. "When he came to town, he wanted to put a boycott on P.D. copper. We would join forces with the farmworkers, with their boycott. But our union guys told us, 'Oh, I couldn't get ahold of so-and-so on the phone, so we're not going to do it.' Now, that was wrong. Every striker was in favor of the boycott, and why not? It couldn't have hurt us, even if it failed.

"It's the same old garbage—these union guys come down here and promise us the moon, but where are they now? I don't think they're used to strikes like this one, that need so much support. In most places you can get a job somewhere else in town while you wait it out. But here, there's only P.D."

Truer words were never spoken. Family budgets had been cut to the bone in the towns where there was "only P.D.," and now the men scattered far and wide in search of a day's pay. Shirley Randall's husband found a job sixty miles away at the Fort Grant Prison, as a security guard—in a position vacated by a man who was now a scab in the Morenci mine. They had essentially swapped jobs.

Shirley, who had been a Steelworker, had some of the same complaints about the unions' conservative strategy for the strike. She was reluctant to criticize the unions publicly, saying that it was like criticism of family members—it ought to stay at home. But even so, she was annoyed by the absence of support from the international union organizations.

"I always look through my husband's Machinist newspapers, and there's never anything about us. There still isn't. I can't understand that, because I think it's been long enough; everybody in this country should have been aware by now—not from the TV stations, but from the union people. Now I read the little newspapers like the *Militant,* and I hate to say it but these Communist and Socialist newspapers, they are more honest than the big newspapers. They truly are.

"I think the unions have made mistakes in the strike; they should have publicized what's happened to us more. We can hold out for however long it takes—if I have to eat beans three times a day, I'll eat beans three times a day. But we need for things to happen in other places too. I am serious about this strike, because if we lose here, the whole country loses. We are being watched."

One of the most valuable union efforts made at the national level on behalf of the Phelps Dodge strike was a campaign that died on its feet. Ray Rogers of Corporate Campaign Inc.—a pro-labor consulting firm—contacted USWA officials in August 1983 with a plan he felt could win the strike. The national strategy centered on a boycott of banks whose credit and stock relationships were vital to Phelps Dodge. The principal targets, which were to be blacklisted by unions and their sympathizers until they in turn blacklisted P.D., were New York Life, whose board was graced by the presence of P.D. chairman George Munroe; Manufacturers Hanover, which had loaned the copper company more than $50 million; and Arizona's Valley National Bank, whose board included two P.D. officials and Governor Bruce Babbitt's brother.

The plan generated some early enthusiasm, but Rogers was not allowed to make it materialize. In a *Village Voice* article in March 1985, Joe Conason suggests that union officials were never completely at ease with the charismatic Rogers, in spite of his impressive record of organizing successful pro-labor campaigns. Also, he points out, USWA president Lloyd McBride died in November 1983, leaving the organization in disarray. Interim president Frank McKee immediately became engaged in a power struggle with Lynn Williams. The USWA never hired Rogers. Much later, the USWA announced that they would be mounting a corporate campaign using a different company— the Kamber group—but this was essentially a public relations effort without enough teeth to threaten an old corporate giant like P.D. In hindsight, the Rogers campaign appeared to be an extremely important opportunity whose knock at the door was ignored because of a domestic squabble going on inside.

Most of the strike supporters had specific complaints about the way union leaders had handled the business of the strike—at both the national and local levels. In defense of the local union officials, many had to be absentee leaders, since they were forced like everyone else to look for temporary work in other towns. Whatever the circumstances, the job wasn't getting done to everyone's satisfaction. There were matters of unpaid bills, and disputes over which union should accept certain responsibilities. Problems between the unions and the auxiliary frequently erupted over relatively minor but significant issues of territory and respect. At one point members of the Steelworkers— incorrectly assuming the Morenci Miners Women's Auxiliary was legally

"their" auxiliary—suggested that only Steelworkers' wives should be alle
the group. (This would have excluded many of its most outspoken members.)
Another time, shortly after the auxiliary had raised and donated $5,500 to
the Machinists, some of that union's leaders asked the women if they had
permission to use the Machinists' Hall for their meetings. There were hard
feelings all around.

"I feel that if we lose the strike," Trudy Morgan said, "the union leaders
are partly to blame. They're getting paid to see what could have been prevented. I'm not afraid to let the union leadership know what I think ought
to be done. The big guys, I mean. It makes it hard on the union guys here.
They're just little people; they don't know. These men have to say, 'We don't
have a check for you,' and then get their asses chewed. I think the international could do more. They've got money. They've got our union dues up
there! They've come into town to give us moral support, but not much more."

Hindsight is naturally blessed with perfect acuity, and it's easy to lay blame
on the union leadership. But some of the complaints were extremely serious;
eventually, seventy-five strikers filed suit against four unions, claiming they
broke promises and used favoritism in arbitrarily doling out strike funds. And
the rift between the unions and the women wasn't just a matter of ruffled
feathers—there were genuine divergences in strategy between the two groups.
Judy Aulette and Trudy Mills, in their *Feminist Studies* article, observed that
the conflicts were often politically motivated:

> The auxiliary was deeply embedded in a community; the local union officials were
> tied to the internationals. Therefore, the conflict being expressed was between
> local rank-and-file strikers, along with strike supporters in the community, and
> representatives of national unions based in faraway Washington and New York. . . .
> The internationals' approach to the strike was legalistic, in sharp contrast to the
> innovative and militant approach advocated by the MMWA [Morenci Miners
> Women's Auxiliary] and some rank-and-file strikers. The internationals' entire
> strategy was to win the strike in the NLRB hearings. Many rank-and-file strikers,
> the MMWA, and leaders like Jorge O'Leary instead attempted to call for more
> widespread national support. At one point, O'Leary went so far as to call for a
> general strike.

This strategic rift was characteristic of a wider problem in the U.S. labor
movement, which began reaching a crisis point in the early 1980s: the
underrepresentation and outright lack of interest in women and their needs.
As union membership was reaching a postwar low, women's participation in
unions had never been higher. Ruth Milkman, in her book *Women, Work,
and Protest*, points out that during the 1970s almost all the growth in U.S.

union membership was among women, not because of sensitive recruitment but because for the first time unions were organizing occupational groups, such as teachers and clerical and service workers, dominated by women. Yet this organizing effort and the rebirth of feminism in the 1960s and 1970s had surprisingly little impact on union priorities and leadership. In 1980, even that traditional bastion of female syndicalism, the International Ladies' Garment Workers' Union—whose membership is 80 percent women—had only two women officers or board members at the national level (7 percent of the total). The nearly half million women Teamsters had *no* women representatives at the national level. More recent figures from a pamphlet published by the Coalition of Labor Union Women (CLUW) Center for Education and Research indicate that gains in this area are slow or nonexistent.

Milkman suggests several reasons organized labor has been slow to become "feminized." It is typical, she says, for men to resist female encroachment on their leadership, and women often have difficulty with the idea of purposefully maneuvering for power within an organization. And in this case, the dominant cultural imagery of union power remains male and blue collar. Union leadership has a long history as a male prerogative, she points out, and the historical union view toward women is as a special group in need of protection—not as a force with an ideological momentum of its own.

Perhaps even more to the point in the case of the Phelps Dodge strike, labor unions in the 1980s are not especially open to radical and populist strategies like those championed by the Morenci Miners Women's Auxiliary. Milkman points out that while trade unionism was once the vanguard of social change in the United States, this ceased to be so after World War II, when McCarthyism and attacks on labor caused a retreat from the "social unionism" agenda of the 1930s and 1940s.

The economic prosperity of the postwar years led labor down the primrose path for a while; management could afford to cede monetary gains, and unions had the luxury of concentrating on economic issues rather than fighting for their lives. In the 1980s, when this changed rather suddenly, labor unions were so far from oppositional politics in the United States that they seemed to lack the flexibility to respond creatively to their own political crisis. It may be that organizations like local women's auxiliaries and CLUW will discover the way to weather that storm.

Berta Chavez, as usual, wanted to roll up her sleeves and fix things herself. "I think the unions could be doing so much more," she said, "and it really makes me want to jump in there. I'd like to get more involved in the union, to have a job with them. I'd like to go around organizing, making people aware of what's happening. This interesting man came to town in April to show us a film called *The Value of the Person*. He's a labor-organizing consultant. He said he grew up in a company town and organized a steel mill. It was a coal mining town. His dad got hurt, and got fired, and they had to live in a tent all summer. He could understand what we're going through.

"But a lot of people don't. These big guys from the top don't realize, when they come here to find a solution to our problem, that we are under a lot of pressure. It's hard to try to tell people on the outside what's happening."

Berta could identify with a labor organizer who had spent part of his childhood in a tent, and she was itching to put her own strike experience to use. Anna O'Leary was also enthusiastic about the women's leadership abilities, but she thought a lot about mistakes they had made along the way.

"Of course, our first and biggest mistake," she said, "was that once we shut the mine down, we let them open it back up again. When we let the scabs come in we lost our bargaining power. If you're a worker, all you've got to bargain with is your labor. If you lose that, you've got nothing.

"But also, we just weren't really prepared for this strike. When Cesar Chavez was organizing the farm workers in California he saw the need for having a strong organization first, before you strike. We did it exactly the opposite. We struck the company without having an organization, so everything practically fell flat. The international has backed us up to a certain extent, but I can just imagine what things would have been like if we'd had a strong union organization within the community *before* things got sour.

"This should be a lesson to all women. Now that my eyes have been opened, I see a lot of people walking around like somnambulists—women who don't work for a cause because it doesn't affect them directly. Not doing anything because they don't need anything right now. I want to say to these women, 'Good grief, wake up!' Sooner or later this lack of planning is going to come down and bear on them—just like it has with us. Three, four years ago we didn't need anything either, but now we do and we're caught with our pants down. Think what we could do if we had started right after the last strike and had time to build up our resources, instead of having to earn from scratch everything that we need."

Everyone had a different theory about why it hadn't been possible to negotiate, badger, or bully P.D. into a settlement. But the strikers agreed on one thing: this last round of negotiations, in which the company was offered everything it had originally asked for, seemed from their point of view to prove that economic concessions had never really been the issue. They had called the company's bluff, and now the cards were on the table. Alex Lopez, chief negotiator for the striking unions, put it this way: "There can be no doubt about it now; P.D. is just out to bust the unions."

When asked directly whether he felt that Phelps Dodge would be better off without the unions, Pat Scanlon replied, "Well, I'm not philosophically anti-union. Unions have their place, and some employers deserve to have unions. On the other hand, there's no question that as a general postulate an employer would prefer to work without a union because then they have a free hand."

This became the new point of reference for the strike. Maybe the strikers couldn't control what Phelps Dodge would give or take, but the union was another matter—its life was in their hands. And several local union officials now began to sense that the "ladies" had the right idea about strategy. They agreed to cooperate with the auxiliary in organizing another rally in Clifton, this time on June 30, to mark the first anniversary of the strike. The women were rightfully proud of having initiated this tactical turn. "We went ahead and had our May 5 rally without union sanction," Fina Roman said, "and I think the attention it got nationwide brought pressure on the union leadership. I can just hear them asking, 'If the women are doing this, what are we doing?' "

Once again the women organized. They slapped out tortillas and made plans, wrote speeches, and invited out-of-town guests. They had word that busloads of supporters were coming from as far away as San Jose, California. The anniversary celebration was going to draw even more support than Cinco de Mayo. The organizers were both excited and nervous—the last rally, which had begun so peacefully, had ended in near-disaster. The auxiliary repeatedly issued statements of their nonviolent intentions for the upcoming rally. They designated monitors to keep the peace and secured a permit to have the highway closed from 3:00 to 5:00 P.M. for their march up the hill to the People's Clinic. In spite of these assurances, a police presence was growing in Clifton, and it was unsettling. Something was up. On her way down Shannon Hill one day, Berta noticed two DPS cars ahead of her; when she looked in the rear-view mirror she saw five more. She remarked to her husband, "If that's keeping a low profile, forget it!"

Anna O'Leary heard that the FBI and CIA were investigating her. She laughed. "If they want my recipe for tortillas, I'll be glad to give it to them," she said, "but I'm afraid I have nothing else to offer. They must think I'm maybe some kind of mastermind. In fact, I *hope* that's what they think."

On June 25, five days before the event, Fina Roman wrote a letter to the

Tucson Union Support Committee. A portion of the letter read: "DPS has already set up a command post inside the Phelps Dodge plant. The governor refused to discuss this with strikers and supporters in his office June 20th. . . . We believe the DPS is planning and hoping for violence since their response to a peaceful rally is greater concentration of officers and riot-fighting/controlling gear. This alone incites strikers' anger, as you know. Only violence can justify their presence in such numbers, therefore, it seems they will insure it. The strikers will again be publicized as the inciters and Governor Babbitt will again be able to use the power of his office to assist Phelps Dodge in union-busting tactics."

On June 29, after an exhausting evening of final preparations, Fina drove home to Safford and went to bed hoping her prophesy would be wrong.

On the morning of June 30 there was tension in the air, but it looked as though the fears might be groundless. The rally looked for all the world like a huge family reunion in Copper Verde Park. Families laid out picnic lunches and talked and listened to music while the kids ran through the crowd screeching and playing tag. Lest anyone forget why they were there, signs and banners proclaimed the strength of the unions and the strike. There were also the usual creatively grotesque caricatures of their nemesis—"The Scab"—and one oversized cartoon of a man on a hospital cart with the caption "June 30, 'Nite 'Nite Scabs." It had been a long year. But the atmosphere was growing more relaxed as the sun climbed to the top of the sky and filled the canyon with hazy heat. Some two thousand strike supporters had turned out for the all-day celebration. If numbers counted for anything, the strike was as strong as it had ever been.

At 3:00 P.M., as planned, some of the participants moved up Highway 666 to the People's Clinic in a happy, boisterous march led by Dr. O'Leary. He stood on top of the clinic and for a few minutes addressed the crowd that had assembled in the parking lot alongside the highway. Then he left. By 5:00 P.M. the crowd had dwindled, most people having returned to Copper Verde Park or gone home.

Some forty people remained, listening to a Mexican band and waiting for what had become a daily ritual: waving picket signs and shouting insults at workers heading home after their shift in the mine. Approximately fifteen people were on the picket line. The others sat back from the road on the low wall and benches in front of the People's Clinic, the nursery next door to it, and the liquor store next to that. When the shift change passed through, traffic flowed smoothly and nothing seemed out of the ordinary (if the two

DPS helicopters circling overhead could be ignored). The picketers shouted
"Scab!" at passersby, who had lately heard this word more often than their
own names.

Two DPS officers pulled up to the picket line in an unmarked sedan and
attempted to speak to the picketers, who, with their usual measure of respect,
waved their signs and jeered. As the officers pulled away, a picketer slapped
the fender of the sedan with his open hand. The officer picked up the
microphone of his two-way radio and gave the order: "Okay, that's it, bring
'em down."

And down they came. If ever a sight on Highway 666 has lived up to that
number's diabolical suggestion, this was it: down the hill, around the bend in
the highway, marched a full formation of two hundred riot troops with
helmets, gas masks, and shields. The sun glinted off their polished black sticks
and boots and faceshields, rendering them inscrutable and frankly terrifying.
Boot heels in the gravel beat a loud, steady cadence, and advancing slowly
ahead of them came the DPS "hard cars" with dark plastic shields over the
windows. The crowd in front of the People's Clinic was struck dumb.

Slowly, people began to crowd out into the highway. The picketers and
bystanders were joined by other strikers who had come up from below, curious
and worried after they saw the highway being sealed off down in Clifton.
They were also joined by reporters and television camera crews; the events
described herein are recorded for posterity on videotape.

An officer warned the crowd through a public-address system that it now
constituted an unlawful assembly. He said it twice in English, then twice in
Spanish, and in the immediate vicinity of where he stood, the warning was
probably audible. The troopers then snapped their gas masks into place and
moved in, banging their batons against their shields in unison. SWAT teams
came forward through their ranks and fired wooden bullets and tear-gas
grenades. The retreating crowd returned fire with a shower of rocks and
bottles, many thrown by youngsters. Several people reported being hurt by
wooden bullets they believe were fired directly at them. A woman was knocked
down when she was hit in the back with a tear-gas canister.

Ricardo and Angelita Delgado, both in their seventies, fled with their
family into the liquor store near the clinic. Ricardo had a pacemaker, and he
and his wife both felt ill from the tear gas. They hid in the store along with
several others, including Alice Miller, the store's owner, who was eight and
a half months pregnant. They watched out the storefront, horrified, as several
of the troops turned sharply out of the column, advanced on the store, and
fired a tear-gas grenade through the window. The store had no back door.

Ricardo and Angelita had to be carried out. Their thirteen-year-old grand-daughter was knocked down as she stumbled out. Alice was grabbed, abruptly questioned, handcuffed, and pushed into the prisoner bus, where there was not very much for her to do but hope she wouldn't go into labor.

In defense of this action, DPS director Milstead said, "If you're going to advance past a point, you don't want to leave somebody behind you." In a July 8 article in the *Arizona Daily Star,* Milstead said he believed demonstrators had been throwing rocks and bottles at troopers and then retreating into the store. (Alice Miller and the others in the store deny that this was so.)

When questioned about his reasons for bringing in the riot troops in the first place, when no unlawful activity had taken place, Milstead said that decision had to be seen in the context of the year that preceded it. "The riot did not start at 5:45 P.M., June 30. It started July 1, 1983, when the strike began." He noted the " 'Nite 'Nite Scabs" sign, and said the DPS feared that the heckling on the picket line would degenerate into assaults later on. The potential for a serious incident after dark, he said, necessitated that the DPS act while it was still daylight. "If we would have gone down there in the dark, there would have been sniping at our officers. There would have been shots fired, and we would have returned fire, and somebody would have been killed."

By nightfall Highway 666 was blocked coming and going. The DPS had set up roadblocks at both ends of town; at three points in between, the enraged crowd had thrown together and ignited barricades of rocks, railroad ties, pieces of steel, and anything that would burn.

Twenty prisoners had been taken to an undisclosed place. Fortunately, Alice Miller wasn't among them. Halfway up the hill, the DPS apparently decided that her arrest might give the officers more trouble than they had bargained for; Alice was let off the bus and taken to a deputy's home, where she was held overnight. Less than forty-eight hours later she would be holding her baby son—named Jorge, after Dr. O'Leary, and widely known as the "tear-gas kid."

The others who were arrested simply vanished up the highway, and their families were wild with worry. "All of us got together and called our union officials," said Gloria Armijo, whose husband was among those arrested. "We were trying to find out where they were at, but nobody knew, nobody knew. We were scared. The people from Morenci were calling us and saying they were hosing down strikers and dragging them into the batting cages at that ball park up there. We were just scared out of our minds. After all, look how far the DPS had already gone. Who knew how much further they would take it?"

As it turned out, after being hosed down in Morenci, the arrested strikers were taken no farther than the Morenci Club, a facility owned by Phelps Dodge. Many spent the night in handcuffs and wet clothes. (Years later, Dr. O'Leary testified in court that some of them suffered nerve damage from being held in plastic handcuffs for fourteen hours.) Most were charged with felonies related to unlawful assembly and rioting.

Meanwhile, the troops had retreated for the night, but they left behind traces of their offensive. The canyon that holds Clifton is narrow and confined, and tear gas does not discriminate. The fumes seeped into the homes of people who had no idea what was going on.

"My house is way over there," said Pat Gomez, "way away from everything, and that tear-gas smoke came in through my kitchen window. My oldest son and his girlfriend were visiting me from Tucson, and they got terribly sick. He had to jump in the shower because it was burning him all over, especially his eyes. He's got contact lenses. There was a pregnant lady over at my house too, not Alice but another one, trying to get away from it all. She was pretty bad.

"I've never been so mad. I saw such things! There was a pretty little girl up near where I live who just passed out from the smoke and gas. We ran over to the Moraleses', and we were washing off the people that were burning and couldn't breathe. Little kids. It was a terrible thing. I got real sick and had to go see Dr. O'Leary. My blood pressure shot way up, and I had to stay in bed.

"Now I'm on the picket line every day. I've never done anything like this in my life, but I'm doing it now. I'm fifty-three years old, and I'm not scared now."

Anna and Jorge O'Leary had left the rally early, hours before the confrontation, because they were tired and wanted to rest. Resting up was a good idea, as it turned out, since they had a long night ahead of them. Their home quickly turned into a refugee camp. All evening, people trailed in seeking solace and treatment for tear-gas burns and other injuries. Later came the second wave: strike supporters from out of town who had come up for the rally and now found there was no way out of Clifton.

"At one time there must have been fifty people in this house," Anna said, waving a hand at her small kitchen. "But things have a way of working out—that's what I've learned. I never think we'll have enough food, but somehow we always seem to manage. I just put a pot of beans on that night, and had some fresh tortillas, and all those kids, the refugees, ate those beans and thought it was the best meal they ever had.

"What really got to me," she said after some consideration, "was the questions that the media people asked. When all these people were hurt and tear-gassed, they came here wanting to know, 'What were you doing with children there?' Like it was our fault that the kids got hurt. Well, it wasn't a planned riot, it was a planned picnic! It was a family thing. I told them, 'Look, these kids were invited. The DPS was not.' "

By this time the people of Clifton had long since given up any knee-jerk notions of their rights and freedoms as U.S. citizens. But people on the outside had not. The June 30 rally shocked reporters, and for the first time, statewide media coverage showed some concerted sympathy for the strikers.

An article entitled "The Anatomy of a Riot," which appeared the following Sunday in one of the state's major dailies, the *Arizona Daily Star*, carefully reviewed the events of the strike and concluded: "On seeing the DPS column advancing down the highway, the first overwhelming reaction among both strikers and their supporters, and among reporters, cameramen and photographers, was, 'What the hell are they doing up there?' The specific provocations cited by the DPS as its reasons for the show of force seem too minor to justify it."

Indeed, the specific provocations sounded rather farfetched. In addition to Milstead's "fears of a nighttime confrontation," he also said that the DPS was carrying out its duty of keeping the highway open. Videotapes of the scene show no obstruction to traffic until Highway 666 was filled from shoulder to shoulder with riot troops marching down the hill in formation—and later, of course, the barricades.

The large number of reporters assigned to Clifton that day were undoubtedly there, in part, because violence was anticipated—an indication of the media bloodthirstiness that irritated strikers—but in the end the reporters' presence did a great deal to vindicate the strikers and point out inconsistencies in the DPS's story. The police implied, for example, that the riot was at least partly instigated by the presence of the firebrand doctor, Jorge O'Leary. But a major newspaper ran a picture of Dr. O'Leary, snapped at the time of the riot—in his home, miles from the scene, treating a small girl whose eyes had been injured by tear gas.

In the following days, National Guard transport trucks were used to bring in even more DPS troops. The occupying force in Clifton—not the "special force" called in when the DPS expected trouble, but the base-line presence—

was now up to nearly three hundred. Governor Babbitt refused to commission an investigation of the weekend's events.

In spite of the June 30 riot, or because of it, the strike's momentum revived. Where hope wanes, anger carries on. The unions vowed to launch their own investigation of the DPS actions. There had been plenty of witnesses—in fact, most of the crucial events were on film. Finally, it seemed, the mainstream media were on the strikers' side. If only the truth could come out, the strikers said, surely every person alive would share their outrage.

# 11

# *If the Truth Would Come Out*

The Steelworkers' Hall on Chase Creek had seen better days, but not busier ones. In fourteen months it had become mission control for the Women's Auxiliary and home-away-from-home for a town full of strikers. The atmosphere was friendly but tired. The pink-painted walls were cracked and peeling. "NO CONTRACT NO WORK" was stenciled in red on the wall here and there under enormous old murals of the Clifton-Morenci area, any of which could be titled "Self-portrait with Smokestacks." The union hall art was contributed by Askie Yazzie, a Navajo man recruited to work in the mine during World War II; during the strike of 1959, he had come down to Chase Creek with his kids every day and painted murals in lieu of picketing.

Askie Yazzie's art was as enduring as Phelps Dodge's intransigence; a summary of the latest contract offer was now written on a chalkboard at the back of the hall, and the bulletin board was papered with handwritten letters from faraway places, all full of hope and solidarity and admiration for the strikers. A "Coal Not Dole" poster from England was tacked near the entrance. Another one next to it claimed optimistically "You can't be punished for insisting on job safety—that's the law," and bore a picture of Karen Silkwood.

It was Labor Day 1984, and the strike was still alive, a fact that had sparked yet another celebratory rally in Clifton. There had been speeches, music, and dancing in the hot street outside. Booths set up by the Women's Auxiliary sold hamburgers, beer, snow-cones, and "I survived" T-shirts memorializing the noteworthy ordeals of the strike. Everyone was eager that today not become another one.

Dr. O'Leary exhorted the crowd from the podium, in an oratory style that had developed noticeably over recent months: "We are going to march and stop the scabs from going in. And we are going to show the people that we are good. We will *not* throw rocks. . . . " He glanced pointedly at a group of teenagers at the edge of the plaza. "We are *not* going to be provoked by the DPS. But we *are* going to march, and nobody can stop us. We don't like the DPS. As a matter of fact, we *hate* the DPS. And we are going to show the people that we don't *need* the DPS."

Fina Roman also addressed the rally, after being introduced by a union official as the president of the "Ladies' Auxiliary." Subtly but unmistakably, she corrected him, and then gave a speech in which she declared that the strikers would not be beaten. "Governor Babbitt himself can put on riot gear," she said, "but even then we will not give up!"

Following the speeches, the noisy crowd marched up the hill and then back down again, waving the usual almost postmodern assortment of placards and banners: American flags (including two stuck behind a dog's ears), a huge placard declaring Clifton to be "Poland, USA," signs saying "Solidarity Forever" and "Labor on the March" and "Scabs Go Home," the Black Eagle flag, and an ornate cloth banner in the traditional Mexican style portraying the Blessed Virgin Mary.

Now several hundred people were crowding into the Steelworkers' Hall for the next event, a performance by Berta's Small Town Breakers. The kids' attire showed individual creativity but uniform toughness: black or olive drab trousers, military caps in mottled jungle camouflage, fake brass knuckles and dog collars, even fake black eyes, applied with greasepaint. Every boy in the group took a turn break-dancing alone or as part of a pair. Some had awkward physiques and self-conscious moves and had to be coaxed on by the crowd's sympathetic applause, but most were lithe and strong and needed no encouragement beyond their own bravado. Some were extremely skilled. One pas de deux began as a carefully choreographed boxing match and ended as something approaching ballet, as the older boy gracefully lifted and spun the smaller one.

The crowd formed a tight circle a dozen layers deep in the hot, unbreathable air of the union hall. At the end of each dance we applauded enthusiastically, even those of us who couldn't quite see. A tall, elderly man allowed me to step in front of him. He was watching with obvious interest, and during a lull he shouted for more. We chatted, and he introduced himself as Eugene Debs Birchfield.

During the next number I pondered the career of Eugene V. Debs, who led the American Railway Union in a successful strike before the turn of the century, was imprisoned repeatedly, and ran for president five times on the Socialist party ticket. (The last time, in 1920, he got nearly a million votes, although he was in prison.) I wondered which of these events might have inspired the christening of a namesake who now stood in the Steelworkers' Hall in Clifton.

After the next performance, by a skinny thirteen-year-old who was very good at spinning around on his upper spine, Mr. Birchfield said to me, "You know, when I was that age I never would have done such a thing. We were shy. Kids now aren't afraid to get up and do something." He considered this for a while longer. "That's good," he said.

His remarks caught me off guard. My mind had wandered from E. V. Debs to the well-worn track of how certain things never seem to change: how the tough, graceful sport of break-dancing was apparently off limits to girls. But then I recalled *High Stakes in Morenci*, the film made in Clifton during the 1950s—the camera-shy children in their slicked-down hair, party dresses, and patent-leather shoes. I suddenly understood that Mr. Birchfield had hit upon a fundamental truth about the difference between then and now. When kids are allowed courage, anything can change.

Later, when the boys and the crowds had returned to the bright outdoors to hear another round of speeches, a small congregation of girls stayed behind in the dimly lit hall. All were younger than twelve or so and dressed in jeans and T-shirts—an unthreatening, but functional, uniform. They made a tight, private circle, and one at a time on the dusty concrete floor, under Askie Yazzie's somber murals, they began to practice some breaking and popping of their own.

The day had been peaceful so far, but as the sunset's shadow moved with the velocity of cool honey down the canyon, nobody was breathing easily just yet. The rally organizers kept their fingers crossed, hoping the town would stay quiet through the night. They had made a deal with the DPS: if the riot troops would stay away from Clifton for twenty-four hours, there would be no riot. The strikers' integrity was on the line now, and it was extremely important that they keep their side of the bargain. Fina was hopeful. People seemed relaxed, she said. Not too angry.

"If we can get through today and tonight," she said, "we have proven that the DPS has been up here for a whole year for nothing, wasting the taxpayers' money."

Everyone's greatest worry was what the kids might do. It's not that they felt their children were out of control, or that they especially disapproved of the rock throwing or police baiting, but it was strategically important that these things not happen now. In wartime, morality gets complicated.

Juanita had two teenagers—a son and a daughter. Her son was a member of the PFC, Puros Firmes Chicanos, a gang of Clifton youths who supported the strike and sometimes roamed around after dark "expressing that support," as Juanita put it. They had been especially expressive on the night of June 30, after the DPS had marched on their rally and stirred up so much ire.

"Two years ago," she said, "if I heard that my son was throwing rocks or making barricades in the street, I would have thought it was terrible. Now I think, well, we're raising these kids to be fighters! Look around at this environment. What can you do about it? They see it, they hear it. They've been part of the picket line. My daughter says, 'This is *wrong*, Mom, we can't let them do this to us.' And so they're fighters.

"But today nobody's going to do it. Today's going to be nice. Everybody talked to their kids and said if anything happens, if they try to provoke, just walk away. There's no need for a confrontation. We have to prove that we can do it. This is another way of winning, I told them."

If this was true, then the people of Clifton won. They held their peace throughout the night, and Labor Day became a day of victory and vindication.

Outside of Clifton, however, the victory was unheralded. Strikers had long complained about a pattern of negative reinforcement by the media—that heads had to be cracked and blood had to flow before the news people would pay any attention to their struggle.

"The news is just a business, I think, like any other big business," Berta explained. "They have to show something, but it doesn't have to be the truth. They say they're objective, but no way. I don't really like the TV cameras to be here because they just pick out certain little incidents, something ugly; they won't show something good. Like the Breakers—I thought sure they would be on, but they weren't. Why does it always have to be ugly? The way they treat us is, if it's not violence, it's not important."

The two previous rallies, both of which had turned violent, had monopolized every major newspaper and newscast in the state for at least a day or two. But coverage of the Labor Day rally was limited. Reporters were assigned to Clifton overnight, presumably on the assumption that if all hell broke loose while the DPS stayed away, it would make good copy. When the peace was unbroken, the fact went practically unnoted. One major daily gave it a couple of column inches on an inside page, tucked between an obituary and a bald eagle census. The strikers' greatest act of maturity and restraint was damned by faint praise.

Since July 1, 1984, the strike had acquired a new sense of urgency. Under federal labor law, striking workers who have been permanently replaced cannot vote in a decertification election held more than one year after the beginning of a strike. Not surprisingly, a move to decertify the unions was now in the works. Phelps Dodge was sending the word to its workers that their interests could be better served by the company than by a union. If the decertification election succeeded, Phelps Dodge would no longer be under a legal obligation to bargain with the unions. The strike, technically, would be over. But like so many serious struggles between people and corporate power, this one was not likely to be decided in court. Fina Roman said, "As long as *one* of us is on that picket line, the union is here and the strike will go on.

"Decertification isn't an easy process," she explained. "You have to be a union member in order to decertify your union, and the majority of the scabs are nonunion, so they can't vote. Most of the union members are on strike, of course, and those who *are* in there are getting a taste of what Phelps Dodge will do without a union. If they can drop wages from ten to six dollars an hour by the stroke of a pen, who will the workers complain to? They might want to create some new union of their own in there, but I don't see them wanting to work without a union of any kind—especially our native scabs, who for so many years have reaped the benefits of a union and understand its value."

But animosities between striker and worker were obviously running high—high enough, most believed, that the outcome of the decertification election was a forgone conclusion. In case any doubts remained, the company sent its employees a letter stating: "You will decide whether you want to stay under control of the unions, or whether you will vote the unions out and give us a chance to work with you on a direct and personal basis without any third party interference." Furthermore, the company said, the vote cast in that election "could well be one of the most important and serious decisions you will ever make during your working life." These workers already knew what the company would do to anyone whose loyalties leaned too far in the union direction. The decision to toe the P.D. line and keep their jobs was one they had already made a long time ago.

The unions sought to delay the inevitable. First, they argued that the election should be postponed because Phelps Dodge had not yet engaged in good-faith bargaining. Second, they said that unless the company could prove that every striking worker had been permanently replaced, the strikers would also vote in the election. The case went before the National Labor Relations Board and was described by Ed Lopez in the *Arizona Daily Star* as being as legally complicated as a messy divorce. Certainly it was not going to be settled overnight.

Meanwhile, Phelps Dodge proceeded on the assumption that the strike was over. At 11:30 P.M. on June 30, the picket shack at the Columbine entrance to the Morenci mine was burned down. Half an hour later, the picket shack at the main gate was bulldozed into the ravine. On August 3, union attorney

Michael McCrory asked a Superior Court judge to allow the strikers to rebuild the shacks. He also cited violence against the strikers—including shots fired into the home of Angel Rodriguez, president of the Steelworkers, and the gun-pointing incident at the May 5 rally—and asked that the injunction forbidding strikers to carry firearms be extended to include company workers in the picket area. The requests were taken under advisement.

The unions also protested P.D.'s policy of paying legal fees for nonstrikers charged with crimes, saying that the practice encouraged violence against the strikers. Edward Comaduran, chief of security at the Morenci plant, said that the men who had shot into Rodriguez's house (one of whom still worked at P.D. by day and slept in prison at night) would be expected to pay the money back. Legal fees were advanced to nonstrikers, he said, on the condition that they not be found guilty.

In an unexpected move, Phelps Dodge announced that it had lost $20 million in the second quarter of 1984 and would have to shut down its Ajo mine. Without warning, five hundred workers in the mining and smelter operations there found themselves out of jobs. (The few employees who remained at the Ajo plant were management personnel, not directly involved with copper production.) A few weeks later Phelps Dodge announced that it would be dismissing one hundred employees at the smaller New Cornelia mine, also in Ajo, including many managers and supervisors. John Bolles, the mine's manager, said that the layoffs were an attempt to save money.

These announcements came as welcome news to the 243 striking families in Ajo, where morale had been flagging. Ajo, a dusty bend in a very long road across the desert, was probably more isolated than any of the other Phelps Dodge towns, and it was difficult for strikers there to feel anything but all alone. Fifteen of them had been arrested, sixty had been fired for strike activity, and many more were fighting eviction, although all but one—the Steelworkers' president—still remained in their homes. Phelps Dodge was no longer permitting strikers or their families (even women having babies) to use its hospital—the only one within 125 miles. If life had been rough for strikers in Clifton, it was running a close second to hell in Ajo.

So when the newly laid-off strikebreakers packed up their cars to leave town, the strikers were there to give them a merry sendoff. "I feel such relief," said Viola Davis at a celebration rally in Ajo. "It was terrible to watch them go across the picket line every day, and now we don't have to put up with that anymore."

The layoffs didn't come as a complete surprise to the strikers. Viola said they had been curious for a long time about Phelps Dodge's finances and didn't trust the company's public disclosures, so she and her friends had bought ten shares of Phelps Dodge stock in order to gain access to the company's financial reports. "But they've even lied to their stockholders," she claimed. "Productivity high, turnover low, is what they put in the stockholders' report, and we know that's not true. Turnover has been really high. They hire somebody, work him a few weeks, and then let him go.

"The main thing now, with the shutdowns, is that we're happy to know P.D. wasn't doing too great without the strikers. We'd been saying that all along, that they cannot function without quality people. It's the same in Morenci. That's a beautiful plant up there—it's huge—and it's a shame the way they've let it go. P.D. has used up a lot of money on these scabs, and they've used up their equipment too."

News of the layoffs was equally well received in Clifton. "Contrary to what people might think, we're not concerned about the loss of these jobs," Fina explained. "Nobody around here has had a wage for fifteen months, so if we continue to be without one, it's not such a big deal. The union is the important thing, and I see these layoffs as a detriment to decertification. The scabs have to be employed to vote.

"Every time there's a layoff, we're just one step closer to a contract, because we're pushing them into a corner. The company is lamenting their loss of profits, but all their skill is down at the union hall."

With the Ajo mines closed, the Phelps Dodge operations that remained in the Southwest were in Morenci, Bisbee, Douglas, and Tyrone, New Mexico. The old Bisbee mine had been closed long ago and the work there reduced to leaching remnant minerals from the mine tailings. The Douglas mine and smelter now had only 350 workers and was scheduled for shutdown in 1988. That left only Morenci, which employed 2,085 workers and was known to be the jewel in the crown—Phelps Dodge's richest and most cost-effective copper deposit. The consensus among strikers was that the company wouldn't shut down the Morenci mine unless the ship herself was sinking. Phelps Dodge said it was not considering any other shutdowns.

But the company was beleaguered, and made no secret of it. In late August, the Arizona Department of Health Services filed suit against Phelps Dodge for violating the Clean Water Act. Chase Creek and Clifton's beloved San Francisco River were rank with dissolved copper, zinc, manganese, and arsenic, and in some areas the acidity levels were equal to those of battery acid. The violations, occurring since 1982, had now earned P.D. a $400,000 fine. Furthermore, if the company didn't clean up its act by December 31, 1984, the state intended to seek a fine of $5,000 per day until the San Francisco ran pure again. Company spokespeople said they simply didn't have the money for the cleanup and, barring the miracle of a rise in copper prices, might have to shut down the Morenci operation.

In early fall, Pete Castañeda told me about a "troop movement" the strikers had witnessed in which the DPS began to amass on the hills around the mine. "We couldn't understand it," he said, "because we weren't planning anything. Later we found out from a friend of ours who's a Clifton policeman that the scabs had gotten wind of a big layoff coming down, and they were threatening to blow up the mine!"

Maggie and Pete knew some victims of the Morenci layoff and guessed that there had been approximately two hundred altogether. Conditions in the mine were generally thought to be poor. The Clifton *Copper Era* reported mine accidents with some regularity, including one in mid-September in which one worker suffered a serious hand injury and another lost a leg. Wages were six dollars an hour for incoming workers. Maggie asked, "Who would come here all the way from Montana or someplace to risk his life for six dollars an hour?"

Meanwhile, the strike was still gaining broad support among union rank-and-file across the country. Maggie's brother, who worked in a San Francisco Bay Area airport, was driving around the runways in a cart emblazoned with bright orange and blue "Support the Copper Strikers" bumper stickers. Relatives and friends had sighted similar stickers from southern California to Montana. The Women's Auxiliary speakers' board was getting ready for round two.

The decertification elections were held in October, but the ballots couldn't be counted as long as the striking unions had an appeal before the National Labor Relations Board. The Steelworkers were still hoping to launch their national corporate campaign to dissuade banks from lending money to Phelps Dodge. Phelps Dodge would then face the prospect of limited finances, just as the strikers had for a year and a half. And if it was going to be a war of attrition, the strikers had already demonstrated that they had staying power beyond belief.

On December 31, 1984, hundreds of strike supporters gathered in Clifton for yet another rally—this one in response to the announcement that Phelps Dodge was shutting down a significant part of its Morenci operation. They celebrated this announcement as a moral and political victory. "Last night was the last shift for all the scabs that are getting laid off," explained Mary Lou Gonzales. "Now they're leaving town. We're out here today to tell them, 'Look, guys, you're leaving and we're still here.' "

"We're all so happy," Berta Chavez said. "This is what we've been waiting for: to see P.D. shut down, to see the scabs get out. We've been saying all along they can't do it without union labor. Now they're closing the smelter, and that's just the beginning. I think they're going to shut down completely. And sometime in the future they'll need to call people back, and the union will still be alive."

The celebrators were undoubtedly overstating the case, but it was hard to argue with the belief that the strike had literally stood its ground and that that in itself was a victory.

"Even if they don't ever call us back," said Berta, "I'd rather not work for P.D. ever than to see them do what they've been doing. That's the way it is. We've beat those scabs at their game, and the company has suffered, and we'll go down in history. For this little town that's pretty good. I love it. I get up singing in the morning."

The DPS had sent 210 officers into Clifton to control the strikers at the "Goodbye, Scabs" rally, but the troops may as well have taken the day off. No provocation could have coaxed a rock or a jeer out of a striker; today all the frustration and anger were on the other side of the fence. There is nothing so sweet as the taste of "I told you so." The prevailing mood at the rally was jubilation.

Liz Hernandez-Wheeler, from Tucson, addressed the crowd. "I'm speaking not only on behalf of the Tucson Union Support Committee," she said, "but also for the many thousands of people everywhere who have heard about your courageous eighteen-month strike.

"This strike is a victory in many ways. It has shown us that unions bring us together. It's ironic and very significant to remember a letter that P.D. sent to the scabs just a few months ago, in which they said, 'We can represent your interests better than a union, and we can secure your jobs better than a union can.' We'd like to ask P.D., Whose interests are you protecting now?"

The lives of the thirteen unions on strike against Phelps Dodge were now in the hands of the National Labor Relations Board, which had not been doing any earth-shaking favors lately for the cause of unionism in the U.S.A. At that moment, nobody in Clifton cared. The crowd released the strings of 450 helium balloons, representing the 450 scabs who had been let go and wouldn't be back. As the red, white, and blue balloons trailed up over the canyon rim and out of sight in the clear winter sky, a mariachi band played taps.

"What we've predicted all along has finally happened," said Fina Roman.

"The scabs believed what P.D. said, but P.D. has a reputation for exploiting employees, and now it's been proven, you cannot believe Phelps Dodge. They used the scabs to get their decertification vote, and when they were through with them they let them go."

The decertification votes would be counted eventually, Fina conceded, and then Phelps Dodge would have ended union representation for its employees in the company for the time being. "But what employees? What company? They may own the wheels, but we make them turn, and if they ever want to open things up again in this state, they've got to know that. P.D. has not busted the union or destroyed the people. The only instrument they had for doing that was the scabs, and they're on their way out. We're celebrating that fact. In the end they didn't bust the unions, they busted themselves."

A truck-rental company that had helped move new hires into town when the strike began was now offering special discounts to help move them out. "Bye, bye!" the crowd screamed gaily each time one of the trucks rolled past. It was a strange victory rally. The outcome wasn't what the strikers had expected, or what they had hoped for, but here they still were in the home they loved, and maybe now they could look forward to enjoying what they needed more than anything else: a little peace.

Jessie Tellez was crying tears of joy. "People have got to realize now, when we hang together we're so great in numbers we can't help but win! Once we realize that, we can turn this world around. It's the workers that keep the mines going, the schools, everything. They've never given us our share of the pie."

Cecelia Morales, Jessie's sister, had come over from Los Angeles to be with her family. She and Jessie were both overcome with the emotions of the day, and the joy of seeing each other, and frequently their sentences broke in the middle while they hugged each other. Cecelia wanted to make it perfectly clear that the people of Los Angeles had heard about this strike. "Some people think it's a lost cause, but I tell them, look, those people are still standing there. You should look up to them!"

Cecelia had helped pull together a busload of union supporters back in the summer, for one of the earlier rallies. "Twelve hours on that bus from southern California, and when they got off up here in Clifton you wouldn't have believed their faces. A lot of them are native Californians; they've never seen a little town like this. They kept looking around for the rest of it.

"We kept going all day long: the rally, then the dance, then we got back on the bus to go home at 1:00 A.M." Cecelia mopped her eyes with the handkerchief Jessie gave her. "We have to hang together or else we're going to hang apart. People are beginning to understand this."

Cecelia said she had never been a joiner, before now. "I have a hot temper," she said. "During the sixties I wanted to join in, but I knew if I did I'd be one of those bombers!"

"But she's trying; we're trying," Jessie said.

"Right. I am trying. Now I'm three-fourths through my life and I know I have to act with a little dignity. One of these days I'll be able to say something without crying."

Jessie laughed, wiped her eyes, and put her arm around her sister. Cecelia went on. "We are *tired* of turning the other cheek. We are not our fathers and mothers, who were brought up humble. And we're not the young union people either, who may have come through the ranks without having fought these terrible battles. You have to hurt a little before you know how to come through tough times.

"The people may be small in power, but they're like a flea: it just keeps biting and biting. There are so many of us, not only union people, but other organizations, minorities, women, even Anglo people who face the same problems we do. We should be able to call them together in just a matter of hours, anytime, anywhere. We're going to have to make an impact with numbers. Just by standing, not even opening our mouths, but just by being there, we can let the corporations know they'd better come to terms with us or we're going to whip their tails!"

Cecelia's and Jessie's faces beamed with this new sense of strength. Other people looking casually into the cauldron of the Phelps Dodge strike might have seen a rather dismal story of a nasty defeat in nasty times. But Cecelia and Jessie were two of about a thousand women who saw something else altogether. They could reach into that mess and pull out the plum of a moral victory.

None of these women expected that the National Labor Relations Board would overturn the union decertification. They weren't naive, and basically they were of the opinion that the government and the product it called "justice" were not worth a tinker's damn, but that was no longer the issue. The issue was that they themselves, empty-handed, simply by virtue of what their hands had done and could do again, were worth something. The currency of female lives in the dusty little towns of Arizona had just gone up on the world market.

Anna O'Leary, who had been elected to give Fina Roman a much-deserved break from the role of Women's Auxiliary president, explained what this meant to her: "It's too easy just to look around you and say, 'Heck, I'm not going to change anything with what I'm doing today.' But it can change things just enough so that other people can come along and keep working at it. You shouldn't get discouraged just because you don't see big changes, because probably you're not going to.

"My mother-in-law always tells the story of the little old granny who's planting fruit trees. The grandkids say to her, 'Abuelita, why are you doing this? You're never going to live to eat the fruit of that tree.' And she says, 'No, but I've eaten the fruit off the trees that other grandmothers planted.'

"In the old days it used to be that the best thing you could do for your kids was to get them a job with the company. Big favor, right? We're not doing that anymore. We're telling them, 'Don't listen to everything the boss tells you. Big companies like Phelps Dodge, look what they did to your father.' It's a lesson that sticks.

"Maybe in the short run Phelps Dodge has shut us out. But every dog has its day, and I see a buildup of these forces. Companies like this are going to be on their way out. It might not be in my lifetime, but someday. And these formerly alienated groups of people—workers, minorities, women—will be on their way in."

Diane McCormick agreed completely. "So many women have been involved in this strike, you know that the next time around more women will be pro-union. Nothing can be the same as it was before." She smiled and put her hands in her pockets. "Just look at us. At the beginning of this strike, we were just a bunch of ladies."

# 12

# Just a Bunch of Ladies

In the summer of 1985 I met Anna O'Leary for lunch at an outdoor cafe in downtown Tucson. She wore a blue cotton dress and gold earrings, and her black hair was pulled back in a tortoise-shell barrette. She did not by any means stand out from the urban, power-lunch crowd as the one woman here whose family had been surviving for two years on tortillas and solidarity; who had grown up the daughter of a shoemaker who believed women didn't need an education; who came from a town so culturally isolated it might as well have been a foreign country. Anna had become a woman of the world.

She was in Tucson to speak to a women's studies seminar about her recent experiences in Nairobi. She had just returned from the conference there marking the end of the United Nations Decade for Women. Her trip was sponsored by the Ford Foundation scholarship program, which had sent thirty-five delegates to the nongovernmental conference.

"They received a total of about four hundred applications for this grant money," she told me, "and I don't know who made the decisions, but they obviously picked out the most radical, the most militant, the most disenfranchised women that you could ever imagine. Some worked with the Native American movement, some worked for clean air, for indigents' rights. There were women working in the South Bronx, women working with Portuguese immigrants—any social action you can think of, they were there. There were even a couple of women who had picketed the Ford Foundation two weeks ago!

"In Nairobi, we actually had a strike on the bus. Apparently there were higher and lower echelons of delegates, and it seems that we who were on grant money got put into a hotel in the red-light district. Not that we minded, but it caused some problems. The conference bus picked us up there, but at the end of the day they left us off at the big Ustani Hotel, where only the richer ladies were staying. Now, this was a place where equality was supposed to be the whole deal. So some of the women started saying, 'Hell, no, we're not taking a taxi back to our hotel; it's ten miles out of this district. We will not get off this bus until you afford us the same treatment that you're affording these ladies with money.'

"Me, I'm thinking, Oh boy, Anna, this is it! I'm in Nairobi, a million miles from home, with no idea what's going to happen to me. But, sure enough, they took us back to our hotel."

Talking about Nairobi brought a sparkle to Anna's black eyes. "This was a new world for me. I was able to pick up a lot of practical information that I had never had access to before. I realized we're just getting up to bat—we've been basically ignorant of sources of grant money, ignorant of how to get it, ignorant of how to use the media to our advantage. I was like a little fish suddenly thrown into another pond. I learned so much."

I would find out the full extent of what Anna had learned later in the day when she addressed the seminar. For now we talked about personal things— our families, our lives, her plans. She reflected on how the strike had changed her.

"Seems like I'm less timid," she said. "Before this strike, I didn't look for the opportunity to maybe draw other people into the boxing ring. Now I just expect them to be there. If people aren't clearly on my side, I wonder if they really care about the struggles of the underdog. Used to be, any confrontation and I'd want to cry because someone was mad at me, or didn't like me. Now I can fight back. I'm not going to make any excuses for who I am or what I think."

Anna is very clear these days on who she is and what she thinks. "You know," she said, "everybody's in tune with what the American woman should be. You pick up a magazine and all you see is Farrah Fawcett-Majors, Christie Brinkley, Cheryl Tiegs. And those of us who do not and never will fit that image? We suffer terribly, and our children do, because their hair isn't blond, because we're brown. So we name our kids Christie and Cheryl after these models, instead of giving them the beautiful names that our own culture has— Esperanza, Consuela, Maria de la Luz—names with very deep meaning. We trade them in for Kristal and Dodi and Gidget, and we think by doing this we're giving our kids something good. What a joke!

"Through the strike, I've learned to appreciate my culture and myself. We used to accept authority just because leaders were authoritarian people. Now we can never take their word at face value anymore; we'll only do what we feel is right. And a part of that is women saying, 'I've been a doormat too long already; I'm tired of your Farrahs and Christies, this is false! Let's see some other people on your magazines and your TV.' "

Anna believes that much good can come from disruptions of the status quo and breaches of traditional roles, like those that have happened in Clifton. "This is exactly what white women were doing with their feminist movement twenty or thirty years ago," she said. "Fighting to get voting rights and that type of thing. All these struggles come from the fact that women's value to society and our contributions to the national wealth are virtually unrecognized. I don't know exactly how to rectify that, through some kind of socialism, I suppose. How would a woman's place in society be different if these things we do actually had monetary value? If instead of sending us a card on Mother's Day, they paid us for being a mother for twenty years, 365 days of the year? I don't have any answers, but at least I do have the questions, and those are some questions, let me tell you.

"I can see that the struggle for women's rights is a long way from being over. White women have gone part of the way, and we have profited from their struggle. Maybe a few Hispanic women like ourselves can pave a bit more of the way. It's hard to tell what's going on with the Mexican male. Maybe they're perfectly content. But we have to think about the generations of women to come. Maybe I'm happy to have a dominant husband, but for God's sake, don't let him come down on the ones coming up—they didn't marry him!"

In the community in which she grew up, Anna said, a woman's closest relatives and friends formed the first line of battle. "First your mother says, 'If this lifestyle was good enough for me, it should be good enough for you. Look at this house, it's a mess.' Then the other members of your own community start to gossip: 'Oh yeah, she's out there preaching her gospel, laying herself wide open for some guy to ask her for a date behind her husband's back.' Or if she's single, it's 'No wonder she's single!' If she's divorced, 'No wonder she can't hold a husband.' Or if her husband starts playing around, making her life miserable at home, then her mother says, 'Why certainly, here you are, why did you have to drive him to that?' *Everything* is sexual, and no matter what, it's the woman's fault."

Anna doesn't really know how her husband feels about what she's doing. He has never told her he is proud of her, although he has said so to newspaper reporters. Anna said she just about fell over dead when he told her it would be all right if she went to Nairobi (though she noted with a laugh that a women's conference would be an unlikely place for her to go "looking for action"). She would very much like to hear him say that he believes in what she's doing, that she has worked hard and accomplished a lot, but she's not waiting around for his approval.

I thought immediately of Jessie Tellez saying, "I told my husband, why don't you wash the dishes?" and of Berta Chavez declaring, "I'm microwave material!" These women had better things to do. It was Anna who had first put forward to me the theory that women had come naturally to their work in the strike because of their experience with domestic organizing: that women were the "egg of the family that holds everything together." A famous man not known for his kindness said that you have to crack a few eggs to make an omelet, and certainly in the mining towns of southern Arizona, eggs had been cracked. I'd kept in touch, and the news from the domestic front was not entirely wonderful. A fair number of the married women I'd interviewed in the last two years were now separated or divorced. They said it was just too hard, after the strike, to stay together.

Some of the problems were economic and geographic—the inevitable drifting apart that happens when the man of the house gets a job in the next county, or another state. There is a saying in Spanish, *"Amor de lejos es amor de pendejos,"* which translates politely to "Long-distance love is very, very stupid."

The other part—and perhaps the greater part—of the problem was that these women had crossed the Rubicon. What began as an extension of domestic servility became a contradiction of it in the end, mainly because the women had altered their perception of what they felt was important, worthwhile, and within their power to do. After the strike, virtually everyone who had been active said that she would do *some* things differently from now on. Many listed jobs or schooling on their agenda, some spoke of new arrangements for household chores, and nearly all said their women friends would continue to be very important in their lives. Gone were the days of the all-male bar; a certain isolation, and the attitude that went with it, were permanently undone. The strike had lasted many months, and these women had had time to do more than simply try on their new role like a department store coat; they had bought it and taken it home. It was a shock. Always before when strikes ended, the status quo had returned.

Historically, the return to business-as-usual in women's lives has been a very typical footnote to strikes in which they temporarily became active. In such excellent books as *Women, Work, and Protest: A Century of U.S. Women's Labor History* (edited by Ruth Milkman), feminist historians have written extensively about moments in time when women held strikes together. But they were only moments in time. As *Salt of the Earth* strike activist Virginia Chacon said thirty years after the famous Empire Zinc strike in New Mexico, "You can't teach an old dog new tricks." In Arizona, in 1985, some dogs learned, and some didn't.

Anna and Jorge O'Leary, happily, were doing all right. "The main thing is,

I'm happy with what I'm doing," Anna said, and this fact is as obvious as anything could be. "I've grown as a person, just by uniting all these issues I was only vaguely aware of before. We never thought much about what the government did, if it was far away from our daily lives. But sooner or later things do affect you. Some people understood that about Vietnam, and the people stopped that war. Now we're seeing the same thing start over in Nicaragua. You think, 'It doesn't affect me, I'm comfortable here.' But all this money that your family is working so hard for, well, one way or another, something close to half of it is going to the government, who uses it to buy arms to fight these poor people over there who have done nothing to us. Instead of using it to help your own community. Instead of improving our health care, or using it for our kids, for libraries or schools or whatever. We mothers are having pathetic little bake sales to buy our kids books, while the government squanders billions and billions of *our* money over there.

"Like so many other things, it comes down to money. The government spent so much on the strike. Bringing in the National Guard. The DPS even bought a new airplane to combat us. Where do you think that money comes from? If people in this country think the war in Nicaragua or the war against the strikers is not hurting them, they're out of their minds. Every time they complain about the poor quality of their kids' education, they should think about that."

Anna's internationalist perspective was shared by her sister auxiliary members, who had on many occasions brought in guest speakers and films that tied their strike, metaphorically and specifically, to struggles in Latin America and elsewhere in the world. Their perspective—knowingly or not—was aligned with a growing rank-and-file rebellion against U.S. labor's mainstream position on international affairs. The AFL-CIO has for decades had a cold-war antagonism toward progressive union movements in Latin America. This approach originated as "bread-and-butter unionism" in the 1920s, which held that the expansion of U.S. influence abroad would be good for workers at home. It may have been true then, but it seems doubtful now, in an era when U.S. plants routinely shut their doors and hop over the border to take advantage of lower wages and economic "free zones." In an article entitled "Solidarity and Self-Interest," Dave Slaney writes that since 1987, the tide within the U.S. labor movement has begun to turn away from the union bureaucrats' steadfast support of U.S. interventionism. The National Labor Committee played a strong role in the 1987 Mobilization for Justice and Peace in Central America and Southern Africa, which attracted 100,000 marchers to Washington, D.C., in spite of opposition from the AFL-CIO hierarchy.

And Ed Asner, president emeritus of the Screen Actors Guild, infuriated the AFL-CIO's upper echelons when he told a convention, "It does not make me proud to see us bolstering the foreign policies of [an administration] whose stated goals include the destruction of our own labor movement." But Asner represented an increasingly assertive part of the labor movement. When AFL-CIO president Lane Kirkland issued a "shunning decree," ordering member unions not to meet with Central American unionists touring the United States, it was largely ignored. The Coalition of Labor Union Women has consistently been among the first to ignore the anti-internationalist policy.

Once during the strike, Ed Asner came to a rally of the Phelps Dodge strikers. In his speech he paid an eloquent, understated compliment to the women. "Security," he said, "is a precious gift we can sometimes give our families, but a much greater gift is showing them we can stand up for what we believe in. Franklin Delano Roosevelt said we have nothing to fear but fear itself—but maybe Eleanor knew more about it. She said that every time you stare fear in the face and live through it, you grow. You must do the thing you cannot do."

Anna and her *compañeras* had done the thing they could not do and had kept on doing it every day for two years. "It's astonishing even to me how we women have changed," she said. "I don't even remember what I did before the strike. What, stayed home? Cooked? A very mediocre type of existence. I never felt like I had anything to say worth listening to. Now it seems like I have so many friends. It's the politicization of the community that's made everything so worthwhile. Our minds are this big; they've been so opened. People might not have any more than a high school diploma, but their concepts of worker-management relationships, of the implications of having a company destroy the union like this, all of a sudden have come together. You can carry on an intelligent conversation with any one of them.

"Before, I don't know what we talked about. Who got married, did you go to the last wedding, who's messing around with who. Now we talk about Nicaragua, about apartheid. It's been in the news that people are rising up in the Philippines against the Marcos regime, so that becomes the topic of conversation. This is women! This is a change for everybody, but especially for us."

Their kids have changed too, Anna said. They recognize names like El Salvador, Guatemala, and South Africa. "For me, these were certainly not familiar terms when I was their age. Morenci was a familiar name," she said, laughing. "And Safford." Anna's youngest daughter, Mandy, had been toted along to the auxiliary meetings since she was ten. "She thinks we're a bunch of crazy women," Anna said. "But just by virtue of being there I know she's learning something. If nothing else, she's seeing women doing something besides cooking.

"I think we have always limited ourselves and our ambitions based on our mothers. My mom never went anywhere or did anything, and really I'm surprised that I've been able to assimilate into the so-called modern American community to the extent that I have. Certainly it hasn't been easy. But my kids will be totally different. They ask me, 'When are you going to California?' I say, 'Let me check my schedule.' Our kids are going to have different expectations. They won't think it's enough for a woman to be fat and married, with nothing else to life.

"This has been our drawback—Hispanics have the lowest numbers of college graduates of any ethnic group in this country, for example. Typically, kids who grow up in our homes aren't even used to seeing books. Years ago I tried putting my kids into school here in Tucson, but they didn't do very well. It was a cultural shock for them. The teacher would show a picture of a man with a briefcase and ask what the briefcase was for, and they would say, 'Well, maybe he could put his lunch in that.' "

Anna is determined that her children will grow up with more open minds than she had. "Already I know my kids will be more questioning of authority. Of course, it's kind of rough right now, because the authority is me. My concern is that they don't have the knowledge yet to discriminate between justified and unjustified authority." She laughed, and shook her head. "I wish they would hurry and grow up. Jorge tells me, 'Oh, you're going to hate having an empty nest.' I tell him I'm willing to try it!"

She said she wasn't ready to abandon Clifton just yet. She still saw it as a striking community, even though the unions had been decertified. Now that people were no longer getting union benefits, there was more need than ever for community services, organizing, and fund raising. "The striking community is my family's life blood," she said. "We support them as much as they support us."

But within the next year or so, the community would gradually change its identity. The strikers would find other jobs, move away, or settle in with a new attitude. People would begin speaking to their neighbors. The vivid orange and blue "Support the Copper Strike" bumper stickers, which once flagged every vehicle as friend or foe, would slowly fade out under the relentless Arizona sun. And then the strike would be over.

When that happens, Anna said, she'll just have to find another strike.

"Four or five years ago, if I had left, it would have been for different reasons. I would have been just a regular person without much to go on except a little personal ambition. If I had to leave, I would just kick the dirt from my heels and turn my back on that stinky little old company town."

Now when she goes, some of that dust will stay in her shoes. She sees a piece of Clifton everywhere she looks. Jorge has talked about going back to Mexico, and Anna says that's fine—it doesn't matter where they go, there will be plenty of work to do. "Just because you cross the border doesn't mean people or the issues are different. They're the same.

"The strike has completely remolded my mind. I was handed a golden opportunity, and I jumped at it. And, of course, I have to remember that I'm not the only one doing this thing. People have been working their butts off for ten, fifteen, twenty years trying to enlighten people's awareness and point out the wrongfulness of the government. This is a world movement, and it's hard work. But it's also good for us. We grow from it." She leaned forward over the table. "I'm not afraid of the future."

The women who came through the strike together shared this sense that they were the lucky ones. They had been given a gift. They had a great many different names for it.

Cleo Robledo put it this way: "Before the strike, I did nothing. That's honestly how I feel. I've learned a lot since then. I don't know exactly how to say it, but it's about people, and . . . " She looked around at the buildings of Chase Creek, then at her hands, then at me. "I just didn't know there could be anything like this. I feel stronger. Before I was just a housewife, now I'm a partner."

Berta Chavez had roughly the same thing in mind, I believe, when she said, "We've won this strike already." It wasn't the victory they'd expected, she admitted, but it felt better than anything they'd imagined; it felt like respect. "I get excited when people want to speak to *me*, ask me for my opinion. Nobody was ever interested *before*. But the thing is, I do have opinions now. I think of myself as a really strong woman; all of us do. We're more likely to speak our minds in any situation, strike-related or not.

"I've gotten letters from people in other states, even in other countries. I talked to a man from El Salvador, and it was unbelievable how much we have in common. He was union too. P.D. has a mine down there, you know. He was trying to organize his union, and he had to leave El Salvador because the government was trying to put all the union leaders in prison, or assassinate them. This strike has made us realize what other people are going through.

We're not alone. We start thinking how amazing it is that P.D. is way out there too."

Berta's sisters said the strike had broadened not only their minds but also their hearts. Diane said, "Before, when we would see on TV something awful happening in some other part of the world, we'd say, 'Oh, how awful, too bad,' and that would be it. Big deal. We're here in this country, where it's safe.

"Now when we hear of something like that, we understand. We know these things can happen anywhere—to them, to us, to any person in this country. We just happened to be the ones that got it—this time."

Berta said she was going to stay in Clifton. Her husband had found a job in Casa Grande—about four hours away—and wanted her to move there with the kids, but Berta had other ideas. "He can come home on weekends," she said. "I'm not going to sell the house; I have plans here. Before, I might have said, 'I can't do that, what would my husband think?' Now I don't worry about that; I just go for it."

Her plan was to become a union organizer. She'd already talked it over with Angel Rodriguez, the president of the Steelworkers. "Even if they close all the mines," she pointed out, "the union's still going to be here. I think they're going to rehire eventually, and you can't have a mine without a union. There will be people that need help. But we're going to make it stronger. There's a need for people to have a better understanding of the union—we lacked that before. I don't feel that this is the end, not at all. I think it's going to be better." If necessary, Berta said, she would start a business to bring in extra income, but her mind was made up about staying.

Berta's sister Diane was ready to try her hand at a new life somewhere else. She and her kids, along with her best friend, who'd just had a baby, would all look for a place together in Tucson.

Other women made plans to leave. Gloria Blase, in Ajo, discussed with her family the idea of moving to the Papago reservation, where her parents had gone after her father's retirement from the mine. Mary Lou Gonzales and Margaret Skidmore both said they would leave Clifton to look for new jobs, preferably union jobs. They felt positive about the future and weren't worried about being destitute. Obviously if anyone had learned anything from the strike, it was how to survive just a little bit longer without a paycheck.

Trudy Morgan's family was still holding on to their half-finished house. Trudy had long ago stopped noticing the sheetrock walls. "The strike has just educated me," she said. "Before, all I ever thought was important was to stay here, get married, have a family, and build a house. Those were my goals, and all I did was stay home. Now I'm ready to go out and get an education and work outside the home.

"It woke me up to a lot of facts. I'm a lot more interested in what goes on in the world. My mom and dad always said, 'Don't stick your neck out,' and I listened. Even after we got married and I was union, I never gave a darn about anybody else's strikes. Now I care, definitely. About the coal miners in England, for instance. It's funny but you always read the paper and think, well, gosh, those idiots, why do they want more money and la-dee-da. Well, I know what it's about now."

Shirley Randall admitted that even though she had been "raised union," she too had always had a tendency to accept antiworker sentiments expressed in the media. "A few years ago, when the news came out about the air controllers going on strike, I believed the TV. And when they had this Miracle Valley Church trouble around Sierra Vista awhile back, with the cops beating up and shooting those black kids down there, I believed the TV. I figured the people must have done something stupid to deserve the treatment they got.

"But when this strike started, and we heard the lies and we *knew* they were lies, I started questioning other things too. Now I wonder about Miracle Valley. And I *know* about PATCO."

Shirley expressed the women's general opinion of the mainstream media. But if they had lost faith in the objectivity of the press, they had lost even more faith in the fairness of law enforcement. Some people might call their outlook cynical; others might call it realistic. It depends on which side of the tear-gas canister you're on.

"We've had a crash course in the school of life" is the way Evelyn Caswell put it. "My view of the way the government is run has really changed. I always thought a person had to commit a crime to be treated like this, but they don't. All you have to do is have an unpopular point of view, and around here, the idea of fighting for a union is very unpopular with P.D. We've always known that P.D. runs Morenci, but we've learned now that P.D. is one of the biggest wheels in the state too—the state gets an awful lot of revenue from the mining industry. Why should we think it's any other way?"

Carmina Garcia, in particular, was sorely disillusioned with Governor Babbitt. "Babbitt is with P.D.," she said bluntly. "He owns property; he's in with the banks and the property owners. I was a big fan for Babbitt before, and all those other Democrats; there wasn't a thing I wouldn't do in the campaign for them here. After this happened I was very disgusted. From now on we're going to look very close at the politicians. You can't just ask, is he a Democrat? That doesn't tell you if he's going to be for the working people. You have to ask them straight, 'Are you with us or are you against us?' "

Some of the younger women, especially, said they didn't think either Republicans or Democrats offered much to working-class people. Some had begun to identify themselves as socialists. And some, like Janie Ramon in Ajo, said they thought a labor party would be a good idea. "It was the working class that voted Babbitt in," Janie pointed out, "but he has blown it now. He blew it by sending in the National Guard. I don't think people here will vote for a Democrat again. And we are definitely not Republicans. What we need is someone who understands labor issues, a working person. Someone who knows what we've gone through."

Certainly, these shifts of allegiance were motivated by anger. But it would be unfair to categorize them simply as blind reactions against the long arm of the law. Fina Roman felt that the political changes she saw in the women around her were thoughtful and deep-rooted. "These women have become involved," she said. "They've become informed. They've been exposed to the true meaning of a union, and the true meaning of civil rights. So they're more outspoken now, but they're also more ready to do research before they make a decision. When they stand up to defend, they're knowledgeable about the subject.

"We don't take anybody's word for *anything*. The National Labor Relations Board was giving us different answers about decertification, so I just instructed the secretary, 'Order a copy of the NLRB bylaws. We'll read it right out of the damn book.' We've grown accustomed to being watched and criticized. We know that once we make a statement, it's not easy to back off. So we just try to make sure we won't have to do that."

If you want to know a woman's world view, ask her what she wants for her children. The answers had changed in the last two years. "My main hope for my kids now," said Jean Lopez, "is that they grow up to be good adults. I don't have high expectations that they be doctors, lawyers, whatever. If that's what they want, fine. But now I just want them to be good, feeling people. I want them to understand causes. I want them to be able to recognize when there's an injustice being done. If they see someone being treated unfairly, to stand up and speak out, tell it like it is. That's what I want."

She's hopeful. She believes that Clifton's gangs of break-dancing, cop-taunting, and occasionally rock-throwing youths are going to make a fine crop of adults. Calloused, maybe, but good-hearted and not easily deceived. And not frivolous. In the year when practically every thirteen-year-old in the nation wanted to look like Simon LeBon of Duran Duran or Madonna the Material Girl, that's saying a lot.

"My son said recently that he wants to be one of those lawyers for people who don't have the money, who fight against discrimination and things like that. A couple of years ago he would have said, I don't know what, a ball player or something."

Another thing Jean had changed her mind about was the U.S. army. "I don't want my son to join the military, no way. I met a lot of Salvadorans when I was on the speaking tour in California, and they told us what the U.S. is doing there, how the government is killing people. I feel very differently about the way this country uses the military now. And, of course, the way they use the police."

Jessie Tellez appeared to be one of the happiest women in town. She was delighted to see the younger women making decisions, looking for jobs, and moving their lives forward, even if this meant some of them would be leaving town. Some day when these women looked back on their lives, she said, they wouldn't face so many regrets.

Jessie herself was married at nineteen, at a time when she was full of ambitions that would never materialize. To this day she mourns that loss, for herself and for every woman her age who grew up without choices. In her day, she said, families were preoccupied with matters mainly sexual—the fear that a daughter would become pregnant and disgrace the family name. Jessie is relieved to see people worrying about things she believes are more consequential. She is elated to hear women talking politics. She has become rather firmly convinced that marriage can limit women, and her advice to her own daughters has been to look for jobs.

"If a woman works," Jessie said, "it can make a big difference in her relationship. Because she can have some independence then, some money, the husband can't control her monetarily. This is just how the world is. You can find some nice guys, but even the nice guys try to control, because of the environment they've grown up in. This world is a man's world. Your leaders, your bosses, even your airplane pilots are male. When we got on the plane to go to California, I said, 'Here we go again—the man is driving, and the women are serving the food.' " Jessie sighed. "Sometimes I just wonder if I belong in the world, really."

She defines herself as a feminist. "I think there are a lot of feminists around here," she said, "especially now. There are some strong women here who won't ever go back to the way things were. Probably there will be some divorces, if the men go to work again and have to behave like the big boys just like before. No matter how you look at it, there's going to be some friction.

"The greatest discrimination here is against women. We are blocked; we have not been able to develop and grow. What I've seen during the strike is that the women have found freedom. They've changed so much. Just recently one of them, she's younger than I am, came up to me at Eastern Arizona College and hugged me. I was so happy. I've been wanting her to go to school for so many years. She said, 'Jessie, I got an A!' And I told her, 'I knew you would.' "

The extraordinary degree of self-assurance these women expressed extended universally to their future plans, most of which included entering, or remaining in, the work force. In a town with a century-old taboo on women's independence, economic or otherwise, this new, almost swaggering approach to the job market was probably the most surprising spinoff of the strike.

In her research on women's attitudes toward work, conducted in the late 1970s, Judith Buber Agassi found several factors that influenced a woman's self-image as a laborer. Some that might seem important—like a supportive mate who lightens the domestic work load or a challenging and satisfying job—tended to count for little. The single factor that most influenced a woman worker's confidence and commitment to her job was her acceptance or rejection of traditional norms concerning the roles of women and their de facto inferior position in the workplace. So perhaps it's not surprising at all that a new bunch of confident women came rolling hell-for-leather out of the strike, for the norms of Arizona's old, stagnant mining camps had been turned upside-down and dumped like a laundry basket.

In 1905, Lucy Parsons addressed the organizing convention of the Industrial Workers of the World with this complaint: "We, the women of this country, have no ballot . . . and have to take a man to represent us. You men have made such a mess of it in representing us that we have not much confidence in asking you."

The subsequent eight decades have apparently amounted to something. On the day I met Anna O'Leary for lunch in Tucson, she was in town to give a talk on the University of Arizona campus. That afternoon I joined about fifty other women in a lecture hall to hear her talk about the conference in Kenya. Anna spoke without notes and looked relaxed at the podium; in a room full of women she was in her element. The things she had to say were very much an elaboration on the eighty-year-old sentiments of Lucy Parsons, but she framed the complaint more assertively. What follows is the greater part of her speech.

"I was one of the lucky persons who attended Forum '85, the conference in Nairobi celebrating the Decade of the Woman. The conference makes a recommendation to each and every government as to the progress of women after the ten years that were designated the Decade of the Woman, ending this year.

"The official U.S. delegation was Maureen Reagan, the president's daughter; Ursula Meese, the wife of the attorney general; and Jean Kirkpatrick. They didn't really listen to us, but fortunately, these women and their views were outnumbered by the whole body of Third World nations, nonaligned nations, and women's movements from around the world. As I talked with all these women I began to see a very necessary link between the struggle of my Women's Auxiliary in Clifton, remote as it is, and all these other struggles. They're all moving toward a more humane and socialistic program and way of life.

"The Maureen Reagan types who were sent by the U.S. had very high concepts of equal pay for equal work, which is fine, but they were representing women who already have the advantage of a job. They weren't talking about women who are functionally illiterate, who are from working-class neighborhoods with no opportunities for education, for employment, nobody to watch their kids for them. As people move progressively forward, women are the ones being kept back from the turning of the world.

"The point of view of the United States' official delegation was very out of sync with the times. They voted very conservatively, against self-determination, against any movement that calls for redistribution of the land. People want clean air and clean water, they want just pay, they want recognition and a value put on the work of women. In the U.S., according to the official delegation, we don't experience these problems.

"We women in the United States shouldn't be led to believe that everything is peaches and cream here, like some people over there in Third World nations think. Many people asked me, 'What country are you from? Your hair is so dark!' One lady asked me if I was 'mixed,' half white, half something else. I told her, 'Well, my ancestors were Indians and Spaniards, so I guess I might be a mongrel of that type.' The U.S. is a nation of tribes, just like Africa. And if we're supposed to progress, in Africa or here, these tribes have to come together and decide for themselves what is the best thing to do. In my opinion, one of these things is to strengthen women's groups that are working for the betterment of our children and the community.

"The work we're doing now in the Morenci Miners Women's Auxiliary is basically support for the families on strike, at a time when the national sentiment is very anti-union, anti-progressive. All national liberation movements and all workers' movements have always been helped by a great majority of women who have not been accorded any responsibility after the struggle is over. When the people put down their arms and those men sit down to decide what is best for the workers and the nation, they tend to totally exclude women. Even now, when we go to the unions and ask for help, the men say, 'Oh, yeah, you girls are just great, just keep making those tortillas and we'll see that you are taken care of.' They're all for us in the abstract, but it's a different story when we want our own place for meetings, when we want to show movies on El Salvador and Guatemala, when we want a place where we can have a newsletter. They say, 'Well, I don't know, there's just not enough money.' They have enough money to send their own guys to Pittsburgh to shoot the breeze over there, but they can't afford five hundred dollars for a copy machine we need.

"So I listened to all these different issues in Nairobi, and I came back, and all of a sudden that light bulb came on in my head: so this is what we're about. Here we are, a group of women trying to raise money for a simple cause; it seems so very clear-cut, but it's really much more complicated. If there's anything Nairobi helped me to do it was to open my eyes and see how we are in the same boat with people in El Salvador, in Nicaragua, our brothers and sisters down there who have been fighting exploitation for centuries. And with the people in South Africa, who are also fighting corporate irresponsibility and segregation and apartheid. We're doing the same thing. In my own times, as recently as that, I've seen the company put us Chicanos on one side and the Indians on the other and the whites in the middle with the better housing. Our unions, which are fighting for their lives now, are the only thing that stands between us and apartheid.

"We are in the same movement with all other people fighting against racial discrimination, against exploitation, against irresponsible companies who pollute our water and air. We're part of a worldwide movement of Third World people—women, working-class and minority people.

"If we want to keep up with the times, I think we should take note of the practices of women. This is not to toot our own horn, but I would really listen to organizations such as ours. Even if it's just helping one kid with school books, or helping one family pay their light bill, we are making a political statement. You might not hear that statement very loudly tomorrow or the next day, but I guarantee you in ten, fifteen years something will come of it. I may not live to see it, but it will be something good.

"If the conference in Nairobi is any indication of what's going to happen in the women's movement, and in the world, it's moving toward more socialistic and humane practices, especially where women are concerned. Women are starting to say, 'Look, we helped you build this world, when are you going to let us help govern it?' It's our lives and our children's lives at stake, but the fact is, most of the time men don't consider the stakes when they're deciding what is best for the country. We see this over and over again. This country is curtailing right now every program that benefits women and children.

"We're not dumb; we can see what's happening. They tell us, 'Oh, we're thinking of your welfare—we're going to take care of you.' I think the time has come to tell them we don't want to be taken care of, because they haven't done a good job in the past. We're going to take care of ourselves now."

# Epilogue

It's impossible to point to a single day on the calendar and declare, "This is when the copper strike ended." By 1987, the National Labor Relations Board had ruled in favor of Phelps Dodge, to no one's great surprise, and the unions had been decertified. The strikers had no more ammunition with which to fight by then, but neither did Phelps Dodge have much reason to celebrate. The company's mining and smelting interest in Arizona—once the youthful, healthy giant among the state's industries—was an ailing skeleton. In order to concentrate its resources on new solvent extraction technology and the purchase of a large mine in western New Mexico, Phelps Dodge had sold a part interest of the Morenci operation to the Sumitomo Company of Japan and had more or less turned its back on the rest of its Arizona mines. The Ajo plant was closed, and the town of Ajo may as well have rolled up its sidewalks. The countdown had begun for closing down operations in Douglas within the year. Although there was plenty of other commerce in that small town, and life would go on, there was a pall over the downtown. The grand old Gadsden Hotel with its marble columns and tiffany glass— built in 1927, when the copper boom still promised the world to Arizona—had never felt emptier: a ghost of good fortune that time forgot. Dust accumulates quickly in the desert.

Morenci and Ajo also had the feel of ghost towns in the making. Chase Creek, once the heart and soul of Clifton, now had a catatonic, staring look from all the boarded-over windows and empty storefronts. The whole town looked weary. Most of the retirees had stayed on in Clifton, and some of the younger families kept up the difficult life of divided households, with one spouse driving to a job in some faraway city.

Terry Benavidez, the first woman mayor in Clifton's history, still foresaw bright prospects. There was talk of revitalizing the town and constructing a levee to prevent a repeat of the flood of 1983; possibly Clifton might even become a tourist attraction—a restored, historic mining town. After all, the town was now famous for what it had suffered and survived. But the population had declined substantially since 1983. Many families had packed up and gone in search of better times in Tucson or Phoenix, or maybe California. The union holdout had progressed like the most dreaded kind of disease: slow, painful, and terminal.

Even so, for some of the families in Ajo, Clifton, and Morenci, the strike had an odd sort of happy ending. In 1987 and 1988, the unions and their advocates won several important legal victories.

First of all, nobody went to prison. Of all the strikers and supporters who were arrested and charged with felonies, only one—Viviano Gonzalez—was ever convicted. He had been charged with resisting arrest when a police officer stopped him from taking cigarettes to his father, who was jailed in Ajo. (The officer, who outweighed Viviano by some hundred pounds, said the defendant was beating him up.) On appeal, Viviano was acquitted. Thus, in spite of all the allegations against the "lawless mob" in Ajo, Clifton, and Morenci, no striker or strike supporter was found to have broken any law. In fact, most were never even prosecuted.

Antonio Bustamante, a Tucson attorney who defended many of those arrested in Clifton at the first Women's Auxiliary rally, believes the state never intended to prosecute them. "This was just a classic case of the use of excessive force to break a strike," he said. "Phelps Dodge didn't even have to pay for it; the taxpayers of Arizona did. The county attorney in Clifton was perfectly willing to use the law in this underhanded way. In the end, the charges against the strikers amounted to nothing, and he knew it."

The U.S. Constitution guarantees a fair and speedy trial to those accused of a crime; one by one, time limits for processing the cases were simply allowed to lapse. For example, many of Bustamante's clients were arrested on May 5, 1984; in November 1985, a judge dismissed the charges because the state had taken no further action beyond the initial arrests. The case against Beverly Cole—who threw a paper cup on the ground at a picket line and ended up with charges of littering, felony fraud, and forgery—was technically still pending more than three years later, only because she had not yet gotten around to filing for a dismissal. No action was ever taken to bring her to trial.

In retrospect, Bustamante felt it was unfortunate that many people had accepted plea bargains. Dozens were arrested and charged with felonies at the June 30 rally, for example, but the state offered to reduce the charges against any who would plead guilty to misdemeanors instead. Because they were working with such limited finances by that time, the weary unions thought it wise to avoid going to court. But some of those who were arrested, like Berta Chavez, with her charge of "assault with deadly fingernails," refused the plea bargains and demanded their day in court. They never got it.

"When anybody persisted, the county attorney dropped them like flies,"

Bustamante said. "The state never took one case to trial. They didn't *dare* take those cases before a jury.

"Obviously, the state knew that these charges were ridiculous. The point is that they didn't care about prosecuting these people; they only wanted to intimidate them. This is a way of controlling a population—it's so easy, so convenient. Just slap them with some charge or other, set a huge bail, and make them sit in jail. Or harass them to the extent that with any move they make they'll accumulate more charges against themselves. Eventually they have to leave town in order to breathe. It's very effective. It doesn't even matter that later the charges will never hold up in court—the damage is already done."

The strategy had been fairly effective. The frequent arrests and excessive bonds drained union and personal resources down to the bitter copper of their last pennies. Some people who were perceived to be leaders of the strike were forced into silence, or forced out of town.

Perhaps the most important effect of all was that the legal offensive helped to turn away public sympathy. Newspapers were crowded for days at a time with accounts of arrests, police actions, and felony charges against the strikers. It is a cultural peculiarity of the United States that we believe our citizens don't run into trouble with the law unless they have done something wrong. Attorney General Edwin Meese said it himself, in 1987: innocent people don't get arrested. At a time when the strikers sorely depended on popular support, the public perception of the strike was skillfully manipulated in the direction of a guilty verdict.

"This was just a textbook example," Bustamante said, "of how the legal and law enforcement systems in this country can be used to break a strike."

Eventually the strikers struck back. Not only had they done nothing wrong, they said, but they themselves had been wronged, and they intended to prove it. The unions launched three separate civil rights suits, each on behalf of many plaintiffs, against the government and Phelps Dodge.

The first suit was filed against Phelps Dodge, Pima County, and Sheriff Clarence Dupnik, on behalf of six labor unions and eleven strikers arrested in Ajo on charges of rioting and other felonies and misdemeanors during August 1983. Among the plaintiffs was Soila Bom, the first person jailed during the strike, who had been arrested for calling someone "scab" over the telephone. Another was Natalie Muñoz, who was arrested in her home, in front of her daughter, and dragged away in her nightgown. (The charge was "rock throwing," and she was acquitted.) A third plaintiff was the striker who was arrested and jailed for not carrying his driver's license.

The suit claimed that Phelps Dodge and Pima County consciously and in concert set out to get the strikers off the streets by overcharging them and setting inordinately high bail bonds—fifteen thousand dollars per person, in most cases, for individuals who were well known by everyone in the community. (One, for example, was a member of the volunteer fire department.) The case also charged that Pima County selectively prosecuted strikers while allowing nonstrikers to commit such acts as cutting a striker's throat (he survived, with a nasty scar) and breaking another striker's jaw with the butt of a rifle. In the former case, there were no charges; in the latter, the attacker was released on his own recognizance and paid no damages to the striker.

"In all, thirty-four incidents were used at the trial showing this discriminatory pattern of law enforcement," said union attorney Michael McCrory. "What we wanted to show was that strikers were arrested no matter how slight the infraction, and scabs were not, no matter how great."

Another interesting piece of history emerged during the trial: the plaintiffs alleged, and documented from several sources, that Pima County had made a list of some thirty strike supporters they wished to charge—*two weeks before their alleged crimes were committed.* McCrory says the arrest warrants and amounts of the bail were prepared and signed by the justice of the peace of Ajo, Helen Gilmartin, and put into a vault. He is convinced this was done at the urging of Phelps Dodge, on the assumption that a good old-fashioned police roundup would do wonders to get things settled down in this little town. If the allegation was true, it wouldn't have been the first time; Phelps Dodge had used precisely the same tactic during the great Bisbee strike of 1917.

After a five-week trial, a jury announced on April 21, 1987, that it was ruling in favor of every one of the plaintiffs. They had been held on excessive bonds, arrested without cause, or discriminated against when authorities ignored similar offenses committed by workers who crossed the picket lines.

The charges against Phelps Dodge were dropped, because the jury felt the evidence of company conspiracy with law enforcement was insufficient (this decision was being appealed). But Pima County and Sheriff Clarence Dupnik were held responsible for the injuries to the strikers and their rights. Soila Bom had been arrested without probable cause, the jury said, and it awarded her $30,500 compensatory and punitive damages. In all, the jury awarded over $200,000 to the plaintiffs and striking unions whose constitutional rights had been violated.

The other two civil rights suits on behalf of the strikers were similarly resolved.

In the second, twenty plaintiffs from Clifton and Morenci charged the Clifton police force, Greenlee County Sheriff Bob Gomez, and the Department of Public Safety with discriminatory law enforcement. The case was settled out of court in 1988, with the DPS agreeing to pay approximately $70,000 damages. The plaintiffs also charged that Phelps Dodge had conspired with law enforcement, but once again it was decided, this time by a judge, that there was insufficient evidence.

The third civil rights case resulted from the rally of June 30, 1984, and was filed specifically against the DPS for its actions on that day. Fourteen of the twenty plaintiffs settled out of court, literally on the eve of the trial, for a total of $180,000. Among these plaintiffs were Ricardo and Angelita Delgado, the elderly couple who had fled into Alice Miller's liquor store and been tear-gassed.

Six plaintiffs did not settle and went to trial before U.S. district judge Charles Hardy. Four of these plaintiffs received judgments that the DPS had falsely arrested them, and each was awarded damages ranging from ten to seventeen thousand dollars. The plaintiffs' attorneys also showed during this trial that police reports had been falsified throughout the strike.

None of the strikers received damages for being wrongfully tear-gassed. The judge said the tear-gassing was an affront to human dignity but that the police were justified in doing it, nevertheless. Thus, Ray Aguilar, whose only charge was that he had been wrongfully tear-gassed, and Alice Miller, the liquor store owner who was gassed and arrested two days before her son's birth, received nothing. A DPS officer testified that he spoke to Alice after she ran out of her gas-filled store (albeit in a confused state) and that he arrested her for refusing to leave the scene of a riot. The judge ruled she had not been falsely arrested but later said he wished to reconsider. Six months later he reversed his position on the "justifiable gassing," saying that DPS Lieutenant Terrence DeBoer should have given those in the liquor store a chance to leave before ordering the use of tear gas. He awarded fifteen thousand dollars damages to Miller and a thousand dollars to Ray Aguilar and two others.

McCrory said he believed that all his Clifton clients might have been awarded much more—possibly an amount in the millions—if they had gone before juries, as the Ajo plaintiffs did. But they were not disappointed by the monetary awards, he said, because their motivations for pursuing the civil rights suits were less financial than ethical. Soila Bom confirmed this sentiment, saying that her main concern was proving to others what the strikers had known all along—that they did nothing wrong and were treated unfairly. The money was just icing on the cake.

"They wanted the police, the DPS, and Phelps Dodge all held accountable for what they had done," McCrory said. "And they wanted to make sure this kind of thing never happened again." The strike supporters definitely accomplished some of their goals, but probably not the one they wanted most—holding P.D. accountable. "I think there was ample proof that P.D. did conspire with law enforcement," McCrory said. "If we had presented the same facts concerning a drug conspiracy, the court would have agreed in an instant. But we have conservative judges here. There is a general hostility in the courts to civil rights cases now—the climate has been moving in that direction for a long time."

In January 1989, the Ninth U.S. Circuit Court of Appeals reinstated the union's suit claiming conspiracy between Phelps Dodge and local law enforcement, citing a meeting at which a P.D. representative allegedly told the Pima County sheriff that he hoped bail would be set high and declared that he "wanted those people off the streets." As of this writing, the suit still awaits trial.

McCrory said his clients felt relieved and vindicated by their victories in court but that the long legal battle had done little to revive their beleaguered faith in "the system," especially because most were never allowed a hearing before a jury. He feels the legal system abandoned the strikers from the beginning—from the moment they were first deemed "undesirables"— and that it's not surprising that they've been left feeling bitter.

"They wanted a chance to go before a jury, and let that jury fairly decide. They would have been better off if they could have abandoned all the legal processes and lawyers' games and been allowed just to stand up and tell their story."

# Bibliography

BOOKS

Agassi, Judith Buber. *Women on the Job: The Attitudes of Women to Their Work.* Lexington, Mass.: Lexington Books, 1979.

*Arizona Statistical Review*, 40th ed. Phoenix: Valley National Bank of Arizona, Economic Planning Division, 1984.

Balser, Diane. *Sisterhood and Solidarity: Feminism and Labor in Modern Times.* Boston: South End Press, 1987.

Brophy, A. Blake. *Foundlings on the Frontier: Racial and Religious Conflicts in Arizona Territory, 1904–1905.* Tucson: University of Arizona Press, 1972.

Byrkit, James W. *Forging the Copper Collar.* Tucson: University of Arizona Press, 1982.

———. *Life and Labor in Arizona, 1901–1921.* Ann Arbor, Mich.: University Microfilms, 1972.

Ewen, Lynda Ann. *Which Side Are You On?* Chicago: Vanguard Books, 1979.

*Financial Times Mining International Year Book 1984.* London: Longman, William Clowes Ltd., 1984.

Granger, Byrd H. *Arizona Place Names.* Tucson: University of Arizona Press, 1982.

John, Angela V. *By the Sweat of Their Brow: Women Workers at Victorian Coal Mines.* London: Croom Helm, 1980.

Jones, Mary Harris. *Autobiography of Mother Jones.* Edited by Mary Field Parton. Chicago: Charles Kerr, 1925. Reprint. Chicago: Illinois Labor Historical Society, 1972.

Kluger, James R. *The Clifton-Morenci Strike: Labor Difficulty in Arizona, 1915–1916.* Tucson: University of Arizona Press, 1970.

Leaming, George. *Labor and Copper in Arizona.* Tucson: University of Arizona Press, 1973.

Milkman, Ruth. *Women, Work, and Protest: A Century of U.S. Women's Labor History.* Boston: Routledge & Kegan Paul, 1985.

Miller, Tom. *Arizona: The Land and the People.* Tucson: University of Arizona Press, 1986.

Nash, June. *We Eat the Mines, the Mines Eat Us.* New York: Columbia University Press, 1979.

Nash, June, and Manuel Maria Rocca. *Dos mujeres indigenas: Basilia; Facundina.* Mexico City: Instituto Indigenista Interamericano, 1976.

Rosenfelt, Deborah Silverton (commentary) and Michael Wilson (screenplay). *Salt of the Earth.* New York: Feminist Press, 1978.

Vallens, Vivian M. *Working Women in Mexico during the Porfiriato, 1880–1910.* San Francisco: R & E Research Associates, 1978.

Zola, Emile. *Germinal.* Translated by Stanley and Eleanor Hochman. New York: New American Library, 1970.

JOURNALS AND NEWSPAPERS

Aulette, Judy, and Trudy Mills. "Something Old, Something New: Auxiliary Work in the 1983–1986 Copper Strike." *Feminist Studies* 14 (Summer 1988): 251–68.

Conason, Joe. "Copper War; A Company and a Union Fight to the Death." *Village Voice,* 19 March 1985,1.

Kingsolver, Barbara, and Jill Barrett Fein. "Women on the Line." *Progressive,* March 1984, 15.

Magnet, Myron. "Phelps Dodge's Lonely Stand." *Fortune,* 22 August 1983, 106–10.

Miller, Tom. "Salt of the Earth Revisited." *Cinéaste* 13 (1984): 30–36.

"The Mining News." *Engineering and Mining Journal,* 27 June 1903, 980.

Slaney, Dave. "Solidarity and Self-Interest." *NACLA Report on the Americas* 22 (May/June 1988): 28–36.

Spalding, Hobart. "Unions Look South." *NACLA Report on the Americas* 22 (May/June 1988): 14–19.

*The Arizona Daily Star* (Tucson), the *Arizona Republic* (Phoenix), the *Copper Era* (Greenlee County, Arizona), and the *Militant* (New York) were among the newspapers that covered the strike continuously. The following articles were particularly helpful:

*Arizona Daily Star*

Brinkley-Rogers, Paul. "Curfew Clamped on Clifton." 5 October 1983.

———— "P-D Fires Doctor Strikers Call 'Saint.' " 8 October 1983.

Mills, Sara. "Ajo Showdown Brings Two-Day Truce." 11 August 1983.

"The Anatomy of a Riot" and "Milstead Says DPS Has Worked Hard to Limit Violence." 8 July 1984.

Volante, Ric. "Strikers Seek to Rebuild Picket Shacks on P.D. Property." 4 August 1984.

*Arizona Republic*

Harris, Don, and Sam Stanton. "Phelps Dodge Struck at 2 Sites." 1 July 1983.

Harris, Don. "Phelps Dodge Expected Strike, Plans to Stick to Guns." 2 July 1983.

Savage, Neal. "Pickets Limited to 5 at Morenci as Company Complains of 'Unruly Mob.' " 4 July 1983.

Stanton, Kathleen. "Phelps Dodge Is Allowed to Reopen Smelter." 19 July 1985.

*Militant*

Miah, Malik. "Solidarity Needed for Copper Strikers." 30 September 1983.

Kopperud, Karen. "Antiracist Fight by Chicanos, Indians Gains through Unions in Arizona." 14 October 1983.

Otero, Josefina. "Steel Union Presidential Candidate Visits Copper Strikers." 3 February 1984.

FILMS

Asseyev, Tamara, and Alex Rose (producers). *Norma Rae.* 16mm, color, 120 min. 1979. Distributed by Films, Inc., Chicago.

Goldfarb, Lynn (producer). *With Babies and Banners*. 16mm, color, 45 min. 1978. Distributed by Cinema Guild, New York.

Kopple, Barbara (producer). *Harlan County USA*. 16mm, color, 103 min. 1976. Distributed by Cinema Five, New York.

Jarrico, Paul, Michael Wilson, and Herbert Biberman (producers). *Salt of the Earth*. 16 mm, black and white, 94 min. 1954. Distributed by Films, Inc., Chicago.

# Index

Accidents in mines, nonunion labor and, 85, 124, 170
AFL-CIO, 180
Agassi, Judith Buber, 187
Aguilar, Ray, 195
Aguilar, Tom, 30
Air traffic controllers strike (PATCO), 123, 184
Ajo, Arizona, 19, 31–33, 35, 48, 100, 168, 191
Ajo mine, x, 13–14, 26, 168, 191
*Altiplano*, Bolivian, 3
Alvin, Cass, 26–27, 46
Amalgamated Clothing Workers of America, 11
American Federation of Labor (AFL), 9, 180
American Railway Union, 164
American woman, media image of, 176
Anniversary celebration rally, 156–62
Anti-apartheid activists, strikers and, 134
Apartheid, Phelps Dodge ties with, 134
*Arizona: The Land and the People*, (Miller), 22
Arizona Copper, 9
Arizona copper strike of 1983
  beginning of, 15–16
  changes in children caused by, 180-81
  changes in women caused by. *See* Women
  contract dispute issues, 44–45
  efforts to close mine, 28–29
  end of, 191–96
  legal victories for unions after, 192–96
  length of, 64, 65, 70

  nonsupporters of, 44
  reasons for, 16, 17
Arizona Criminal Intelligence Systems Agency, 42
*Arizona Daily Star* (newspaper), 127, 159, 161, 167
Arizona Department of Health Services, 169
*Arizona Republic* (newspaper), 16, 26, 43
Armijo, Gloria, 49, 52–57, 62–63, 120, 125, 159
Armijo, Macy, 53, 55, 62
Arrests, 33, 35, 48, 59–61, 130–33, 148–49
  activism of women due to, 102
  during anniversary rally, 159–60
  Cinco de Mayo rally and, 147, 148–49
  as intimidation strategy, 192–93
  at Morenci mine, 42
Arrest warrants, 60, 194
Arsenic fumes, lung damage from, 81
Arvant, Deni, 121
Asarco, 15
Asner, Ed, 180
Assets, Phelps Dodge, 45, 46
Aulette, Judy, 113, 153
Auxiliary work. *See* Women's Auxiliary

Babbitt, Bruce, 30, 31, 35–36, 38, 39, 56, 136, 152, 157, 162, 164, 184
Balser, Diane, 143
Banks
  national corporate campaign against, 170
  Ray Rogers's plan for boycott of, 152

Baray, Mike, 7, 10, 11, 13, 113
Baray, Stella, 20, 113
Barter, use of, 104
Bathroom facilities for women miners,
75
Benavidez, Terry, 191
*Beneficio propio*, 68
Biases of author, x–xi
Birchfield, Eugene Debs, 164–65
Bisbee, Arizona, 19
Bisbee deportations, 9
Bisbee mine, 6, 169
Blase, Gloria, 19, 31–33, 89–91, 100,
112, 183
Boland, Dick, 26
Bolivian mining region, 2–3, 5
Bolles, John, 31, 56, 168
Bom, Soila, 33, 193–95
Bonds, excessive, 33, 61, 193
Boston, rally in, 134
*Boston Transcript* (newspaper), 143
Boycott of banks, Ray Rogers's plan for,
152
Boycott of Phelps Dodge copper,
Chavez's suggestion of, 151
"Bread-and-butter unionism," 179
Bromley, Wesley, 124
Brookside mine in Kentucky, 1973 coal
strike at, 4
Bustamante, Antonio, 192–93
Byrkit, James, 6, 9, 65
*By the Sweat of Their Brow* (John), 5–6

Calcine, dangers of, 82
Casey, Cindy, 58–60
Castañeda, Maggie, 61–62, 69–70,
113, 170
Castañeda, Pete, 69, 70, 170
Caswell, Evelyn, 103, 111–12, 184
Celebration rally in Ajo after
shutdown, 168
Chacon, Virginia, 20, 178
Chaco War, 5
Chavez, Berta, 27–29, 34, 40, 42, 43,
51–52, 57–61, 104, 107, 108,
112–13, 118, 120, 127, 128,

129–32, 143, 146, 147, 154–55,
164, 166, 171, 177, 182–83, 192
Chavez, Candy, 51–52, 58, 60–61
Chavez, Cesar, 151, 155
Chavez, Placido, 121
"Childhood Friend" (Tellez), 122
Children
arrests of parents, effect on, 58, 59–
62
attempted arrests of, 132–33
Christmas celebration and, 119–20
Cinco de Mayo rally and, 146–48
courage of, 165
hopes for, 71, 117, 181, 185–86
Labor Day 1984 rally and, 163, 164–
66
lessons for, 174
mistreatment by nonunion labor and
officers of, 57
National Guard occupation, effect
on, 35, 39
Small Town Breakers, 106, 164
strike, effect on, 106, 112, 115–18
tear gas use and, 160
"Chilean wheel," 7
Christmas celebration during strike,
118–20
CIA, 156
Cinco de Mayo rally, 140–41, 145–48
CIO, 10, 12, 78
"Citizens for Justice," 40–41
Civil rights, defense of, 47–48, 71–72
Civil rights suits against government
and Phelps Dodge, 193–96
Clean Water Act, violation of, 169–70
Clifton, Arizona, 1, 3, 19
anniversary rally in, 156–62
atmosphere of community, 22–24, 47
attachment of residents to, 65–70,
97–98
changes after strike, 181
Christmas celebration in, 118–20
curfew after flood in, 56
DPS special force in, 127–33
endurance of strike in, 64, 65, 71
eviction war in, 100

flood in, 49–58, 62–63
independence from Phelps Dodge, 23
Labor Day 1984 rally in, 163–66
National Guard occupation of, 34–39
after strike, 191–92
women's growing responsibility in,
101–3
*Clifton-Morenci Strike, The* (Kluger), 9
Clifton police force, civil rights suits
against, 195
Clothing exchange, 105
Coalition of Labor Union Women
(CLUW), 180
Center for Education and Research,
154
national convention of, 138–39
Coffeen, Bill, 148
Cole, Beverly, 137, 149, 192
Comaduran, Edward, 168
Communication Workers from Tucson,
119
Communism in unions, accusations of,
12
Community
attachment to, 64–72, 97–98
expansion of notion of, 107
isolation and strength of resistance
in, 65, 71
politicization of, 180–81
Company housing, 8–9, 68
evictions from, 42, 99–101, 126,
131, 132, 140
Company towns, 22–23, 26, 65, 121.
*See also* Ajo, Arizona; Morenci,
Arizona
Conason, Joe, 47, 152
Confidence gained by strikers, 176, 187
Confidence of women miners, 87, 94,
95–96
Congress of Industrial Organizations
(CIO), 10, 12, 78
Contamination from flood, 54
Continental Airlines, 123
Contract, working without, 92, 95
Contracts offered by Phelps Dodge, 44–
45, 85–86

Conventions, speaking at, 136–39
Convergent evolution, 20
Copeland, Betty, 14
*Copper Era* (newspaper), 85, 121, 170
Copper-mining towns of Arizona, 19–
20. *See also* Ajo, Arizona;
Bisbee, Arizona; Clifton, Ari-
zona; Douglas, Arizona; Mor-
enci, Arizona
Copper Queen mine (Bisbee), 6
Corporate Campaign Inc., 152
Cost-of-living allowance (COLA), 45
"Cross training" for job combinations, 65
Culture, women's role in Mexican,
108–9, 144–45
Curfew in Clifton, 56

Daily life, effect of strike hostilities on,
112–13
Damages collected in civil rights suits,
194, 195
Davis, Viola, 100, 151, 168
Death rate for miners, 4
DeBoer, Terrence, 195
Debs, Eugene V., 164
Decade for Women conference in Nai-
robi, U.N., 175–76, 188–90
Decertification, union, 166–68, 170,
172, 173, 191
Decision to strike, 44
Delgado, Angelita, 58–61, 158–59, 195
Delgado, Ricardo, 51, 158–59, 195
Delgado sisters, 24–25. *See also* Casey,
Cindy; Chavez, Berta; McCor-
mick, Diane
Democratic system, doubts about, 38–
39
Department of Public Safety (DPS), 26,
35, 37, 38, 103
in Ajo, 31–32
anniversary rally and, 156–62
arrests by, 35, 48, 59–61, 130–33,
147, 148–49, 159–60
Cinco de Mayo rally and, 146–48
civil rights suits against, 195
cleanup after flood and, 56

cost of, 179
excessive show of force by, 48
"Goodbye, Scabs" rally and, 170–71
Labor Day 1984 rally and, 165
in Morenci, 29–30, 127–33
occupation by, 15
special force of, 127–33
surveillance by, 129–30
Diaz, Porfirio, 6
Disabling injuries, 4
Discrimination
  against Mexican-Americans, 6–8,
    11–12, 67, 68, 79
  against women, 187
  housing, 12–13, 189
  in law enforcement, 104, 128, 193–
    96
Divorce, differences over strike and,
    112, 114, 178
Doctors, company, 89. See also Medical
    care
Domestic labor, escape from, 107
Douglas, Arizona, 19, 26, 70–71
Douglas, James, 9
Douglas mine, 169, 191
Drucher, Bert, 29-30
Dual wage scale, proposed
    establishment of, 45
Dupnik, Clarence, 193, 194
Duval Corporation mine, strike at, 64–
    65

Eagle Creek, people driven from, 66
Economics, safety and, 4
"El Corrido de la Huelga" (ballad), 64
El Salvador, 189
El Salvador mine, 182
Emergency aid after flood, 54, 55–56
Emergency food bank, 57, 104
Empire Zinc strike (1951), 5, 178
Environmental Protection Agency,
    violations of Morenci smelter
    agreement with, 124
Epperson, Joe, 146, 148
Escalante, Merci, 70
Europe, support for strikers in, 125

Evictions from company housing, 42,
    99–101, 126, 131, 132, 140
Family(ies)
  closeness of strikers', 117
  conflict over strike within, 112, 114–
    15, 137–38
  reactions to women miners, 87, 93,
    94–95
  struggle for women's rights and, 177
  support system for strikers', 104–7
  See also Children
Fathers, women miners' respect for
    their, 18, 91–92
FBI, 156
Federal disaster aid after flood, 62–63
Federal Market, picket at, 41–42
Feminism, unionism and, 143
Feminist movement, 176–77
Feminist Studies (Aulette & Mills), 113,
    153
Finances, management of, 108
Financial Times Mining International Year
    Book, 45
Fink, Officer, 60
Firearms
  injunction against, 103–4, 168
  nonunion labor carrying, 103–4, 116
Firing of strikers, 32–33, 42, 90–91
Flooding of San Francisco River, 49–
    58, 62–63
  losses from, 53–56, 62–63
Floorwalker, job of, 1
Foner, Philip, 9
Food bank, 57, 104
Ford Foundation, 175
Forging the Copper Collar (Byrkit), 9, 65
Fortune magazine, 46
Friendships, strike and, 113–18, 122
Fullen, Janet, 44, 70
Fund raising, speaking tours and, 136,
    137
Furnace explosion, 86, 88–89

Garcia, Carmina, 27–28, 30–31, 34,
    65–68, 101, 112, 137, 184
General Motors, 1937 strike against, 4

German documentary on strike, 125
*Germinal* (Zola), 5
Gilmartin, Helen, 32, 194
Gomez, Bob, 195
Gomez, Pat, 160
Gonzales, Mary Lou, 80–86, 91–92, 170, 183
Gonzalez, Viviano, 192
"Goodbye, Scabs" rally, 170–74
Government, civil rights suits against, 193–96
Greyhound Bus, 123

Halloween, celebration of, 120
Harassment
    by DPS and National Guard, 35
    by nonunion labor, 111–12, 129–30
    on picket lines, 128–29
    sexual, 11, 21
        of women in mines, 73–74, 76–77, 87, 89
    *See also* Hostility between strikers and nonstrikers
"Hardhats," 121
Hardy, Charles, 195
*Harlan County USA* (film), 4
Health and safety issues, 89–90
Hernandez, Brigham, 17
Hernandez-Wheeler, Liz, 47, 171
Hicks, Clifford, 35
Hicks, Nancy, 35, 42, 57, 100, 148
*High Stakes in Morenci* (film), 141–42, 165
Hispanics. *See* Mexican-Americans
Hostility between strikers and nonstrikers, 111–22
    in daily life, 112–13
    racial character of, 113
    violence, 120–22
    *See also* Harassment
Houses, attachment to, 99–100
Housewives, transfer of skills as, 107–9
Housing
    company, 8–9, 68
        evictions from, 42, 99–101, 126, 131, 132, 140

discrimination in, 12–13, 189

Ice, Duane, 33
Incas, 2, 3
Indecent exposure by nonunion labor, 103
Industrial Workers of the World (IWW), 9, 187
Industry, negotiating standard set of terms throughout, 14–15
Injunctions
    against firearms, 103–4, 168
    against strikers, 26, 36, 40–43
Injuries
    mining, 4, 67, 88–89
        accidents involving nonunion labor, 85, 124, 170
    of strikers, 103
Inspiration Consolidated Copper, 15
Insurance
    *beneficio propio* of Mexicans, 68
    lack of flood, 54
International Chemical Workers Union Local 703, 31
Internationalist perspective gained by women, 179–80, 189–90
International Ladies' Garment Workers' Union, 154
International support for strikers, 125
International union leadership, difficulties with, 125–26, 151–52, 153
International Union of Mine, Mill and Smelter Workers, 10–11. *See also* "Mine-Mill"
Interracial marriage, 79–80
Isner, Ray, 46, 48

Jackson, Jesse, 134
Jamaicans in mines during World War II, 10
Jerome-Verde Copper Company, 7
John, Angela V., 5–6
Johnson, Bob, 124
Jones, Annie, 64

Journalism
  fundamental myth of, x
  objectivity and, x–xiii
  *See also* News media

Kamber group, 152
Kennecott Company, 15
Kirkland, Lane, 180
Kirkpatrick, Jean, 188
Kluger, James, 9
Knott, Lydia, 18, 35, 92–93, 99, 131

*Labor and Copper in Arizona* (Leaming), 9
Labor Day 1984 rally, 163–66
Labor movement, U.S.
  1980s as turning point, 123
  rank-and-file rebellion against mainstream position on international affairs, 179–80
  underrepresentation and lack of interest in women, 153–54
  *See also* Union(s)
Ladd, Jack, 150
Law enforcement
  discriminatory, 104, 128, 193–96
  loss of faith in, 184–85
  use of system to break strike, 192–93
Layoffs at Ajo and New Cornelia mines, 168–69, 170
Leadership in Women's Auxiliary, 99
Leadership of national union, difficulties with, 125–26, 140–41, 151–53
Leaming, George, 9
Legal system, loss of faith in, 196. *See also* Law enforcement
Liquor, ban on, 56
Locker rooms, segregation in, 13–14
Lone, Jack (fictional name), 86–87
Lopez, Alex, 156
Lopez, Ed, 167
Lopez, Jean, 17–18, 37–40, 42, 48, 69, 132–33, 136–37, 139–40, 185–86
Lopez, Marta, 64
Lubrication helper, job of, 73–74

McBride, Lloyd, 152
McBride, Pearl, 43
McCormick, Diane, 24, 25, 29, 33, 34, 40, 43, 48, 52, 59, 60, 112, 118, 128, 130, 183
McCrory, Michael, 168, 194–96
McKee, Frank, 126, 152
McWilliams, Tom, 16
Magma Copper, 15
Magnet, Myron, 46
Manufacturers Hanover, 152
Marquez, Eduardo, 8, 11, 12–13, 30, 56
Marriage
  divorce and differences over strike in, 112, 114, 178
  interracial, 79–80
Martin, John, 5
Martinez, David, 119
Martinez, Terri, 57, 121–22
Maternity leave for women miners, 75–76, 77
Media. *See* News media
Medical care
  company monopolization of, 89–90
  coverage for strikers, 55
  "People's Clinic," 105
Meese, Edwin, 193
Meese, Ursula, 188
Men
  complaints about Women's Auxiliary, 141–43
  effect of strike on, 106–7
  respect between women and, 144, 145
Mexican-Americans
  as crucial component of union movement, 9–13, 14
  discrimination against, 11–12, 67, 68, 79
  marriage between Anglos and, 79–80
  segregation of, 6–9, 12–14, 67, 98
  women on picket line, 102
Mexican society, role of women in, 108–9
  industrialism and, 6

women's changing role in strike and, 144–45

*Militant* (newspaper), 151

Milkman, Ruth, 153–54, 178

Miller, Alice, 158, 159, 195

Miller, Tom, 20

Mills, Trudy, 113, 153

Milstead, Ralph, 127, 159, 161

"Mine-Mill" (International Union of Mine, Mill and Smelter Workers), 10–12, 79

Mining
accidents, nonunion labor and, 85, 124, 170
dangers of, 4, 86, 88–89
history of, 3, 21
   Bolivian mining region, 2–3, 5
   Mexican-Americans and, 7, 9–13, 14
   segregation and, 6–9
   union organization, 9–21
   Victorian era, 5–6
   women and, 4–5, 10–11, 13–21
injuries, 4, 67, 88–89
pollution from, 69, 169–70

Miracle Valley Church, 184

Mobilization for Justice and Peace in Central America and Southern Africa (1987), 179

Morales, Cecelia, 172–73

Morenci, Arizona, 3, 19, 22–23, 191
discrimination and segregation in, 67
DPS special force in, 127–33
during flood, 52
Mine-Mill organized in, 11–12
National Guard occupation of, 34–39

Morenci Club, 51, 57, 160

Morenci mine, x, 3, 169
arrests and terminations at, 42
first days of strike in, 25–26
history of Mexican laborers in, 6–8
opening to women in 1970s, 13–14
partial shutdown, after strike, 170–71
recruitment of replacement workers for, 46–47

shutdown, in beginning of strike, 29–31
psychological effect of, 46–47
ten-day cooling-off period and, 33–34

Morenci Miners Women's Auxiliary, 15, 17, 21, 71, 116, 132, 189
changes in, 39–41
eviction war and, 101
flood relief and, 55
food bank organized by, 57, 104
growing independence of women in, 102–3
leadership in, 99
management of finances of, 108
meetings, 106
men's complaints about, 141–43
new level of economic consciousness for women working in, 107–10
new role of, 143–44
program of speaking tours, 134–39
revival of, 24–25
rift between union leaders and, 126–27, 140–41, 152–53
support system for striking families, 104–7

Moreno, Arlene, 80–86, 88, 91

Morgan, Trudy, 36, 113–18, 153, 183–84

Muñoz, Natalie, 193

Munroe, George, 152

Murillo, Vicki, 93–96

Nairobi, U.N. Decade for Women conference in, 175–76, 188–90

Nash, June, 2

National Guard
anniversary rally and, 161
Governor Babbitt and decision to send in, 36
occupation of Clifton and Morenci by, 15, 34–39
cost of, 179
effects of, 39–44, 48
return of helicopters during flood, 52

return to Clifton after Cinco de
    Mayo rally, 148
National Labor Committee, 179
National Labor Relations Board, 123,
    167, 170, 171, 173, 185, 191
National Organization for Women, 138
National support for strikers, 125
National Union of Mineworkers in
    England, auxiliary of, 125
Navarrette, Frank, 42
Navarro, Ed (fictional name), 54–55,
    63, 79
Navarro, Flossie (fictional name), xii,
    1–2, 3, 10–11, 36–37, 54–55,
    63, 78–80
Negotiations, 14–15, 123, 150–52,
    155–56
New Cornelia mine, layoffs at, 168–69
News media
    anniversary rally coverage, 158, 161,
        162
    antiworker sentiments expressed by,
        184
    Labor Day rally coverage, 166
    negative reinforcement by, 166
    portrayal of flood victims by, 56
    portrayal of strikers by, 16, 42–43,
        85–86
    public perception of strike and, 193
New York City, rally in, 134
New York Life, 152
Nicaragua, 189
Norma Rae (film), 4

Objectivity, journalism and, x–xiii
Occupational Safety and Health
    Administration (OSHA) inspec-
    tions, 81
Occupation by National Guard, 34–39
    cost of, 179
    effect of, 39–44, 48
O'Leary, Anna, 108–10, 125, 128,
    138–39, 144–45, 155, 156,
    160–61, 173–82, 187–90
O'Leary, Jorge, 105, 128, 145, 153, 157,
    161, 163, 166, 177, 178, 182

O'Leary, Mandy, 180–81
Operating engineer, job of, 77
Operating Engineers Local 428, 46
Oruro, Bolivia, 2, 3

Pachamama (goddess), 2, 3
Paine, Thomas, 72
Papago Indians, 19, 80
Parsons, Lucy, 187
PATCO, 123, 184
Pattern bargaining, 17, 45
Patterson, Rosie, 10
"People's Clinic," 105
Permanent replacements of strikers, 46–
    47, 150. See also "Scab labor"
PFC (Puros Firmes Chicanos), 165
Phelps Dodge Mining Company
    advertising, image in, 45
    civil rights suits against, 193–96
    company housing of, 8–9, 68
        evictions from, 42, 99–101, 126,
            131, 132, 140
    company towns and, 23, 26, 65, 121
    contracts offered by, 44–45, 85–86
    costs of strike to, 124–25
    decertification election and, 166–68
    development of Arizona copper indus-
        try, 6
    discrimination against Mexican-
        Americans, 6–8, 11–12, 67, 68
    disputes over health and safety issues
        with, 89–90
    driving people from Eagle Creek, 66
    El Salvador mine, 182
    employment of women during World
        War II, 1
    financial status of, 45–46
    flood relief from, 56–57
    history of labor conflicts with, 9–21
    injunctions against strikers and, 26
    layoffs at Ajo and New Cornelia
        mines, 168–69
    negotiations with, 14–15, 123, 150–
        52, 155–56
    operations of mines during strike,
        25–26, 27

payment of legal fees for nonstrikers charged with crimes, 168
pollution from mines, 69, 169–70
recruitment of nonunion labor, 27–29, 36, 46–47
relocation of families by, 68–69
resistance in Ajo to, 31–33
scare tactics against women picketers, 61
shutdown of Ajo mine, 168
shutdown of part of Morenci operation, 170–71
start of 1983 strike against, 15–16
after strike, 191
strike in 1955 against, 141
terminations of strikers, 32–33, 42, 90–91
ties with apartheid, 134
union busting
 as goal of, 156
 tactics, 46, 47, 124–25
Picket line
 consequences of holding, 25
 after flood, 57
 harassment on, 128–29
 injunctions ruling on, 40
 women on, 40–43, 102, 103
Pima County, civil rights suits against, 193–94
Police brutality, 136. *See also* Arrests; Department of Public Safety (DPS); Harassment
Police force, civil rights suits against, 195
Politicians, loss of faith in, 184–85
Politicization of community, 180–81
Politics, women's shift of allegiance in, 184–85
Pollution from mines, 69, 169–70
Powerhouse pumpman, job of, 82–83
Pregnancy of women miners, 75–76
Press. *See* News media
Protective clothing, 81
Puebla, battle of (1862), commemoration of, 140
Puros Firmes Chicanos (PFC), 165

Race, hostility over strike and, 113
Racial equality issue, 79
Rainbelt, Alison, 44
Rallies
 in Ajo after shutdown, 168
 anniversary, 156–62
 Cinco de Mayo, 140–41, 145–48
 "Goodbye, Scabs," 170–74
 Labor Day 1984, 163–66
Ramon, Janie, 14, 31, 32, 48, 91, 185
Randall, Shirley, 21, 86–89, 103, 104, 113–18, 151, 184
Ray, Arizona, mine, "Strike of the Mexicans" at, 9
Reagan, Maureen, 188
Reagan, Ronald, 123
Recruitment of nonunion labor, 27–29, 36, 46–47
Red-baiting, 12
Red Cross relief during and after flood, 51, 54, 55
Refrigerated Cave (bar), 80, 81
Religious groups, aid after flood from, 54
Relocation of families by Phelps Dodge, 68–69
Replacements for strikers, permanent, 46–47, 150. *See also* "Scab labor"
Resourcefulness of women, 106
Resources of women during eviction war, 99
Respect between men and women, 144, 145
Restraining orders, 26. *See also* Injunctions
Reverberatory furnaces, jobs in, 82, 93–94, 95
Rights
 civil, 47–48, 71–72
 knowledge of, 42, 133
 women's struggle for, 176–78
Riot troops at anniversary rally, 158–61
Robledo, Cleo, 35, 41, 43, 120, 131–32, 182

Robledo, Ernie, 119
Rodriguez, Angel, 47, 89, 128, 137, 168, 183
Rogers, Ray, 152
Role model, father as women miners', 91–92
Roman, Fina, 15, 17, 38, 40, 47, 49, 50–51, 52, 55, 57–58, 71, 125, 134–35, 143, 156–57, 164, 165, 167, 169, 171–72, 185
Roman, Renaldo, 121
"Rustling shift," 12

Safety issues, 89–90
    economics and, 4
Salt of the Earth (film), 5, 20, 178
San Francisco River
    flooding of, 49–58, 62–63
    pollution by Phelps Dodge of, 169–70
Santa Cruz, Roy, 12
"Scab labor," 25–29, 44, 46–47
    carrying firearms, 103–4, 116
    Cinco de Mayo rally and, 146, 147–48
    cruelty to flood victims by, 57
    dangers of mining for inexperienced, 85
    displacing strikers during eviction war, 100
    divorces among, 114
    DPS protection of, 127, 128
    during flood, 51, 52, 55, 56
    growing experience of, 123–24
    harassment by, 111–12, 129–30
    layoffs of, 168–69, 170
    mining accidents, 170
    recruitment of, 27–29, 36, 46–47
    sexism of, 103
Scanlon, M. Pat, 13, 17, 26, 27, 33, 45, 46–47, 100–101, 121, 150, 156
Schoolbooks, soliciting money for children's, 105–6
Schools, segregation in, 67, 98
Schwartz, Baby Doll, 73–78, 91, 122

Segregation of Mexican-Americans, 6–9, 12–14, 67, 98
Self-assurance gained by women, 187
Sexual harassment, 11, 21
    of women miners, 73–74, 76–77, 87, 89
Sharp, Vicky, 15, 16, 112
Silkwood, Karen, 163
Sisterhood and Solidarity: Feminism and Labor in Modern Times (Balser), 143
Skidmore, Margaret, 54, 80, 81, 83, 85, 183
Skills, transfer of housewife, 107–9
Slaney, Dave, 179
Small Town Breakers, 106, 164
Smokestack, job of cleaning, 81
Snipers, 41
Social Club of Clifton, 23–24
"Solidarity and Self-Interest" (Slaney), 179
South Africa, 134, 189
Spaulding, Stuart, 55
Speaking tours, women on, 134–39
Springsteen, Bruce, 105
St. Vincent de Paul, 54
Stress workshop, 106
Strike in 1967, 12–13
"Strike of the Mexicans" (1915), 9
Strikers
    Arizona population's distrust of, 36
    defense of civil liberties, 47–48, 71–72
    national and international support of, 125
    news media portrayal of, 16, 42–43, 85–86
    sentiment among, 48
    support system for families, 104–7
Strikes, documentaries of historic, 4–5
Sulfur dioxide
    emissions at Morenci, 124
    lung damage from, 81
Sumitomo Company of Japan, 191
Sun Valley Mennonite Church, 54
Supay (ancient god), 2, 3, 7

Support system for striking families, 104–7
Supreme Court ruling on replacement workers, 47, 150
Surveillance of picketers, 42
SWAT teams, 35, 158–61
Szady, Matt, 121

Tallant, Chandra, 35
Tear gas, use by riot troops, 158, 160
Tellez, Fillmore, 118
Tellez, Jessie, 71, 97–99, 101–3, 104, 106–8, 122, 133, 137, 172, 173, 177, 186
Ten-day cooling-off period, 30–31, 33–34
Terminations of strikers, 32–33, 42, 90–91
Territorial showdown between women and DPS, 133
Thurgeson, Stan, 121
Tohono O'odham, 19. *See also* Papago Indians
Truth, Justice and the American Way, doubts about, 38–39
Tucson, Arizona, 19
strike-support rally in, 135
Tucson Union Support Committee, 47, 171

U.S. Constitution, 192
U.S. Steel Corporation, 126
Undercover agents, 42
Union(s)
belief in necessity of, 91–92
conservative strategy for strike, 151–52
criticism by rank-and-file of, 151–53
divergence of women's strategy from, 153–55
early history of organization of movement, 9–21
Mexican-Americans and, 9–13, 14
women and, 10–11, 13–21
efforts made at national level, 152

health and safety issues and, 89
help with bail from, 61
help with food bank, 104
offer of June 8, 1984, 150
strength of loyalty to, 70, 71
stress workshop organized by, 106
underrepresentation and lack of interest in women, 153–54
women miners and, 76, 77–79, 83–84, 91–93, 95
Union busting
as Phelps Dodge's goal, 156
tactics of Phelps Dodge, 46, 47, 124–25
Union decertification, 166–68, 170, 172, 173, 191
Unionism
"bread-and-butter," 179
feminism and, 143
after World War II, 154
Union leadership, difficulties with, 125–26, 140–41, 151–53, 157
Union rank-and-file, support of national, 170
United Auto Workers, 123
United Nations Decade for Women conference in Nairobi, 175–76, 188–90
United Steelworkers of America (USWA), 26–27, 76, 79, 126–27
national convention in San Francisco, 136–37
United Transportation Union, 13
Unity Council, 12–13
USWA Local 616, 47

Vallens, Vivian, 6
Valley National Bank, 152
*Value of the Person, The* (film), 155
Vega, José, 121
Velasquez, David, 10
Victorian era, women in mines during, 5–6
Vietnam veterans among strikers, 38
*Village Voice* (newspaper), 47, 152

Violence
  in Ajo, strike suppression and, 35
  between strikers and nonstrikers,
    120–22
  See also Arrests; Harassment;
    Hostility between strikers and
    nonstrikers

We Eat the Mines, the Mines Eat Us
  (Nash), 2
Weisen, Ron, 126, 140
Western Federation of Miners, 9. See
  also Mine-Mill
White Mountain Apache reservation,
  22
Wildcat strike of women during World
  War II, 11
Williams, Lynn, 126, 152
With Babies and Banners (film), 4
Wives of Workers (WOW), 100–101,
  116, 121
Women
  altered perceptions after strike,
    178
  attachment to community of, 70, 71
  author's reasons for writing about, xi
  changes in due to strike, 20–21,
    176–90
    attitudes toward work, 187
    broadening of understanding, 182–
      84
    hopes for children, 71, 117, 181,
      185–86
    internationalist perspective gained,
      179–80, 189–90
    loss of faith in law enforcement,
      184–85
    political, 184–85
    politicization of community and,
      180–81
    self-assurance, 187
  contributions to mining history,
    4–5
  discrimination against, 187
  divergence in strategy from unions,
    153–55

early history of union movement
  and, 10–11, 13–21
exclusion from mines, tradition of, 2
forces demanding strike participation
  of, 5
growing responsibility of, 101–3
growth in union membership due to,
  153–54
independence from husbands,
  growing, 102–3
influence over men's decision to
  strike, 44
media image of American women,
  176
organizing for strike, 99, 155
respect between men and, 144, 145
role in Mexican society, 108–9, 144–
  45
role in strike, changing, 143–45
on speaking tours, 134–39
union underrepresentation and lack
  of interest in, 153–54
Women, Work, and Protest: A Century
  of U.S. Women's Labor History
  (Milkman), 153–54, 178
Women and the American Labor
  Movement (Foner), 9
Women in mines, 73–96
  in Appalachian coal mines, 3
  confidence of, 87, 94, 95–96
  family reactions to, 87, 93, 94–95
  harassment of, 73–74, 76–77, 87, 89
  lessons learned from strike by, 95–96
  men's resentment of, 81–82
  opening of mines in 1970s to, 13–14
  percentage of work force, 78
  pregnancy and, 75–76
  reasons for employment in mines,
    84–85
  respect for their fathers, 18, 91–92
  six-day work week for, 78
  supportiveness among, 82
  unions and, 76, 77–79, 83–84, 91–
    93, 95
  during and after World War II, 1–2,
    5, 10–11, 78–80

working through strike, 121
Women's auxiliaries, statewide network of, 64. *See also* Morenci Miners Women's Auxiliary
Women's movement, trend toward more socialistic and humane practices in, 190
Women's rights, struggle for, 176–78
Wooden bullets, riot troop's use of, 158
Work, women's attitudes toward, 187
Work schedules for miners, 78, 84
World War I, 9

World War II
    employment of women in mines during, 1–2, 5, 10–11
    union organizing limited by, 10
    women in mines since, 78–80
WOW (Wives of Workers), 100–101, 116, 121
WPA, 66
Wright, Laura, 121

Yazzie, Askie, 163

Zola, Emile, 5

## ABOUT THE AUTHOR

Barbara Kingsolver is a fiction writer, journalist, and human rights activist. Her novel *The Bean Trees* won enthusiastic critical acclaim, as did her second book, *Homeland and Other Stories*. A full-time writer, Kingsolver has contributed feature articles and reviews to the *New York Times* and many other publications. She grew up in eastern Kentucky and now lives with her family in Tucson, Arizona.